W9-BUD-582

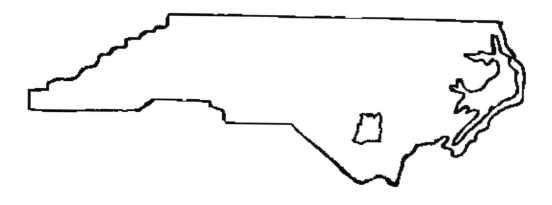

Chrysthine

Portrait Of A Unique
North Carolina Girl
Up From The Sharecrop Fields

An 83-Year Memoir
and
An 83-Year History of North Carolina's Number One
Agricultural Income County
Written 1997-1998

Chrysthine

Portrait Of A Unique
North Carolina Girl
Up From The Sharecrop Fields

Christine Whaley Williams

663 East N. C. #11
Pink Hill, N. C.
28572
252-568-3391

Pentland Press, Inc.
England • USA • Scotland

NEW HANOVER COUNTY
PUBLIC LIBRARY
201 CHESTNUT STREET
WILMINGTON, N C 28401

PUBLISHED BY PENTLAND PRESS, INC.
5122 Bur Oak Circle, Raleigh, North Carolina 27612
United States of America
919-782-0281

ISBN 1-57197-150-5
Library of Congress Catalog Card Number 98-068269

Copyright © 1999 Christine W. Williams
All rights reserved, which includes the right to reproduce this book or
portions thereof in any form whatsoever except as provided by the U.S.
Copyright Law.

Printed in the United States of America

Chrysthine

Foreword by Melvin Williams

Chrysthine is the story of a loving, courageous girl, whose life story will be an inspiration to every reader of this book.

Did she have ambition? Definitely! A tremendous amount of ambition was necessary to rise from such humble beginnings to achieve the success she has enjoyed.

Hers is an admirable kind of ambition which never hurt anyone as she strove to attain success.

In fact, it is remarkable how much of her life she has spent helping other people.

While we were growing up, our devoted mother frequently entertained us by relating intriguing stories about various periods of her life.

However, it was not until I read *Chrysthine* that I learned some of her most private experiences. This was especially true of her heartbreaking romance.

Most history books only tell about what state and national leaders have done. My mother's combination of Memoir and History book tells about life as it was lived by the "real" people in the era of harvesting of long leaf pines, the heyday of the railroads, and the laborious conditions of sharecropping.

Her accounts of life in the rural south during much of the 20th century will bring back memories to her contemporaries and will be a revealing education to young readers.

Her memory of details of early 20th century life is even more remarkable when readers learn that, as a child, she never made notes nor kept a diary.

Reading *Chrysthine* will be a fascinating journey for readers of all ages.

Overview

My Fourfold Purpose In Writing This Book

To inspire readers to understand and believe that:

1. Regardless of the circumstances of one's birth and childhood, it is possible for children to set goals, build dreams and develop a life of discipline and order in spite of road blocks of poverty, family illnesses, bereavement, and lack of educational opportunities.

2. Having to endure nights in cold, drafty sharecrop houses and long days in sharecrop fields with the hot sun, dust, wind, and rain prevailing can be not only stettings for children to establish goals for a better financial existence but they can be fertile soil for developing a love for and an understanding of all kinds of people, regardless of their lowly employment and status in life. Work in sharecrop fields surrounded by a loving family and the wonders of creation can provide not only food for the body but balm for the soul and a deep appreciation for whatever better circumstances come in the future.

3. Family love, loyalty, and appreciation for work efforts can make up to little children for the lack of better financial resources and help them cultivate a happy outlook on life.

4. Above all, it is my purpose to share with readers how I have found that when problems and circumstances come in one's adult years such as your life's unfulfilled romance, a failed marriage, and other tragedies too big for us to handle alone, it is only through having developed a faith and dependence on a power greater than we are that we can survive, achieve and serve others. It has been this faith and dependence that have enabled me to rise above disappointments and, in my 83rd year, to still be of service to my family and to others in spite of having come from a short-lived family.

Advance Praise for

Chrysthine

Portrait Of A Unique North Carolina Girl Up From The Sharecrop Fields

"Christine Williams walks barefoot out of the Carolina tobacco fields straight into the reader's heart—full shod in success."

Jo Cameron Jones, Reporter
Warsaw-Faison News

"Christine writes a true and inspiring story of a girl growing up in the rural south under almost primative conditions and of her early and present day successes in life. This is real history and records facts which would otherwise be lost."

Adelaide and Milton Rice

"Christine's book weaves the tears and joys of her life into past and current history of her beloved County. Her life's success story is an inspiration for all ages."

Ruth W. Wallace

Christine Williams takes the reader on an eighty-three year journey of her inspiring life enmeshed in Duplin County and North Carolina History.

From the beginning path to the final chapter, the traveler is presented a circuitous life gathered into a fragrant bouquet.

The traveler will laugh with her and shed tears with her but will never be bored on the journey with her.

Scarlette Williams
Retired High School English Teacher

As teenage siblings living close to Mrs. Christine Whaley Williams, we have watched her book unfold telling about how she worked in sharecrop fields and about overcoming the odds of a young girl living in poverty. Also, by becoming the first woman ever to be elected to a public office in the biggest agricultural income county in our state.

We can hardly wait for her book to arrive in our school library so other students can enjoy the stories of how our ancestors lived in the yester-years of North Carolina and managed to thrive on a low income.

We believe her book will educate the young people of today on how times have changed. We have also come to believe that in spite of the many circumstances of a persons' childhood, if they are true to themselves and their families, things will just work out.

Jennings and Krystal Smith

Christine Williams is real. Her story is real, woven from strong threads of vivid memory with keen insight and attention to detail. She has written a remarkable account of life and times in a rural area where roads have taken her from toil as a proud sharecropper's daughter to one of the highest and most demanding elective offices in county government—the first woman to hold such an office.

Laced with great humor as well as lessons life teaches and challenges that must be met, Christine Williams' book makes for honest-to-goodness, down-to-earth good reading.

Mrs. Sammie W. Carter, Editor
The Wallace Enterprise
The Warsaw-Faison News
The Richlands-Beulaville Advertiser News

Dedication

To my parents, Mack and Genett Whaley, who provided me with a rich childhood in poverty. They always let me know I was loved and shaped me into what I became as an adult.

To my son, Melvin Williams, who prodded me since I retired in December 1988 to write this book, who served as my advisor and who talks with me by telephone most every day and ends every good-bye with, "Remember I love you."

Special Thanks

I am deeply grateful for all the assistance, encouragement, and interest in the preparation of this writing. Special thanks to those who have given "hands-on" help with information and verification of data. If your name does not appear on this list, please know that your help and encouragement was meaningful and appreciated.

Alma Anderson

William Blanchard

Sarah Bolin

Lois Britt

Judy Brown

Sammie Carter

Stephanie Childers

Ed Emory

Jeraldine Hill

Dr. Dallas Herring

Jo Ann & Cletus Jones

Jo Cameron Jones

Reverend Gene Lakey

Etlar & Lounell Mainor

Edd Dudley Monk

Hardy Parker, Jr.

Dennis Pittman

Mr. & Mrs. Melvin Pope

Cynthia Potter

Dr. & Mrs. Corbett Quinn

Ada & Elwood Revelle

Adelaide & Milton Rice

Beatrice Sheppard

L. H. Sikes

Reverend Brad Simpson

Sonya & Anthony Smith

Linda Smith

Essie Cooke Taylor

Remus & Gaynelle Teachey

Betty Whaley Thornton

Narcie Turner

Geraldine & Russell Tucker

Lee Tyndall

Rosamond Tyndall

Pat Vinson

Ruth Wallace

Sabra Waller

William Warren

Dr. Donn Wells

David West

Pearl West

Robert L. West

Melvin Williams

Scarlette Williams

Billy Wood

Contents

Part Seven: 1961-1987

Part Eight: 1989-1998

Mack and Genett Whaley, my parents, told me story after story about how my life began in the town of Magnolia and on sharecrop farms in rural Duplin County, North Carolina. Twenty-two years of living with them filled my memory with intriguing tales about how our lives unfolded a decade and a half into the turn of the century. Now, eighty-three years later, I reminisce about the fragrant-sounding town called Magnolia and the landscapes of the sharecrop farms where so many memories were indelibly etched in my mind.

Part One

1915-1917

Magnolia

Mack Whaley Earns a Living at Fred Pickett's Livery Stables and Sets His Sights on Emerging Sharecropping

Mack Whaley reached for the hollowed-out gourd drinking cup hanging from a rusty nail in Mr. Fred Pickett's livery stables. He used the stables' pitcher hand pump to get himself a big, fresh drink of water to fill the void in his stomach—a void caused by the absence of the lunch he hadn't brought to work today. Genett, my mother, had been too preoccupied to prepare the usual biscuit with a piece of sausage or other meat which was his daily lunch fare. She had instead delivered me—an eleven-pound baby girl—earlier in the morning with the assistance of the midwife, Jane Barden, whom Daddy had fetched on one of the stables' hacks. Her fee was only a fraction of that charged by Dr. Robert F. Quinn, the only family doctor in Magnolia.

As Daddy stood in the crisp Magnolia air drinking the refreshing water this Thursday, 28 October 1915, he wondered how things were going at our little rented three-room house two blocks from the center of town. He couldn't leave the stables to check on us today because he was by himself. Mr. Fred was taking care of important business at Carolina Manufacturing Company where he was vice-president and general manager. Daddy had to feed and groom the horses and polish the rental hacks. Plus, he had to take care of the drop-in customers.

While feeding the horses, Daddy said aloud, "Chrysthine," as he thought about Mother naming me after a beautiful little curly-headed girl she had read about in a storybook. He could still see Mother carefully spelling "Chrysthine" for the midwife and he could see Jane writing my name on my birth certificate.

"She'll be fine," Daddy uttered, still half in a daze, "what with Jane spending the day with Genett." Daddy remembered how Jane was just at their house eighteen months earlier to deliver their eleven-pound son, Milton. As he performed his stable chores, he pictured Milton toddling around the house today wondering about the arrival of me, his new sister.

With two children already and the almost surety there would be more, Daddy seriously questioned how he could make a good living for his growing family on his meager pay of five cents an hour at the livery stables.

He polished another rental hack and reflected on his father, William Whaley, who had also worked as a stable hand for Mr. Fred Pickett. Granddaddy Whaley had died before Daddy, the youngest of five children, was old enough to go to school. Daddy went to work at the stables as a little boy to help support his sickly Mother. He never attended a single day of school. He always signed his name with an "X," but he could make astounding calculations in his head.

His lack of formal education did not affect his character development, his aspirations for a better life for his family, or his ability to work hard.

Lean and rangy, a powerhouse of disciplined energy, Mack Whaley went about his livery stable duties in his ironed but aging gingham shirt and worn bib overalls. He whistled while he worked the long ten-hour day.

Daddy followed the sound of footsteps to the front of the stables where he smiled warmly from a clean-shaven face to his third customer of the morning. In the course of the seemingly longer-than-usual-day, he not only greeted this customer from Pender County, but many others on their wagons and carts from such distant counties as Sampson, Onslow, Lenoir, and Wayne selling tar, pitch, turpentine, and longleaf pine lumber materials in Magnolia to be shipped on the railroad running through the center of town. Many of these materials were shipped as naval stores for use in building wooden ships and boats. Of course, some would be used for home and commercial buildings.

An article in the May 1962 edition of *The State* read: "An early 19th century map of eastern North Carolina shows the principal towns to be Wilmington, New Bern, and Stricklandsville, as Magnolia was then called." The same article stated: "Magnolia was larger than Kinston." The article continues: "In addition to being engaged in lumbering and manufacturing of naval stores, Magnolia had also become a tobacco auction market for early leaf farmers who brought their cured tobacco in hogsheads pulled by carts over the sandy or muddy roads."

In 1915, traveling salesmen, called *drummers*, who rode the train from Richmond, Virginia, New York, and other northern manufacturing locations to take orders for their goods from the several thriving Magnolia merchants called on Daddy, too. Magnolia became the drummers' headquarters because it was the trading center of eastern North Carolina at the time.

After the drummers showed their wares to the thriving Magnolia merchants, they rented two-horse hacks from Daddy at the Pickett stables or from Mr. Groves' livery and took their sample goods to Wallace or to the big G. B. D. Parker General Store in the little unincorporated village of Chinquapin. They spent the night with Mr. Parker in his great big house or stayed at the only hotel in Wallace. Sometimes they came back to Magnolia to sleep in one of its four two-story wooden frame hotels: Southerland, Matthews, Hamblin, and Middleton House.

Automobiles were uncommon then, and there was no such thing as an automobile rental. None of the few automobile owners would dare think of renting such a fragile treasure to drummers who came in on the train. The sandy or muddy roads had surfaces too poor for anything as temperamental as the early cars.

The most interesting of all the livery stable customers Daddy encountered was a dashing young shoe salesman from Richmond, Virginia who visited him this spring. He had been quick to tell Daddy he was Lewis L. Strauss, the son of the vice-president, sixteen years old, and on his first trip as a shoe salesman for Fleishman, Morris & Company. Strauss opened his two big trunks of shoe samples, each holding eight trays, and showed the array of shoes to Daddy, who was greatly impressed. Then he rented a two-horse hack from Daddy to take his line of fine shoe samples to the G. B. D. Parker General Store at Chinquapin.

Daddy never dreamed he would see the son of the vice-president of the United States selling shoes in Magnolia, much less renting a hack from the livery stables he tended. Lewis L. Strauss had said he would be back in October. The month was nearly gone and Daddy was looking for Strauss any day. He might even come today, Daddy believed.

Later, Daddy learned that Lewis L. Strauss was the son of the vice-president of Fleishman, Morris & Company in Richmond, Virginia, and not the son of the vice-president of the United States. Daddy wasn't too far off, though, for Strauss did become advisor to four men who became presidents of the United States. He retired his shoe-drumming days at age twenty-one to become engineer Herbert Hoover's personal secretary. Later, he became best known as chairman of the United States Atomic Energy Commission for Presidents Roosevelt, Truman, and Eisenhower, for which he received the Medal of Freedom.

In addition to drummers like Strauss renting hacks from Daddy, turpentine farmers who brought their raw turpentine to the three large turpentine stills in Magnolia to be distilled, barreled, and shipped by rail often left their animals at the stables overnight.

It was in this thriving and progressive atmosphere that on 28 October 1915, Mack Whaley was weighing all aspects of his family's situation and attempting to chart their future.

Working for Mr. Fred Pickett had been good for Daddy, especially since Mr. Pickett couldn't be at the stables much because of his growing duties at Carolina Manufacturing Company. This had given Daddy more and more experience at managing affairs at the stables. This was how he earned his reputation for dependability and stickability. Mr. Pickett knew he could always depend on him.

However much Daddy liked to work for Mr. Pickett, he also realized that the sales and uses of horses and mules were beginning to decline as the era of automobiles was growing. There was talk that the Horne family in Magnolia would soon establish the Horne Motor Company and sell Fords. Predictions abounded that the shipping of tar, pitch, turpentine, and lumber products would diminish with the looming scarcity of longleaf pines and the coming of metal and fiberglass boats.

Later that evening at home, Mother and Daddy discussed how the jobs at the three sawmills and the three strawberry crate factories would be secure, but there were no hopes of better wages than the present five cents an hour.

Even the greatly expanding flower bulb farming offered the same five cents an hour for workers in the flower fields and in the large warehouses where the bulbs were graded, cured, and stored for shipping on the railroad. It would be interesting to watch Magnolia become known as The Flower Town, America's Bulb Metropolis, advertising that ninety-eight varieties of bulbs could be supplied. But as late as the early thirties, flower bulb wages would stay at five cents an hour for bulb workers.

As Daddy and Mother talked that night, they discussed all known options for more income. Mother had already been assembling wooden strawberry quart cups at home by using tacks and the metal quart cup mould the local crate factories supplied to all Magnolia homes. The pay for tacking the wooden quart cups together and putting them in stacks of thirty-two each was seventy cents per thousand. Most ladies could tack five hundred in a day by working all day, which earned them thirty-five cents. When Mother had a whole hour, she could do one hundred, earning seven cents. But she would have less time now with two children to care for. With Daddy's nimble hands he could really turn them out fast, as many as one hundred fifty in an hour. He decided he would just have to extend his day on into the evening and assemble quart cups until they could make new arrangements.

Of the few choices he had to care for his growing family, Daddy decided for sharecrop farming which was just beginning to grow in popularity. At least, the harder he worked, the more profit he would make.

The sharecropper furnished labor, tools, mules or horses. The landlord provided the land, fertilizer, and seeds. Crop proceeds were divided equally between the landlord and the sharecropper. The sharecropper was allowed to grow all the vegetables, chickens, and hogs he needed, and he could have a milk cow.

He decided to talk his situation over with Mr. Pickett, whom Daddy loved. He had been Daddy's only father figure for so long. They had mutual deep-seated respect and admiration for each other. Mr. Pickett had been good to him and taught him much.

Daddy would miss the close contact with his two brothers and two sisters and their families once they moved to a farm. Yet, he and Mother felt they were preparing for better days ahead. "I'll start looking for a good landlord with a big farm where I can work extra hard, honey. We'll have a garden and won't have to buy many groceries. We'll make ends meet and perhaps save some."

"I'll look forward to working in the garden and giving you a hand with the farm chores," Mother added.

They both agreed the farm would be a good place to teach the children to work. Mother was a thrifty housewife who cooked and made clothes without patterns. She had Grandmother Thomas's pedal sewing machine which hummed like a softly twirling top.

"In the meantime, while I'm still working for Mr. Fred, I'll be looking for a repairable farm wagon, a mule, and some used plows so we can be ready to go to work when we find our farm," Daddy offered.

"You know Mr. Pickett takes the weekly newspaper, *The Duplin Record.* You might want to ask him to look for a wagon for sale in the want ads if one doesn't show up at the stables," Genett suggested.

As Daddy continued to muddle through his past and sort out the problems he, Mother, and we children faced in the future, he remembered Mother telling him about Christmas Eve in 1910 when her father, William Thomas, age sixty-six, and her Mother, Jane, fifty-nine, sold their fifty-five-acre farm near Beulaville for fifteen hundred dollars to I. J. Sandlin, the big general store merchant in Beulaville. Mr. Sandlin was just beginning to amass a fortune in farms, mostly from his "time" customers.

Mother's six brothers and sisters had already married and settled around Beulaville, leaving only Mother, sixteen at the time, to move to Magnolia with her parents.

Daddy figured if Mother's parents at their advanced ages, in 1910, could make the eighteen-mile move from Beulaville to Magnolia to live near the railroad line to realize their dream for a better life, then he could move his little growing family to a farm with hopes to work hard and make a better life for them. (The railroad line running through Magnolia, the 161-mile Wilmington-Weldon Railroad, opened 9 March 1840, and merged with the Atlantic Coast Line at the turn of the century.)

Grandfather Thomas loved to talk about how he had served in the Civil War, reared his family, and longed to live in the thriving metropolis of Magnolia. Thank goodness my Thomas grandparents decided to move to Magnolia. Otherwise, Mother would never have met my good-looking and affable Daddy.

It was love at first sight for both of them, but they dated for two years. Then on 14 December 1912, they sent by John Brown, a rural mail carrier who had one of the few automobiles in town, to the Duplin County courthouse in Kenansville to purchase a marriage license. True to Daddy's story, the completed marriage license on file in the Duplin Courthouse shows that Mack Whaley and Genett Thomas married on 15 December 1912. It is signed by

John Brown as "affiant and license purchaser" and by Geo. Edwards, J. P. as "Officiating Officer."

Grandfather Thomas was fascinated by everything in Magnolia. It was so much bigger and had so much more to see and enjoy than the little village of Beulaville. He swelled with pride every time he walked to the handsome red brick train depot to watch the trains come in and depart. Grandfather Thomas first saw the depot in 1910 when it was seventeen years old. Melvin Pope, former mayor and lifelong resident says he sadly watched it being demolished in 1985 when it was ninety-two years old.

The Magnolia where my grandparents settled in their later years and my parents fell in love was a place "where sweet magnolias blossom 'round everybody's door," as described in a popular song back then. The town has a fascinating history which has been described in texts like *Flashes of Duplin's History and Government* by Faison and Pearl McGowen in addition to Daddy's recollections.

The McGowens write that the town of Magnolia was located on a farm given by David Carlton to his daughter, Tabitha Strickland. Consequently, when the railroad was constructed through the farm, the trains stopped there at what became known as Stricklandsville, the McGowens recount.

Two years later, in 1857, a May 1962 edition of *The State* records that "one of the most beautiful and popular young ladies of Duplin County, Miss Maggie Monk, daughter of J. B. B. Monk, a leading citizen of the time, got married." The citizens of Stricklandsville changed the name of the town to Magnolia as a wedding gift for the bride, and the town was officially reenacted as Magnolia.

The State article on Magnolia goes on to say: "At the time the town was reenacted by state law as Magnolia, the streets were lined with shady, umbrella-like elm trees. Later, a disease ravaged the elm trees and, as they died, residents replaced many of them with magnolia trees, which became seen in abundance."

Through the years, the word "magnolia" has become disassociated with the beautiful bride of 1857 and replaced with the popular southern magnolia tree, native from North Carolina to Mississippi. These trees are held in high esteem in some southern states where they have the proud distinction of being the state flower or state tree. Its dark green, wax-like leaves and its shapely nectarous white blossoms always seem to bespeak love and romance. Today, silk magnolia flowers are seen gracing homes in all parts of the United States. Their unusual blossoms are also widely used as subjects by artists.

So, it was among these snow-white magnolia blossoms which speak of love and romance that Mack Whaley and Genett Thomas, my Mother and Daddy, sealed their vows of commitment to each other. Their lives together wouldn't be without many struggles, though, because they faced poverty and all the hardships of a rural economy still very much in its earliest adolescence.

In 1912 to 1917, after Daddy and Mother married and lived in Magnolia, there was little social life in the town except the great train excursions to Wilmington and its beaches, fifty-five miles to the southeast. Ordinary residents, as well as the more affluent ones, saved their money for these excursions.

Daddy didn't have much opportunity to leave his livery stable duties to go on the train trips. My parents only went once. But on the weekends, Daddy and Mother often walked the two blocks from their little home to be a part of the large crowds assembling at the train station to see the travelers off to Wilmington and to welcome them back home.

The magnificent pre-Civil War, seventeen-room wooden structure which had served as a boys private school had been moved next to the depot on Railroad Street where it had become the home of John R. Croom, Magnolia's most wealthy and outstanding citizen. At its new location, this historic building could be admired by the railroad passengers who, as they came through Magnolia, would be roused to ooh and aah at its magnificence. (This building has been abandoned for many years and stands as a monument to a glorious bygone past. It has now been purchased by an out-of-state couple who say they plan to restore it to its original elegance.)

Aside from the social activity at the train depot, opportunities to socialize with others centered around traditional institutions like churches and schools. The Missionary Baptist Church, organized in 1835, housed the largest congregation in Magnolia and had the finest building.

When I was born there in 1915, there was a well-designed brick public school building with an auditorium. It had just been completed in 1914 and was first used in January 1915.

The three saloons in Magnolia, which had existed prior to North Carolina enacting alcohol prohibition in 1909, had been replaced by at least a dozen bootleggers who, under cover, delivered alcohol to the four hotels, the livery stables, blacksmith shops, barber shops, flower bulb warehouses, and anywhere else men frequented. It was generally known that one bulb warehouse used part of its storage space for making bootleg whisky. However, the other large bulb warehouses provided play areas for children during their out-of-season times when bulbs were not being stored.

This was also the period in United States history when the burgeoning railroad system affected population growth. Residents living in towns and cities which were not on waterways where they could ship their products had to grow up around the railroads in order to engage in commerce. There was no freight movement at all by trucks and tractor-trailers in the early 1900s.

The pre-Depression and Depression years ahead of Daddy and Mother would test their best intentions and serve as tremendous challenges for the whole family as they would leave their beloved Magnolia and launch out into sharecropping.

But like the magnolias which had risen from the ashes of the disease-ravaged elms when Stricklandsville was reenacted as Magnolia, Daddy and Mother would find a way to rise above the paltry wages and rural poverty which overshadowed them as the curtain rises on the second decade in the twentieth century.

Milton and Chrysthine

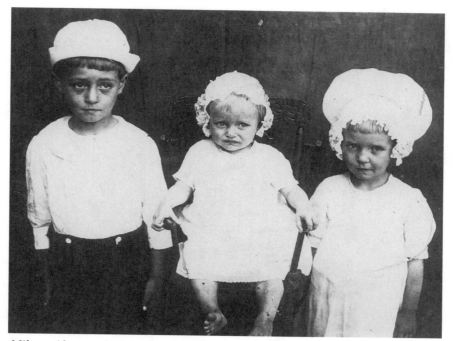

Milton, Alma and Chrysthine wearing clothes made by Genett. Alma was sick with malaria the day the roving photographer came by.

Sketch of a typical turpentine still in use during the 1915 era in the Magnolia-Chinquapin area.

A sketch of the wooden quart cups and 32-quart wooden crates manufactured at Magnolia and used for shipping strawberries on the train and for selling them at the local markets.

Part Two

1917-1921
Chinquapin

1917

The Landen Farm

By the fall of 1917, Daddy had saved enough money to buy a used farm wagon, a mule, and some secondhand plows. He packed his pregnant wife, Milton, me, and all our belongings into his wagon. On the Monday after Thanksgiving we drove the nineteen miles over the deeply rutted, poorly kept roads to the little unpainted sharecrop house on the Dr. J. F. Landen farm. It was located a mile from the unincorporated village of Chinquapin and less than a half mile from the Northeast Cape Fear River. It was at the intersection of what is now Highways N.C. 41 and N.C. 50.

As we moved from Magnolia and settled on the Landen Farm, Daddy and Mother were excited about the prospect of a better life for their growing family. Daddy knew he would miss the kindly and protective Mr. Fred Pickett who had been his only father figure since he was just a little boy. He knew, too, he would greatly miss the horses and mules at the livery stables. They had been such an important part of his life and he loved them. He would miss his daily contact with his mother, Lucy Whaley, who had stayed at Magnolia with his brother, Dave, and his family. Mother would miss her parents, too, but she was glad to make the change for the prospect of a better future for the family.

Milton and I were really excited at having a big yard where we could play tag, hopscotch, hide-and-seek, ring around the roses, jump rope, and just be free to run without the restraining limits we had known in our little Magnolia yard. Daddy made us two swings by tying a rope to a tree limb and using small scrap boards for the seats. Milton and I pushed each other in our swings. But what a treat it was when Mother or Daddy pushed us because then we could swing higher.

It was at the Landen farm that I first remember the nightly family devotions during which Mother read from the Bible and prayed for all of us. Then she would play hymns on her used pump organ that she had bought really cheap by making wooden strawberry quart cups after her family had moved to Magnolia. Daddy would play his "juice" harp along with Mother's organ and we would sing along with them. Both played by ear.

On 2 March 1918, Dr. Landen came to our house to deliver Alma. She was a frail six pounds and unhealthy from her start. She was especially susceptible to the malaria that came from the mosquitos which infested areas around the river which ran between our house and Chinquapin. There had never been any river drainage; therefore the mosquitoes were a plague on the area. Since this was before the days of antibiotics, Dr. Landen used Groves Tasteless

Chill Tonic for treating the chills and fevers which came with malaria. All of us contracted malaria at some point, but Alma was sick most often. The malaria problems would eventually be the reason for our family leaving Chinquapin five years later.

One day at the Landen farm, Milton and I had been climbing up on an empty nail keg and jumping off when I landed on my right wrist and broke it. Dr. Landen came, jerked it back into place, applied a wooden splint and a bandage, and gave me a dime because I didn't cry. He was a very kindly gentleman and did not charge for the visit because we were sharecroppers on his farm.

Growing tobacco became the center of our farm life. Growing this crop back before there had been research and studies on tobacco was a laborious, tedious, and time-consuming operation from the time the plant seed beds were prepared in December until the last golden leaf was graded, tied, and prepared for market at Wallace twelve miles away the last of November. There were no chemicals to kill grass and weeds or worms and suckers. Every step in the planting, cultivation, and harvesting was done exactly as it was when the first settlers came to this country. But Daddy persevered and Mother helped, while Milton and I looked after Alma.

When the Wallace tobacco warehouse owner first inspected Daddy's tobacco, he declared that it was among the finest he had ever seen. Daddy's reputation for growing and marketing quality tobacco was established that first year.

The possibility of growing cotton was out of the question at the Landen farm because there was not room in the farm pack house to store the picked cotton until it could be taken to the cotton gin. The pack house would barely store the cured tobacco until it could be prepared for the auction market.

At the Landen farm in the fall of 1918, Daddy experienced his first luxury of going hunting in the woods, where he killed his first squirrels and his first wild turkey. From that day on, his family looked forward to his hunting and the cornmeal dumplings that would be enhanced by the taste of the boiled squirrels he shot in the woods. Mother also learned to prepare a delicacy from the squirrel meat rolled in flour and fried.

When Daddy was fortunate enough to shoot a wild turkey, he would twist its head off, let it bleed and then take it home where he doused it in hot water, defeathered it, took out the insides, and gave it to Mother to prepare for roasting for a family feast. Back then, fresh meat had to be cooked the same day it was killed because we had no ice or refrigeration.

Milton turned six in April 1920, and when school opened that fall he was ready to enter the public school at the Little Cavenaugh one-room schoolhouse about a mile down the road from us toward the town of Wallace. School opened the last of September. I was not old enough to start school, but Mother and Daddy thought it would be safer for two of us to walk to school together than for Milton to walk alone. I was very eager to go with him to school because we had been inseparable. Daddy contacted the teacher and she said that the school had some empty seats. If I would be quiet and not disturb the other children, she would let me attend, though I was not yet old enough. She said the rule about appropriate school age was not a law, but just a policy at that time.

Quiet I was, listening carefully and meditating on everything I saw and heard. In the classroom, there were a few children from each of seven grades.

I took my turn sweeping the floors and dusting furniture, just as Milton took his turn bringing in firewood for the old wood-burning heater. We had no idea that this experience would give me such a jump-start on learning when added to the reading and writing Mother had been teaching at home. Mother only went through the fourth grade, but she had continued reading everything she could get her hands on. She especially read the Bible regularly.

1920

Living One Year in the Center of Chinquapin

In December 1920, after Milton and I had entered the Little Cavenaugh school, we moved to the center of Chinquapin in order to live in a larger house. There simply wasn't enough room in the Landen house. Our new house had a big room for us to play in and another big room where we could store harvested cotton.

School Experiences

Our first chore upon arriving in the village of Chinquapin was for Daddy to take Milton and me in the farm wagon to the large Chinquapin school to get us enrolled. The petite Chinquapin first grade teacher, Miss Daisey Burnham from Warsaw, told Daddy that I was too young to stay in the first grade, having just turned five in October. But she agreed that since I had already been attending the Little Cavenaugh school, she would let me stay on in the first grade because the school was very short on students. So the arrangement was approved, provided my parents and I understood that they would allow me to repeat the first grade the next year.

I soaked up everything that was going on in the first grade for the rest of that school year. By repeating the first grade the following year, I was able to help Miss Daisey tutor the other children in reading and learning numbers. This early learning gave me such a good foundation that all the way through school I made top grades and was able and willing to help tutor students. I always thought this foundation helped me to meet the demands of life even after I graduated high school at the bottom of the Depression in 1932.

As soon as we moved into the village of Chinquapin, pretty fourteen-year-old Isabelle Wood next door began coming to our house on Sunday mornings to walk Milton and me to the Shiloh Baptist Church for Sunday school and worship services. Everything we saw and heard at church fascinated us. "Jesus Loves Me" was a new song for us. When we sang it in Sunday school, it seemed to be meant just for us. We couldn't help singing it on the way home and singing it for our parents after we returned home. Soon Mother was playing it on her organ for us to sing.

I remember Isabelle holding our hands as we walked and how she would pick me up on her hip to carry me around any mud holes in our path as we walked to church. These are some of my most poignant memories. She and her daughter, Eva, and I have reminisced about this throughout the years. It was the beginning of lifelong experiences of people caring for me. I marvel at how, from that time forward, so many of my memories have been involved with people helping me and my family in the most meaningful ways.

The Flu Epidemic

It was at our house in Chinquapin where every member of our family but me had influenza. One of my most indelible memories is walking to the edge of our front porch and picking up pans of food covered with dishtowels. The food had been brought to our family by caring neighbors who were afraid to come into our house for fear of catching the flu. We would eat the food and I would return the empty pans to the edge of the porch.

Except for Mother, all of our family completely recovered from this bout with influenza. She was left weak and sickly, often having colds and many attacks of pneumonia. She kept a recurring cough throughout her life. The flu had left her with a disease called bronchiectasis. Much later on, after World War II, doctors told us that there had been no experience with lung surgery until World War II when shrapnel had to be removed from wounded men. They told us that had anything been known about lung surgery after Mother had the flu, it would have been possible for the edges of her lungs to have been removed and she would never have suffered so much.

The Turkey Shoot

In spite of our worry over Mother, we had happy times.

In 1920, the Sunday just before Thanksgiving, there was a turkey shoot at a vacant field near our house. We heard the rifles go "tacrang, carong, carong, tacrang." We smelled the gunpowder that was fired as it penetrated the cool, crisp air. A few days after the turkey shoot, a young soldier named Lloyd Thigpen, who lived near us and who had served in Europe during World War I, had been discharged from the army and had come home to stay. Our friends and neighbors welcomed him and talked about his participation in the war. Milton and I didn't really understand what it meant for Lloyd to have participated in a war. We could detect from adult conversations that a lot of shootings of guns had been involved where he had been. In our little minds, we decided he must have been off participating in turkey shoots like we had heard in the field near our house.

Fun in the Cotton Storage Room

One big room in our house was used to store the harvested cotton until Daddy could get an opening at the local gin to have it processed. During its storage in our house, Milton and I had fun pretending that it was snow and had "snow fights" throwing cotton and rolling one another in it. One day we almost covered little Alma with too much cotton and Mother would not let us play in the cotton any more for fear we might get stifled.

1921

The Lude Quinn Farm

In the fall of 1921, while I was repeating the first grade in Miss Daisey Burnham's classroom at the big Chinquapin school, Daddy thought the family would be better off if we moved further away from the river with its continuing mosquitoes, chills, and fevers, to a still better house on the Lude Quinn farm. That farm was out from Chinquapin toward Beulaville. We were a lot more comfortable there. Of course, none of our houses had running water and all three of our pitcher hand water pumps had been located in the yard outside our houses. All of the houses had outdoor toilets.

While living at the Quinn farm, we would still attend the big Chinquapin school. We were close enough to the schoolhouse that we could walk unless there was rain. In that case, Daddy would take us in the wagon. We had to walk by the train station where the train would many times be parked across the highway and delay us while longleaf pine logs were being loaded at the station.

One day we became impatient. We stuck our heads under the loaded log cars to crawl under them to the other side. Without warning, the train gave a jerk. We quickly pulled our heads back just in the nick of time to avoid being hurt or killed.

On 2 January, after we moved to the Quinn farm in the fall, Daddy awakened us early in the morning, helped us get dressed quickly and took us next door to the home of Mary and Joy Wood. Now we just loved to go there because they had no children and they petted us. But we thought it strange that Daddy helped us get dressed and took us so early while Mother stayed in their bedroom and didn't help. That was just not like her.

We were keeping our eyes on our house and we saw Dr. J. F. Landen enter with his big black satchel. We had been told that doctors and midwives brought babies in black bags, so we decided we must be getting a new baby. We became concerned that a new baby in that black bag might have trouble breathing but when we were finally allowed to go home, what a relief to see that our new baby brother, Rdell, was just fine.

It was while we lived at this house that I got on the train at Chinquapin with Mother, Daddy, and my baby brother and rode through Beulaville and through Pink Hill to Parrott's Hospital thirty-six miles away in Kinston to have my tonsils and adenoids removed. I had assumed Mother and Daddy would be spending the night in the hospital with me. I will never forget the utter desolation and loneliness that I endured the whole night long when I faced the reality that my parents and Rdell would be required to spend the night at a boarding house across the street from the hospital while I awaited my morning surgery.

Another time during that year, Daddy took the family in our wagon to Beulaville, seven miles away, to visit my widowed Aunt Nora Smith and her five children. We loved to go there. My parents had promised they would leave me at Aunt Nora's for the coming week and so they did.

When Daddy came alone in his wagon to take me home at the end of the week, there was torrential rain all day long. On the way back to Chinquapin, when we came to Muddy Creek, we saw that the swift flowing water in the creek had washed out the wooden bridge. We could see parts of the bridge lodged against the creek shoreline where they had floated downstream.

A man at the creek told us the bridge would not be replaced until the following day. There was no way we could drive through the stream to the other side. There was no alternative except to go back to Beulaville to spend the night at Aunt Nora's and return to Chinquapin the next day. There was no phone system in our area and we had no means of contacting Mother and the three children at home. What a miserable night we had and how glad we were to get home the next day!

This was during the era when each county was responsible for the building and maintenance of its roads and bridges. Since 1868 in North Carolina, the county boards of commissioners had the authority to appoint a man in each locale within the county to be responsible for road and bridge maintenance. The man we talked to at the Muddy Creek bridge site had the responsibility of quickly getting a new wooden bridge built.

It was not until 1929 that North Carolina's State Legislature became the first one in the United States to pass an act enabling the establishment of a statewide system of highways. But the minutes of the Duplin County commissioners reflect that actually the statewide system was not put into effect in Duplin County until 30 June 1931.

Automobile travel was increasing as the early 1900s ended and the 1920s began. This brought increased demand for better roads. Duplin County borrowed large sums of money to build roads and bridges. When I became register of deeds and clerk to the county board of commissioners in 1952 and for several years thereafter, Duplin County was still reborrowing most of this road and bridge building money it had borrowed during the 1920s instead of paying as the debts came due. It was felt by our county commissioners that this had to be done in order to provide enough funds in current county budgets to cover current county expenses. This re-borrowing was the same plan that was being used to pay off the debts made by the county in the 1920s when the new consolidated brick schools were built. It was called "refunding."

During the 1921-22 school year when we were at the Quinn farm, tobacco sales had been extra good and while in Wallace at the tobacco warehouse, Daddy had found a good used two-seater family horse-drawn buggy. There wasn't a top on it, but we were all excited about the prospect of not having to sit on a quilt spread out in the back of our old farm wagon.

Aunt Ruth's and Uncle Will's Vendue

Nineteen twenty-two was the year Mother's oldest sister, Ruth, and her husband, Will Gresham, who were considered to be very well off, had a widely publicized vendue at their farm and home near Muddy Creek, between Chinquapin and Beulaville. (A vendue is a public auction). They sold almost everything they owned, including the farm, furniture, horses and mules, and farm tools. They packed their family into their big Chrysler touring car and set out for a new life in Decatur, Alabama.

The vendue was advertised on signs for about a month all around Chinquapin and Beulaville. When the big day finally came, we were beside ourselves with excitement because this was our first vendue. There was a band, pig barbecue, and a hot dog stand. There was a block of ice. A man stayed busy shaving ice into glasses and pouring tea, lemonade, or canned pineapple juice over the ice. Hundreds of people came from miles around.

Among Aunt Ruth's possessions, she had found two tall sterling silver iced tea spoons and since she did not have a full set to sell, she gave these to my cousin, Norman Smith, and me. We thought we were rich! Mine remained among my treasures for a long time until after I was married and it was among the things I lost in a house fire.

Aunt Ruth's folks had decided to seek their future in the good road building opportunities booming in Alabama. Uncle Will was industrious and knew how to effectively apply his talents and attention to the new career of asphalt road building that was catching on in Alabama where he prospered greatly.

The Gresham family had made the decision to move away because their oldest daughter, Gincy, who was the same age as my mother, had married a man who was very abusive. Because of the continued treatment inflicted upon her, Gincy and the child born of this marriage had moved back home with her parents, but the husband persisted in harassing them. Their move proved to be a wise one and Gincy's son grew to be a fine young man. He gave his life for his country in World War II.

The Greshams usually made annual trips back to North Carolina later after we had moved to the Hines farm near Kenansville. Their visits to see us were always special occasions. They enjoyed our homegrown food. When they were at our house, we slept on quilts on the floor in Mother's and Daddy's bedroom and let the Greshams have our two bedrooms. Correspondence has always been carried on between the families. The Gresham grandchildren still visit and write.

Chrysthine

Five years ago, I rode with a friend to Decatur, Alabama, to visit a Pink Hill neighbor who had moved there. While in Decatur I called two of Aunt Ruth's grandchildren. Even over the phone we slipped right into laughing over recollections of past visits and I wished I had been driving my own car to Alabama so I could have visited them in person.

A Vice-President's Son Visits Chinquapin

From the Book *Men and Decisions*

The book, *Men and Decisions*, by Lewis L. Strauss, is very fascinating. It is part memoir and part history of the United States during the first fifty years of the twentieth century. It was loaned to me by Hardy Parker, Jr., who was born in Chinquapin in 1948, a grandson of G. B. D. Parker.

Not only did Strauss direct the Atomic Energy Commission under Presidents Truman and Eisenhower, but he served as advisor to Presidents Hoover and Roosevelt as well as to Truman and Eisenhower. He was associated with towering figures in science, politics, diplomacy, and business, including Einstein, Baruch, Forrestal, Taft, and many others.

On the first two pages of his book, Strauss tells how from age sixteen until twenty, he was a traveling salesman, called a "drummer" back then. He sold shoes at wholesale to merchants in the Carolinas, Georgia, and West Virginia. He tells how, when calling on a merchant for the first time, he started out by introducing himself as the son of the vice-president and then he would say that he would like to show his fine line of shoes.

Strauss writes that it never occurred to him how this must have sounded, until one occasion when he had driven many miles from Magnolia in a two-horse rented hack over the sandy roads east of the Atlantic Coast Line Railroad to see a storekeeper in a little unincorporated village called Chinquapin. He states the man ran a big store, the only one for miles around.

Strauss describes how, when he opened with his introduction, the merchant looked at him and replied, "Well, sir, I must say that this is a great honor. Imagine it, you, the son of an honest-to-goodness vice-president, coming all the way back into the sticks to see common people like us!" The merchant then called to his clerks, "Come on up here! Come on up here and meet a big man from Richmond."

Strauss wrote: "By this time, like Alice in Wonderland, I had shrunk to about two inches, and must have shown it. He pulled my leg a little more and then said, 'Well, son, I can see you are a new one. Show me your samples.'"

Lewis L. Strauss would gradually learn that the seemingly blunt sarcasm and dry fried humor that this merchant displayed on Strauss' first visit were his trademarks and that he was actually friendly inside, but just firm. Strauss relates how the merchant bought a sizable order and was a loyal customer for as long as he traveled and a friend as long as the merchant lived.

Then he writes: "His name was G. B. D. Parker."

The
G. B. D. Parker Family
at Chinquapin

During my official first grade at the big Chinquapin school in the 1921-22 school year, there was a teacher named Miss Mary Belle Royal. We loved to watch fifty-eight-year-old bachelor G. B. D. Parker bring Miss Royal to school in the mornings. He would walk around his boxy looking Ford Coupe to her door and open it to let her out. He was always there in the afternoons when school let out, waiting to take Miss Royal to Dr. Landen's house where she boarded and roomed. She was from Salemburg in adjoining Sampson County. This was our first experience observing a courting couple and we were impressed by all of Mr. Parker's attention to Miss Royal.

Milton and I walked to school the mile from the Lude Quinn farm, past the G. B. D. Parker mansion, some other homes, and the railroad station. We enjoyed watching this, our first romance, bloom and develop into what local people called a very surprising conclusion after Mr. Parker's long bachelorhood.

The Duplin County marriage license shows that on "8 April 1922, G. B. D. Parker, age 59, of Duplin County, married Mary Belle Royal, age 33, of Sampson County, at the home of Dr. Landen." Reverend W. P. M. Currie, Presbyterian Minister, signed the marriage license as Officiating Officer. Three witnesses who signed the license were Grover C. Quinn, W. C. Hodgin and Gardner Edwards, Mr. Parker's trusted store bookkeeper from 1914 to 1931.

G. B. D. Parker's big general store sold almost everything the folks in the Chinquapin area needed. It was the hub of Chinquapin about which everything else seemed to revolve when we lived in that area from 1917 to 1922.

One corner of the store served as the Chinquapin Post Office. Justice of the Peace court was held once a month in the store. The late Joshua James, Superior Court Judge, often said that he first became interested in the law as a small boy observing the court held in Parker's store.

Parker's store was the only place most area people ever shopped. It was here that I first saw women's high-top button shoes on a trip to the store with Daddy. I wished my mother had some, but she wore shoes that were only ankle high.

All kinds of staple groceries were available. Parker's customers knew that he killed a beef to sell in the store every Friday. It was whispered around that whatever part of the beef didn't sell was the part Mr. Parker had cooked at his house. There was no refrigeration, so all fresh beef had to be sold in one day. Each family had their own cured pork and their own live chickens, which walked around in their yards.

There was a livery stable adjacent to the store where carriages and buggies were sold. Later, Mr. Parker sold some Ford cars.

The Great Depression Affected Parker's Customers and then Affected Him, Too

As the Great Depression escalated, farm prices went down during the late twenties and early thirties. Farmers could not pay their accounts to Parker's store. He foreclosed on more than one hundred farmers who lost their land, crops, farm implements, all their possessions, their spirits, and their hopes. Some lost one hundred to four hundred acre farms with nice homes for such debts as six hundred to one thousand dollars.

Most of these foreclosed farmers were left penniless. Many stayed on their once-owned farms and became sharecroppers. Some sought out employment at the few lumber mills left from the days of the harvest of the longleaf pines. Some found work on the highway, and some remained on the farms and became laborers for Mr. Parker.

At one time, the Parker estate owned 33,000 acres of land, a hotel at Wallace, and part interest with A. R. (Sonny) Bland, Sr., in a general merchandise store and livery stable at Rose Hill.

Then came the time when Mr. Parker could not pay his own fertilizer accounts and his debts to other suppliers, because his customers could not pay him. Because of low prices, he could not make any profit from crop sales on the lands he had acquired by foreclosures. He amassed a debt of over one hundred thousand dollars that he could not pay and had to go into receivership. L. R. Hagood from Columbia South Carolina was hired as receiver and farm manager.

Mr. Parker died in 1932 at age sixty-nine after only ten years of marriage. Mrs. Parker later moved to Raleigh where their three children attended college and married.

When the receivership was finally settled, Mr. Parker's family was left with 15,000 acres of rich farmland at forty-two different locations to divide among his three children.

G. B. D. Parker Shot

Stories about G. B. D. Parker and his family have remained fascinating topics of conversation for the people of the Chinquapin area throughout the years. They love to tell how Mr. Parker worked long hours all of his life. The story goes that his long working hours started back when he worked as a boy at the store his father, Buckner Parker, founded in 1830 about a mile from where G. B. D.'s store stood. Buckner died in 1879.

G. B. D.'s habit of going to work early continued throughout his lifetime. One morning when he was walking the short distance from his home to his store, about four o'clock, he saw a young, neighboring ex-serviceman squirrel hunting on his property. Parker asked the hunter not to shoot on his property ever again.

Soon, G. B. D. was again walking to work in the pre-dawn hours on a below-freezing morning, all bundled up in his hat and scarf, double-breasted cowhide overcoat, and cowhide gloves.

A shot rang out from the small caliber pistol of the same young man Parker had ordered not to shoot in his woods. The bullet hit the Chinquapin merchant in his chest and he fell to the ground. A neighbor heard the shot, found that Parker had been struck, and galloped his horse, pulling a buggy, to get Dr. Landen.

Dr. Landen's outside car crank would not start the motor, which was often the case with the early automobiles on a freezing morning. The doctor jumped into the buggy and rode with the man to the scene of the shooting.

To their amazement, they found G. B. D. Parker sitting up where he had fallen when he was shot. He was stunned, but otherwise unhurt. The bullet had not penetrated the double-breasted layers of his heavy cowhide leather coat.

The community was glad Parker had escaped serious injury, but all were shocked by what had taken place and saddened about the tragic aftermath: The young man who shot him had run deep into the woods and had immediately committed suicide by shooting himself. The story handed down through the years is that the young man had been suffering anxiety attacks.

Hardy Parker, Jr., tells how he owns the pair of cowhide gloves that his grandfather, G. B. D. Parker, was wearing that tragic morning.

Hardy Parker, Jr.'s Chinquapin Office

A Trip Back to the Days of the Long Leaf Pine

A visit to Hardy Parker, Jr.'s office takes a guest back in time to the important period in the history of Eastern North Carolina after the turn of the last century when the density of longleaf pines was the state's trademark. The harvesting of longleaf pine materials was the main industry for many years. The longleaf pine has always played a great role in the history and symbolism for the entire state.

As late as 1957 when our State Legislature adopted our State Toast, the legislators agreed on the one composed in 1904 by Lenora Martin and Mary Burke Kerr. It speaks to the romance and importance of the longleaf pines in the history of our great state.

The State Toast

Here's to the land of the long leaf pine,
The summer land where the sun doth shine,
Where the weak grow strong and the strong grow great,
Here's to "Down Home," the Old North State!

Here's to the land of the cotton bloom white,
Where the scuppernong perfumes the breeze at night,
Where the soft southern moss and jessamine mate,
'Neath the murmuring pines of the Old North State!

Here's to the land where the galax grows,
Where the rhododendron's rosette glows,
Where soars Mount Mitchell's summit great,
In the "Land of the Sky," in the Old North State!

Here's to the land where maidens are fair,
Where friends are true and cold hearts rare,
The near land, the dear land whatever fate,
The blest land, the best land, the Old North State!

It is significant that through the years and to this day, the highest honor that a North Carolina governor can bestow on an individual is the Order of the Longleaf Pine, which states:

In REPOSING SPECIAL CONFIDENCE IN THE INTEGRITY AND ZEAL of the individual is to confer THE ORDER OF THE LONGLEAF PINE with the rank of Ambassador Extraordinary privileged to enjoy all rights granted to members of this exalted order, among which is the special privilege to propose the following North Carolina Toast in select company anywhere in the free world:

> *Here's to the land of the longleaf pine,*
> *The summer land where the sun doth shine,*
> *Where the weak grow strong and the strong grow great,*
> *Here's to "Down Home" the Old North State!*

Colorful certificates conferring this honor bear the Great Seal of the State of North Carolina and the personal signature of the governor. Individuals who receive this honor usually frame their certificate and consider it to be among their treasures.

Hardy's office sits across the highway from the long-abandoned general store of his grandfather, G. B. D. Parker. It was built above a large pad of rosin left from one of the three early turpentine stills in Chinquapin when the gathering, distillation, and selling of tar, pitch, and turpentine were the main activities in the Chinquapin area back when the great forests of longleaf pines thrived in Duplin County.

Against the wall in front of Hardy, Jr.'s desk stands a carefully preserved five-foot portion of a longleaf pine tree, which expertly shows how turpentine was gathered. The aged cuts show signs of how the turpentine drained to the bottom of the tree's cuts into what was known as "the box."

The "boxes" were cut in the longleaf pines every spring to catch the turpentine as it drained. They were slanted in such a manner as to direct the drippings to the center of the "box." Collections were made several times during spring, summer, and fall. This was sticky business.

The raw turpentine was cooked in a tremendous boiler. The steam from the boiling turpentine entered a long, curved pipe called a "worm." As the steam cooled down, it changed into liquid turpentine to be sold for use in such medicines as Vick's VapoRub and for many other purposes.

The rosin deposits left in the boiler had some uses, too, such as to be rubbed on ropes and fiddle strings to make them slick and pliable.

In Hardy, Jr.'s office, an antique metal container hangs above the tree portion. It holds some rosin pieces the size of baseballs. The balls, hardened by long years of time, look more like golden marble. Samples of the official tools of the turpentine trade either lean against the tree portion or stand against the wall by it. The tools are no longer sticky with turpentine, but are clean and polished.

Hardy, Jr., has evolved not only as the historian of the Parker family but he is a student of all aspects of the history of the Chinquapin area and eastern North Carolina. He loves to explain about the period when the great forests of longleaf pines were so plentiful that some wealthy gentlemen owners, who had acquired their land grants from the State of North Carolina, leased trees for fees to poor, uneducated turpentine farmers who "farmed" the trees.

This was hard, muscle-straining labor, which produced little profit for the turpentine farmers, but provided good incomes for the landowners.

After the building of the railroad from Wilmington to Weldon in 1840, rosin, tar, pitch, and turpentine from the Chinquapin area were hauled to Magnolia for shipping.

Then came the massive timber cutting days and the network of small logging railroads which were built with their rails closer together than standard rails. Small train engines ran on these tracks to transport the logs to the great numbers of small sawmills which dotted the countryside. These small trains were called "trams."

Later, during the heyday of the small sawmills, a railroad was built from Chinquapin to Beulaville to Pink Hill and on to Kinston. It was used mostly for shipping logs and longleaf pine materials but during a few years it also carried passengers.

It was on one of these train cars that I rode with my parents when I was five years old from Chinquapin through Beulaville and Pink Hill on to Kinston for my tonsils and adenoids to be removed at Parrott's hospital.

As the longleaf pines were cut from a location, the sawmill and the small logging railroad with its little train engine would be moved to a new location. One of these small trams ran from N.C. Highway 11 near the present B. F. Grady Elementary School by Scott's Store on to Mt. Olive. This old train bed is now Secondary Highway 1500 and is officially named The Tram Road. D. L. Scott, Jr. remembers his Grandfather Scott telling him about serving as the engineer on this Tram Train.

The longleaf pine stumps were dynamited and burned, and small farms were hewed out of the land where the pine trees had been cut. Many of the small farms were purchased from people who had obtained land grants before the pines were cut. The new purchasers became farmers. Today these small farms are gone and their memory is fast fading, lost forever to the computer age, technical farming, and contract growing of crops and raising animals.

Hardy Parker, Jr. was born at Chinquapin in 1948. He lives with his family at Wrightsville Beach in New Hanover County where his parents moved when he was a toddler. He fondly remembers, as a boy, leaving his family to spend the summers with his Grandmother Parker at Chinquapin.

As soon as he was old enough, his Grandmother allowed him to drive a Farmall Cub tractor to get cropped tobacco leaves out of her fields. He and his little Farmall Cub also helped fill two corn silos with cut, green corn stalks several summers.

His family still own 2,700 acres of farmlands at Chinquapin and he maintains his farm office there.

Large, handsome portraits of his father, Hardy, and his grandfather, G. B. D. Parker hang on his office walls along with a picture of G. B. D. and several other people made in 1920 on the front porch of his then thriving general store.

Hardy, Jr. has a lovely teenage daughter, Ellie, who has caught his love for Chinquapin and its history. She often comes with him to his office during the summer.

Chinquapin Son Invented Pepsi-Cola

When we lived in Chinquapin from 1917 to 1922, one of Daddy's best friends was Vann Bradham. He had a son, Killis Bradham, with whom we played. Vann was from the same family as the famous Caleb Bradham who had invented Pepsi-Cola in 1898.

In preparation for the 100th Anniversary of Caleb Bradham registering his Pepsi-Cola drink with the State of North Carolina on 28 August 1898, Leon H. Sikes, who is evolving as Duplin County's historian, wrote the following article. It appeared in the August 1997 issue of *Footnotes*, the official publication of the Duplin County Historical Society. This article is reproduced here by permission of Leon H. Sikes.

From Chinquapin to Fame

Far from the crowds in the southeastern corner of Duplin County, the small community of Chinquapin has existed quietly for generations. Situated on the east side of the Northeast Cape Fear River, Chinquapin had its start in the early to middle 1800s as shipping point on the river for the naval stores industry—tar, pitch, rosin and turpentine, the products of the longleaf pine. The word chinquapin is of Algonquin Indian origin, and is the name of a shrub-like tree in the beech family.

In the flow of history, Chinquapin has neither a long nor unusually exciting history, but it does indeed have a claim to fame. Records show that Chinquapin had a general store as early as 1849. The first post office opened its door on 21 February 1850. However, its mark in history was made by a native son years later.

On 27 May 1867, a son was born to one of the community's early families, George Washington and Julia McCann Bradham. They named their firstborn Caleb Davis Bradham.

A man of many talents, George W. Bradham lived, worked and with his wife, Julia, raised their family in Chinquapin. In addition to being a farmer, he owned and operated a retail grocery and ran a turpentine still near the river's edge. Caleb grew up in the small, close community, no doubt helping his father in the store, learning and experiencing life. But destiny would take Caleb away from his roots in Chinquapin and on to fame.

In 1886, at age nineteen, Caleb entered the University of North Carolina. A desire to attend medical school prompted him to leave UNC after three years to enter the University of

Maryland medical school. Financial problems back home made it necessary for him to leave medical school in 1891 after only two years. He soon found a teaching position in New Bern.

In 1893, a pharmacy was up for sale at the corner of Middle and Pollock St. in New Bern. Without hesitation, Caleb seized the opportunity to put some of his medical school pharmacy training in practice. He purchased the drugstore and on the front window in large letters Bradham's Pharmacy was painted. He was in business.

Mixing syrups and flavorings were a daily part of a pharmacist's life and Bradham loved to experiment with different flavor mixtures. From behind the curtains in the back room of the pharmacy one particular mixture was a real hit with the drugstore crowd. They named it "Brad's Drink." It was such a good mixture that he registered it with the state on August 28, 1898, under a new name that was soon to become a household word. When accepted and registered by the U.S. Patent Office on 16 June 1903, the young man from Chinquapin had officially created Pepsi Cola for the world.

The Whaley Family Leaves Chinquapin

    Living at the Lude Quinn sharecrop farm had not solved the problems of mosquitoes, malaria, chills, and fevers. The use of Groves Tasteless Chill Tonic escalated as the number of children had grown to four. Our parents decided the only solution was to move away from the river area. The Hines sharecrop farm near Kenansville on N.C. Highway 24 was vacant. Daddy and Mother decided we would try our fortune there. So, in December 1922, we made our move to the Hines farm with great expectations!

    A neighbor used his horse to pull our wagon, which was piled high with our furniture and belongings. He drove along with us to the Hines farm, twelve miles away. We enjoyed the luxury of our buggy and gleefully talked about a new life away from the river, most particularly that there would be no more Groves Tasteless Chill Tonic!

Exhibit of portion of a long leaf pine tree showing box and tools used for collecting turpentine. Now in the office of Hardy Parker, Jr. at Chinquapin.

Billy Wood of Warsaw with scale model made by his late father of the small steam trains used in eastern North Carolina during the 1915 era to haul long leaf pine logs from the forests to the main railroads.

Above: A 1997 view of the abandoned G. B. D. Parker store complex at Chinquapin.

Left: Caleb D. Bradham who grew up at Chinquapin and invented Pepsi-Cola in 1898 at Newbern, N.C.

Above: This turn-of-the-century wagon delivered Pepsi to individual homes.

Left: First Pepsi-Cola delivery truck in the Carolinas—1908.

Part Three

1922-1937
The Hines Farm

1922

Kenansville-Warsaw Highway, North Carolina

At the Hines farm, dollars were scarce, but dreams were plentiful. We had the promise of no malaria, no Groves Tasteless Chill Tonic, big fields to work in, a big yard, and pine thickets to play in, Cooper's Mill Pond to fish and swim in, and a railroad about four hundred yards from the house where we could watch the train go by twice a day and walk on the rails and cross ties. What more could there be to enjoy?

The "L" shaped wooden frame house had been built facing the old Kenansville-Warsaw Highway and parallel to the railroad. The railroad was still in place, but the old road was abandoned and the new road ran behind our house and pack house. It was a dirt road when we moved there in 1922. But in 1929 the North Carolina State Legislature passed enabling laws to create the first statewide highway system in the United States. In 1930 the state paved the highway behind our house from Kenansville to Warsaw even though it did not take over our entire county road system until later.

Daddy's sharecrop arrangement at the Hines farm was the same as at Chinquapin. Mr. Hines would furnish the land, fertilizer, and seeds. Daddy would furnish tools, labor, the mules, horses, and other animals. The crop sales proceeds would be divided in half.

Our house at the Hines farm had four big rooms and two porches, but no closets, no bathroom, and no insulation. The walls and ceilings were unpainted tongue and groove ceiling boards. Mother's and Daddy's bedroom had a chimney with an open wood burning fireplace that provided the only heat in the house, except for the wood burning cookstove located in the combination kitchen and dining room.

Alma and I had an unheated bedroom, as did Milton and Rdell. Nails were driven into the walls. Our clothes were put on coat hangers and hung on these nails.

The outdoor toilet was near what had been the front porch of the house before the old road had been abandoned and the new road built behind the house. Now the pitcher hand water pump was in the front yard next to the front porch. What had been the front porch of the house was four feet high and we immediately spotted it. It would serve as a fine playhouse for us when it was raining.

A smokehouse for use in storing our cured meat was now situated in the front yard.

We had a four-legged iron skillet which was placed on the wood coals in the fireplace to keep warm water for our baths. We took our baths in a white enameled wash pan. A kettle of water always stayed on the cookstove.

Mother and Daddy had six clay bricks which were kept in front of the fireplace to be warmed on cold winter nights, wrapped in little blankets, and put to our feet as they tucked us into our feather beds for our prayers and good night kisses.

The Kenansville School

Our first assignment upon moving into the Hines house was for Daddy to take us to the one-room schoolhouse on Rutledge Street, where Miss Audrey Farrior from Rose Hill taught the first through third grades. She was a master teacher and Milton and I felt right at home, because the children were so friendly. Milton was in the third grade and I joined the second.

On the first day at the one-room school in Kenansville, the boys and girls in the second grade seemed eager to tell us about the wondrous spring of water near the courthouse in the center of Kenansville. They seemed to think new people needed to know all about the spring. The children said we had to go by and see it on our way home and just taste the water and see how it "just keeps on coming out of a hill through a pipe." When we started home after school, Milton and I detoured a block to go by this wonder of nature the students had felt so compelled to tell us about.

We couldn't believe what we were seeing! The water really was gently flowing through the pipe out of the hill with nothing pumping it! It just came calmly and regularly pouring out. When we got home, we excitedly told our parents about the water "that just keeps on coming out of the hill and never stops!" Daddy and Mother found our story hard to believe until they went to see this reported phenomenon for themselves. We returned there many times. Our schoolteachers took their classes to the spring for class picnics.

As I viewed this spring on my first day of school in Kenansville, I never dreamed that later on I would spend forty-four years and eight months of public service in buildings adjacent to this spring, or that I would eat many lunches at the tables under the shade trees surrounding the spring.

All Duplin County historical accounts relate how in 1784 when Duplin and Sampson Counties were divided into their present areas, the site for the Duplin County Courthouse was chosen solely because the ever-flowing spring was thought to be a perfect location for a county courthouse. For many years it was the only source of water for the people and their mules and horses which brought them to the county seat to attend to court affairs and other county business.

Kenansville—A Town with Great Interest in Education

As we settled down on the Hines farm, we found that we had moved close to a town where there had always been great interest manifested in education. An act of the 1785 North Carolina State Legislature had created Grove Academy for the education of youth in the Grove neighborhood of Duplin County. Though it was a public school, it was for boys only.

Parts of the 1909 bulletin advertising the Grove Academy gives the following description of the town of Kenansville. This description still fits the town and its people as we knew it in 1922 when we arrived at the Hines Farm:

> There is no village in North Carolina east of the mountains that compares in beauty and picturesqueness with Kenansville, the county seat of Duplin.
>
> Its trees are beautiful and symmetrical; its culture and refinement are not excelled anywhere.
>
> Unique in its records and rich in colonial history, the little town stands out pre-eminently as a place of interest and antiquity.

1922

Fifteen Years at the Grove Presbyterian Church in Kenansville

On our first Sunday at the Hines farm, our parents allowed eight-year-old Milton to drive our mule and buggy, with Alma and me, to Sunday school and church services in Kenansville. Mother and Daddy told us to stop at the first church as we came into town, regardless of what kind it was.

Milton proudly tied our mule and buggy to one of the many pine trees at the Grove Presbyterian Church, just inside Kenansville. This church was founded in 1736 and was the first Presbyterian congregation in North Carolina. The first Grove Presbyterian Church building was at Golden Grove just outside Kenansville. Colonel Owen R. Kenan donated land for a new Church building on 12 May 1857 on which the present Grove Church was erected.

The first thing that impressed us as we went inside the church was a marble plaque dedicated to Reverend James M. Sprunt, who had served as pastor from 1851 until his death in 1884. It looked so freshly completed, but we were later told that the pastor's wife had just recently used black paint to touch up the letters on the plaque.

This was the same James M. Sprunt who had been headmaster at James Sprunt Institute. He had also served as Duplin County Register of Deeds from 1865 to 1880 to supplement his income during the time when the Grove Church's congregation was small. The present James Sprunt Community College located in Kenansville is named for Reverend Sprunt, this most famous pioneer in religion and education in Duplin County.

We had arrived at Grove Presbyterian Church that first Sunday when Mr. Chauncey S. Carr was ringing the bell which hung in the belfry. We imagined that he was ringing the bell especially to welcome us. Mr. Carr had served his county as Register of Deeds from 1903 to 1906. He looked the image of a Southern gentleman and when he shook our little hands we did feel welcome.

As we entered the church Mr. R. V. Wells, our county's clerk of court, and his wife, Mrs. Laura Wells, greeted us. We thought "Mmm, this surely is a friendly place." Each time I entered this church for the next fifteen years, the same warm feeling came over me which I had experienced on that first day.

Mrs. Wells taught us in our primary Sunday school class. We would stop by her house some afternoons on our way home from school to recite our Sunday school memory work to her. When we had completed an assignment she would place a gold star the next Sunday on the 12" x 20" posters which stayed in our classroom at the church until we had finished the whole poster. Then we took the posters home and decorated our bedroom walls.

Mother taught us both the Presbyterian children's catechism and the older children's catechism. After we had recited them to her, we then stopped at Mrs. Wells' home and recited them again. After reciting the children's catechism, we were awarded a black leather New Testament with our name on it in gold. A full-size, black leather Bible with our name in gold was presented during a Sunday morning worship service following the recitation of the older children's catechism, which was actually named the shorter catechism.

It was in Mrs. Wells' Sunday school class, when I was nine years old, that I signed a "total abstinence" card, which she said meant that I would never touch alcohol. This vow, along with Mother's teachings, sealed any desire I might have later developed for alcohol.

Mr. and Mrs. R. V. Wells had a son who was much older than I, but a daughter, Louise, was in the second grade when I moved to Kenansville in 1922. She and I continued in the same school grade throughout elementary and high school. Since her father had a steady job as clerk of court, she was able to go to college and become a schoolteacher. Later, she moved back to Kenansville and served as the organist for many years at the Grove Presbyterian Church. She still lives in Kenansville and is one of only six remaining members of our eleven member high school graduating class of 1932. It is always a real treat to talk to her.

Mr. Wells served as Sunday school superintendent, clerk to the session, and taught us in the junior Sunday school class.

Every summer, the three churches in Kenansville combined for their Bible school and for the annual Sunday school picnic at White Lake, fifty miles away. One year I recall that we rode to the picnic with the wealthy Mrs. Lucy Jolly, in her black Buick sedan. That was the day when most of the parents were sitting on the pier, watching the children swim, when a speedboat ran into one of the pier's pilings, causing the whole pier to lose its footing and gently sink into the lake. The parents who had been sitting on the pier were slowly eased into the water. The clothes they were wearing were the only ones they had brought with them. A few of the children had been swimming under the pier at the time it fell, but it had fallen so gently they were all able to get out from under it. No one was hurt, but none will ever forget that picnic!

We drove our mule and buggy to the church for about six months. Mr. Early Carr Newton, a widower and member of the church, had been left with three children the same ages as Milton, Alma, and me. Mr. Newton said he would like to start coming out to our home and pick us up for all the church activities. He was an unassuming and gentle man who made his living as a carpenter and later worked in the county school bus garage as a mechanic. His children were in the same public school classes as we were and we knew them well. He never failed to come for us, until I was fourteen. That was when Daddy purchased a used Studebaker touring car, which Milton could drive to church. The Presbyterian young people met on Sundays at five o'clock in the afternoon and we were always there.

Cocky, young Vance Gavin from the Baptist church attended our Sunday evening youth meetings to be with his girlfriend, Reba Pickett, whom he later married. Vance usually gave the prayer on these occasions. I recall his embarrassment once when he prayed, "And, Father, we ask you to bless us in the past as you have done in the future." However, Vance grew up to be considered the most successful attorney-orator in our area.

When I was fourteen and entered the girls intermediate Sunday school class, the church had no one to assume the responsibility of working with this all-girl group. Mr. Wells, the superintendent, insisted that I do this. It was a surprise that working with the intermediate girls proved to be so rewarding. They were interested, energetic, and enthusiastic about the Bible lessons and special projects, such as visits to the County Home where the aged indigent citizens of the county lived. The residents were always delighted to see the beaming faces of these teenagers, hear the singing, recitation of Scriptures and poetry, and enjoy the little goodies we took for their refreshment. The Southerland twins, Ellen and Eleanor, were in this class. I never did learn to tell them apart. I worked with this class until I married and moved away when I was twenty-two.

Our family had been the recipient of many visits from Mrs. Louise Boney and some other ladies in the church who had often remembered us during Mother's frequent bouts with pneumonia and other illnesses, and later on during Rdell's sickness. It was Mrs. Boney who usually delivered the fruit baskets and such. She was a delightful sight driving into our yard with her car windows down, a gaily colored scarf blowing in the wind, and her long hair tied in a knot at the top of her head.

Reverend Miller was the pastor when we moved to Kenansville in 1922. On Sunday mornings as I listened to his sermons, I envisioned a halo behind his head and I was fascinated by everything he said. Then came the Reverend Frank L. Goodman who was a down-to-earth man who explained the Bible in such easy to understand terms. His explanations always supplemented what Mother was teaching us from the Bible at our nightly family devotions and the memory work she and Mrs. Wells were drilling into us.

Soon after beginning to attend the Grove Presbyterian Church, I begged my parents to let me join the church, because I really wanted to be a part of everything that was going on. But, beg as I might, Mother stood fast in her belief that since Jesus was twelve years old in the Bible's first account of his visit to a temple, that children should not join a church until they were twelve years old. When I finally became twelve, I couldn't wait to join. I will never forget when it was time for me to be baptized. I was wearing a wide-brimmed brown hat with a nearly flat crown, held on by a rubberized band in the back. Mrs. Ella Gooding, the wife of our local doctor, kindly helped me remove the bobby pins from the band that was holding my hat on my head.

While our parents never attended the Grove Presbyterian Church, they always saw that we were there for every function. When we would bring home our rewards for achievements for memorizing Scriptures and the catechisms, the pride of our parents showed in their faces and let us know they felt rewarded for their efforts in encouraging us to be active in the church.

It was a combination of our experiences in the Kenansville Grove Presbyterian Church, the constant guidance of our parents, and the influence of our schools that taught us to believe in and rely upon a source of strength beyond our own. These three influences worked together to develop integrity and give us the moral compass needed to serve and care for all kinds of people.

Now, every Sunday morning as I listen to Dr. Bain, the pastor at the Pink Hill Presbyterian Church deliver his sermon, every word he speaks is meaningful to me and takes me back to my fifteen years at the Grove Presbyterian Church which so affected my life and beliefs.

1923

Life at the Abandoned James Sprunt Girls School in My Third, Fourth and Fifth Grades

The year I entered the third grade, all eleven grades of the Kenansville schools were consolidated at the main building of the abandoned James Sprunt Institute for Girls in Kenansville. Milton and Alma also went to this school. We continued there while I was in the fourth and fifth grades.

Reverend James M. Sprunt had been the principal when it had been a private boarding school established in 1896 by the Wilmington Presbytery for the Christian education of girls.

Fourteen acres of land on which this building was located also contained a girls dormitory which was now used for rental apartments, and the headmaster's residence rented as a family dwelling. None of the James Sprunt Girls School property was any longer used for a girls private school.

During our years there, Mr. Pate was our principal. My main memory of him is how he tried to make all of the boys believe that any of them could be president of the United States, or anything else they wanted to be, as long as they were willing to start working toward such a goal. He especially tried to motivate the laziest boy in our class, but he never could. At that time it seemed to me that our principal and some of the teachers had not caught on to the idea that it was important to try to encourage girls to succeed!

Our principal and the teachers often reminded us how lucky we were to be experiencing the grandeur and atmosphere that had been a part of the former James Sprunt Institute for Girls.

We started every day with chapel assembly. One of the teachers led us in singing such songs as "America," "America, the Beautiful," "The Old North State," and other songs from the *Golden Song Book*. These were followed by a devotional led by the principal or a local minister. Then we returned to our classes where we usually sang, "We're all in our places with sunshiny faces, for this is the way to start a new day."

It seemed that most of our reading books and our instruction was geared around the farm. I recall once in the third grade that our whole class had to recite in unison a poem that began, "When the frost is on the pumpkin and the fodder's in the shock and you hear the gobbling of the strutting turkey cock."

An Engraved Wedding Invitation

When I was in the fourth grade, I saw my first engraved wedding invitation. Mr. and Mrs. Fred Pickett, Daddy's former boss at Magnolia, mailed us an invitation to attend the 6 December 1924 wedding and reception of their daughter, twenty-eight-year-old Alice Mae Pickett, to thirty-one-year-old John R. Croom, the son of Mr. and Mrs. John F. Croom. The Pickett-Croom wedding and reception was to be held in the Methodist Church in Magnolia. This marriage would unite the two most prominent families in Magnolia.

I remember rubbing my fingers over the raised letters on the invitation and marveling at the beauty of a real wedding and reception communication. We all dreamed of going to a wedding of rich people. This was the main topic of conversation at our house for days. We just wondered what such a wedding would be like.

Of course, Mother had to write and mail our regrets because we still had an open family buggy and we could not depend on the weather in December to accommodate our family even though we would be bundled up. However, it made all of us feel proud of our daddy, that Mr. Pickett would want him and his family to be there at such a momentous occasion in the lives of the people of Magnolia.

A New Boy Comes to School

When the banks began to fail, a new boy joined our class. His father's bank had failed in a distant city and his father had committed suicide. The boy's Mother and her two children had moved to Kenansville to live with relatives. The boy was apparently bitter and called nearly everyone a son of a bitch. When he called me that one day, I asked Mother what it meant. She said it wasn't something nice, but to just feel sorry for the boy, because he was frustrated and that this was a good time to learn that when you are called an ugly name, it does not really change what you are at all, so just feel sorry for whoever does it.

Our First Yeast Bread at the James Sprunt School

Some school students began to carry sandwiches for their lunches, made with white yeast bread that they called "light bread." We only had homemade buttermilk biscuits made with homemade lard. Milton and I begged Mother to let us take a dozen eggs from our own hen nests to the nearby store and trade them for some of this new light bread. She gave us a little basket with twelve rich, brown eggs. I agreed to tote the eggs to the store. Milton would make the purchase when we got there.

On our way to the store we realized we did not know what denominations the light bread was sold in, so we really didn't know what to ask for. We had quite a discussion about what we were going to tell the storekeeper. Finally we agreed what it had to be. I set the basket down on the counter next to the cash register and Milton proudly told Mr. Penney, "We want to trade you this dozen eggs for a ton of light bread." Mr. Penney said, "Son, I don't think you really want a ton. What you want is a loaf."

Collard Stealing

The only pranks that seemed to be known during this period for teenagers to execute were collard stealing on "Old Christmas Night," 6 January, or watermelon stealing in summertime.

Collards are the most favored of all the green vegetables throughout the South. They remain green in the gardens throughout the year. They were treasured by the people who had them in their gardens.

While we were at the old James Sprunt School, two of our high school teenage boys from some of the most prominent families went collard stealing on Old Christmas Night. They took the stolen collards to the school auditorium, lifted the top of the school piano and stuffed four big collard stalks, root, dirt, and all, into the inside of the piano and put the top back down.

When Mr. Pate determined who stuffed the collards into the piano, he announced at the next morning chapel program that the responsible boys would be sentenced for an extended period to perform janitorial duties after school.

Did the boys' parents support Mr. Pate? You bet they did! The boys grew up to be great citizens.

Supporting the Family at the Hines Farm

Daddy and his mule could plant or cultivate only one row of crops at a time. He never owned a watch, but he could tell by the position of the sun when noon came and he was always on time for lunch.

He approached every task with great energy and total tenacity. He made work fun and exciting. We were always happy to be by his side helping with the work, such as replanting corn, chopping weeds from the crops, harvesting tobacco and cotton, bringing wood for our cookstove and fireplace, milking the cow, and feeding the other animals.

In spring, we picked strawberries for a nearby farmer for a half-cent a quart.

In June, Cora Miller, who lived on the farm adjoining us, took Alma and me into the woods with her children to pick wild blueberries in ten-quart buckets. When Mother canned as many blueberries as we needed, we sold berries to the local stores for five cents a quart to make extra money. Picking the "big blues" was fun; eating handfuls of the meaty, juicy berries was more fun! But before we left the woods, the teeny, weeny red bugs that infested the straw, wood mold, and debris we had stood on to pick blueberries had already seized in on our feet, ankles, and legs. We started scratching like mad. Nothing helped until we got home and Mother used her bottle of kerosene to rub on our red bug bites.

Sharecropping—Long Hours, Tedious Work

At the Hines farm, Daddy built on the reputation he had established at Chinquapin for marketing high quality cured tobacco from the eight acres he tended each year. During every six-week tobacco harvesting season, we spent two days a week helping Daddy crop the tobacco leaves and get them into the log flue-cured barns. Then we spent one day a week either hand-topping the flower from the tobacco stalks, breaking suckers which grew between each leaf and the stalk, or picking green horn worms from the leaves and stomping them dead.

This left two days a week for us to work for the Taylor family near Warsaw where we earned fifty cents a day working in their tobacco harvest. Mrs. Taylor didn't work in the harvest so she gave us lunch. She always had fresh butter beans and other delicious food to satisfy our hunger.

Cotton, corn, and hogs were also important in Daddy's plans to support his family. One half of the cotton sales went to Hines, but we paid no share from the corn crop or hog sales, nor from selling pork barbecue, corn bread, and cabbage slaw on the Warsaw streets on fall and winter Saturdays.

Picking cotton in the fall was the one farm chore I disliked to a point of dread. It took about one hundred pounds of cotton to fill up the big burlap bag we hung around our neck by a two to three inch wide strip of cloth Mother would cut for us and help us attach to our bag. We would drag the bag down the cotton rows as we picked the little white sections of cotton from their prickly burrs which became more prickly as they dried out and cold weather came. We would empty our bags several times into a bag which sat at the end of each of our rows. I thought I never would be able to pick one hundred pounds in a whole day, but finally I did. Etlar Monk, who sometimes helped us, could almost pick one hundred pounds by lunch time.

Winter Trapping for Wild Animal Hides

Daddy brought in extra income in the winter by setting baited steel traps in the nearby woods along the creek to catch otter, mink, raccoon, fox, and beavers to sell the dried fur hides to Mr. Floyd Strickland at his Warsaw hardware store.

Trapping was encouraged when we were growing up. Daddy checked the steel traps early every morning before daybreak using his swinging kerosene lantern for light. He killed the animals at the traps and put them in his big burlap bag to bring home.

With his very sharp pocketknife, he made a slit in the center of the hind legs of each animal. Then he very carefully inserted his trusty knife, with the skill of a surgeon, between the animal's skin and flesh, turning the skin inside out as he cut toward the head. The skins were then stretched on boards Daddy had shaped to fit the various sized animals. Each board had a small hole in its top to use in hanging the hides in our meat smokehouse to dry for two weeks. Then they would be ready for the trip to Mr. Strickland's hardware store for sale.

This was the day when fur coats, fur scarves, and fur stoles were the top status symbols for ladies. The love of furs in the South was still prevalent in the 1950s when financing statements covering ladies furs were still being recorded in the Duplin County Registry.

Mrs. Laura Gavin, our postmistress during my childhood, had a teenage daughter. When the daughter went away to college, Mrs. Gavin bought her a new mink neck piece and gave me her old one. It was made from three small mink fur hides. I have never felt so regal as when I donned the mink scarf for Church or other dress-up occasions.

Peanuts

The peanuts we planted in springtime were purchased in the hull and we always had a peanut shelling before planting time. One spring night each year our neighbors, including the young people, came for a shelling. We soon finished our task and played games in the upstairs of our pack house where we had the shelling. We would attend peanut shellings held by other farms, too.

When the peanuts matured in the fields, Daddy turned the roots of the peanut hills over with his plow so we could pull them up and make field stacks where they stayed until they dried. Then we picked the nuts off the vines, some were sold to the local stores and we kept enough for our year's supply of eating. Landlords did not get half of a sharecropper's peanuts.

Chickens

In those days, most farm families counted on raising around a hundred chickens a year so there would be one for every Sunday dinner, some to set on nests three weeks and hatch baby chicks, and some to lay eggs to sell throughout the year to the stores in exchange for groceries. Each family always kept at least one rooster to crow early in the mornings to awaken the family and to fertilize the eggs for hatching baby chicks.

The family chickens always had the run of the yard around the house. Our yard was sandy and one of our Saturday morning chores was to sweep the yard with brooms made of small branches cut from little trees and bushes. We had to be sure that all the week's chicken droppings were covered by sand when we finished sweeping. Few farm families back then tolerated grass in their yards.

Hog Killings

Hog killing day was one of the biggest annual events on the farm. A lot of judgment and planning was needed to pick a very cold day on the shrinking of the moon. It was believed that fresh pork cured better, that lard rendered better, and sausage and liver pudding, stuffed in casings that had been made from the hogs' intestines, cured better when the hogs were killed during the shrinking of the moon. We swapped work with other families for help in the hog killings. The salted hams, shoulders, and other cuts were packed with the skin side up on the ground over a thick canvas which covered the naked soil in the family smokehouse. Fresh sausage and tenderloin were canned in glass jars for our family's use.

Gardening

A year-round vegetable garden always had some kind of greens like collards, mustard, and turnip greens with roots, cabbage, and rutabagas even during the winter.

Sweet potatoes were cured by piling a three-foot high hill of potatoes on pine straw on the ground. The potatoes were then covered with pine straw. Finally, the hill of sweet potatoes and pine straw was covered with six to eight inches of packed dirt. A small opening for use in retrieving the potatoes was made on the side of the hill. This was covered with a piece of thick wood and pine straw was banked against it.

Then came spring and the garden would produce shoots of greens, garden peas, beets, and so forth.

So, together with our hills of cured sweet potatoes, spring and winter vegetable gardens, and the canned food Mother put up, we were well fed. Of course, we always had a milk cow with fresh sweet milk every day, butter, buttermilk, and clabber.

Squirrel and wild turkey on our table were welcome winter treats.

The Fourth of July—A Big Day

Every Fourth of July was a big day for us. Not only was it our country's Independence Day, but it was also Daddy's birthday. He always pulled the first ripe watermelon on the fourth of July. Every year, we would try to find a melon before then that we were real sure was ripe. But Daddy would thump it with his special thump and announce: "It will be just right on the Fourth," and sure enough, it would be! After the Fourth of July, our family sold both watermelons and cantaloupes from an old table under the shade of our big roadside oak tree. Daddy kept the two grocery stores and the two filling stations in Kenansville supplied with melons during the season. No other farm around had such good sandy loam which grew the sweetest melons imaginable helped by Daddy's early planting and tender loving care. Melons became my favorite food for a lifetime, both in season and out.

We could keep all of the money from the melon sales.

Other Aspects of Our Life at the Hines Farm

Daddy kept a sheet of cowhide leather to repair our shoes. After we children had gone to bed at night, he would sit by the fire and repair our shoes, resoling them, using his iron shoe last, which had three shoe sizes on it. We always had just one pair shoes which we wore to school and church. The shoes we usually wore at home were our old shoes and sometimes were a bit small.

When we needed jackets, shoes, and warm clothing which Mother could not make, we ordered them from the Sears catalog, because she seldom went the seven miles to Warsaw to shop.

Mother was limited in getting about because of her frailty. The habit of ordering clothes through catalogs has stayed with me throughout the years, as I have always found so many other things to do with my time instead of going shopping. And catalogs usually give such a wide choice of sizes and selections.

Along with our daily chores of bringing in firewood, we cleaned and trimmed our oil lamps. Electricity was not brought to our area until 1930 when Carolina Power and Light Company began to serve the Kenansville to Warsaw Highway residents. Many people not living on the main highway still did not have electricity for quite some time. We still used our pitcher hand water pump and did not have a washing machine or any electric appliances, except the refrigerator we bought as soon as we got electric power.

There was one clear glass electric light bulb hanging from the center of each room, which had to be turned on and off by a pull cord. There were no electric receptacles in the walls.

Our refrigerator was plugged into a double socket in the electric light outlet hanging from the kitchen ceiling. We still had our outdoor privy, using old Sears catalogs, *Blade and Ledger* monthly newspapers, correspondence, and other paper documents for toilet tissue.

To reward us for working hard, Daddy would take us swimming to nearby Cooper's Mill Pond. There he taught all of us to swim to the other side of the pond where we would sit on a big log. We often took our reed fishing poles and a hoe to dig some earthworms so we could catch red-breasted perch. These were plentiful in the creek that flowed into the mill pond. Our catch provided tasty fried fish for supper.

Our family ate all our meals together and discussed family affairs at the table. There was just one strict rule against giggling during a meal. The rule was that if we could not stop giggling, we had to leave the table until we could "straighten" our face, then we could come back and finish our meal. I never understood why it was so easy to start giggling at the table during a meal. But it seemed that's when we shared the funny incidents of the day and they just seemed very, very funny, even more hilarious than when the incidents occurred.

It was considered good discipline to spank children when we were growing up. If we were not good for Mother, she would always say she would talk to our Daddy about our behavior when he came to the house. She always said she never felt strong enough to spank us. When she told Daddy how we had misbehaved, he always said, "Now, I hate to do it, but if you do this again, I'll have to spank you." The disappointed look on Daddy's face helped us to remember not to do this same thing again.

One day when Rdell was picking up rocks in the yard and throwing them, he made a straight hit at the head of a young fryer-size chicken and killed it. He twisted the chicken's head off to let it drain blood properly and took it to Mother. When Mother asked what happened, Rdell replied, "The chicken just jumped in front of a rock."

We always had plenty of chewing gum from the gum trees adjacent to the yard. Daddy "tapped" the trees to assure a continual supply. This was comparable to the way sugar maples are tapped to get the maple sugar. The gum from the trees would harden rather quickly. This chewing gum, together with the "toothbrushes" we made from pulling off the little twigs from the sweet gum trees and using them for brushing our teeth, kept our teeth in good condition. We never went to a dentist.

Our clothes were mostly homemade on Mother's pedal sewing machine. During the Depression, we could buy cloth for making garments at ten cents a yard. Mother crocheted caps and dresses and knitted our winter socks. Once she ordered a small knitting machine with a hand crank, which could knit our socks and stockings as she carefully turned a handle to be assured of the right size. For several years, Daddy would buy chicken feed in pretty printed cotton sacks from which Mother could make nice school dresses. It took two of these sacks to make a dress for Alma or me and one to make a shirt for Milton or Rdell. The quality of material used for these feed sacks was equivalent to that of the ten cent material which could be bought at the store.

Hair clippers ordered from the Sears and Roebuck catalog, along with Mother's scissors, gave all of us the haircuts we needed. She never cut her hair, but wore it in a ball at the back of her head.

Our Dream of Having a Pony

A sample *Blade and Ledger* tabloid-size monthly newspaper came in the mail to our family. It contained a big advertisement stating that boys and girls who acquired a certain number of "points" for selling subscriptions to the *Blade and Ledger* would receive a "beautiful and gentle Shetland pony." This monthly paper contained interesting family-oriented articles on medical and other subjects of family interest. Milton and I had been enjoying our wide open spaces around the farm and we had done a lot of thinking about how grand it would be to have a Shetland pony. The subscriptions to the *Blade and Ledger* newspaper were only one dollar a year. The newspapers were mailed once a month from Chicago, using a special bulk mailing permit.

This particular spring, our excitement was uncontrollable at the thought of having our own Shetland pony. Every Saturday for several weeks we took our sample *Blade and Ledger* and walked into Kenansville and visited every home in town. We also visited those homes between Kenansville and our house, and all the people we came in contact with along the way, asking them to subscribe to the *Blade and Ledger*. I would lie awake many nights thinking of the day the Shetland pony would arrive.

Our excitement began to diminish as we realized that we would end up with only about one quarter of the points needed to qualify for the Shetland pony. But later we decided the experiences we had in contacting people and learning to sell a product gave us the impetus we needed for many later efforts.

Our little brother never understood why we didn't get the pony!

The Railroad Tracks

Our house was about the distance of a city block from the railroad tracks which ran the seven miles from Warsaw to Kenansville. One of our favorite activities was to run down the hill to the railroad tracks to watch the log train and freight trains go by. When the engineer would see us watching on the hillside, he would blow his whistle for a long distance just to please us. The track repair crew had a little hand-pump car they rode on up and down the tracks when making repairs. It was exciting to see this unusual vehicle go by. We sometimes walked on the rails to see how far we could go without having to step off. Sometimes when we were going with Daddy for our swims at the mill pond, about a third of a mile from our house, he would let us walk on the rails. We loved to stand on the cross ties over the trestle at the mill pond and watch the water drain into the stream that carried away the gushing mill pond water.

The Big Snowstorm

During the rare two-foot snow that came to eastern North Carolina 3 March 1927 we had to stay home from school a whole week before the snow melted. This was our first experience in making snowmen to decorate our yard. Every day while the snow remained we made snow cream using our own sweet cream from the family cow, Lucy.

When school reopened, Daddy had to transport us to and from school for a week while our still-unpaved highway dried out from the slush and mud created from the melting snow. So, we not only appreciated the delightful snow because we could make snowmen and cream, but it's the only time we had enjoyed a whole week of buggy rides.

My First Part-Time Job Away from the Fields

By the time I was in the seventh grade in school, I began to wish I could go in to Warsaw on Saturdays with Daddy and be a salesperson in one of the two thriving general merchandise stores or the ladies' dress shop owned by the Assyrian, Fred Maroon. There was no age limit then for working and I was a big girl. Mr. Maroon said I could start working on Saturdays that fall when the farmers started selling tobacco. That's just when Daddy would start going in to Warsaw with his barbecue, slaw, and bread.

This store is where I first heard the expression "window shopping." Some ladies would come in the shop, examine, and feel every garment, decline any help, and say: "I'm just window shopping."

While I was working there on Saturdays, charming Virginia George from Kinston married Graham Phillips. She also worked there on Saturdays. When I wasn't busy, I spent some time talking to Virginia and enjoying her beautiful manners.

Warsaw Street Social Life

During my high school days the biggest social life in Warsaw and the communities in the area was the gathering of the young people on the two main business blocks on Railroad Street on Saturday afternoons. They would socialize, visit in the stores, buy five cent Coca-Colas and five cent hot dogs, or five cent honeycomb squares of ice cream made up of layers of vanilla, strawberry, and chocolate.

This is where Milton met his future wife, Ella Taylor, and her twin sister, Mary. Most of the young people did not have their own cars, but were dropped off and picked up by their parents.

The Pesky Crows and One Adventurous Toad Frog

As Daddy's planted corn kernels sprouted and peeped through the soil in spring, they were attacked by the crows. Coveys of these sleek black birds seemed to sit in the trees and watch for the sprouting corn.

As the crows descended on the tender corn hills and had their feasts, they didn't seem to be deterred by the scarecrows we had carefully placed in the fields. We dreaded to watch them enjoy their fun because we knew every tender hill of corn they ate would have to be replanted by a little hole dug with our weeding hoes and covered with a pat of dirt. This was one of the children's duties.

Sometimes we had to go over the cornfields two or three times to replant the hills devoured by the crows. As we replanted corn, we often chanted the poem:

> Caw, Caw, called the crow
> Spring has come again I know.
> Just as sure as I am born
> There's the farmer
> Planting corn.

Our most exciting corn replanting experience came one day when Milton, Alma, and I were replanting a field for the second time when Milton began jumping up and down, screaming and quickly shedding his denim bib overalls as fast as lightning.

An adventurous toad frog had jumped up the right leg of his overall pants, became frustrated, and instead of jumping down, was frantically making his way upward.

Milton wanted to stomp the rescued frog but he couldn't dare do it, because though it was ugly and intrusive, he knew it existed on flies and other unwanted insects.

Tramps and Gypsies

During the Depression years unemployed tramps frequently came along our highway. Many of them stopped at our house, because our large pack house and stables were between our house and the highway, and they could see good prospects of a place to spend the night sleeping in the hayloft. The tramps seemed to know and understand they would always be given some food and allowed to sleep on the hay in our pack house. They never caused us any trouble and Mother and Daddy always pointed out to us that their situation could come to any person. None of them could afford smoking tobacco, so we didn't have to be concerned about hay fires.

During July and August for several years, three or four families of gypsies would come in their worn-out cars and ask to pitch camp in the pine thicket across the road from our house. They used water from our pump. There were rumors that gypsies would steal, but we never encountered any problems with them and our parents again reminded us these wandering tribes could be God's people just as we were.

Milton, Alma, Rdell, and I were absolutely charmed by the gypsy children, with their light brown skin, long hair, brown eyes, fancy beaded jewelry, and the girls' long dresses. The boys usually had on canvas cloth knee pants and they loved to shoot with bows and arrows.

All of us loved to play with the gypsy children. The year that Alma was ten, there were four gypsy families camping in the pine thicket. One family had a ten-year-old girl named Mary. Alma loved to play with Mary. She had the same kind of creative mind Alma had. Alma was devastated when Mary got blood poisoning in a leg sore and died. Her parents put her body in a casket, boarded the train at Warsaw and took Mary's body away for burial. Mary's parents rejoined the other families in about two weeks.

The gypsy men would go out during the day and sell small woven rugs.

The gypsies' visits brought back memories of the American Indian stories we had read and we envisioned that these gypsies might be their offspring, but our parents believed they were offspring of some Biblical tribe.

Visits of Cousins

We were blessed with a total of thirty-eight first cousins on Mother's side and eighteen on Daddy's side. We often visited the cousins who lived in Beulaville and Magnolia and they loved to come to our house.

Once, two boys who were our teen-aged cousins from Beulaville thumbed rides on the highway to our house, making a change of rides in Kenansville, where they said they bought two of the biggest yellow oranges they had ever seen. The "oranges" were about six inches in diameter, but they said they were so sour they could not enjoy them. Actually, they had purchased grapefruit, thinking they were oranges.

When our cousin, Paul Duff, married Fannie Morton at Beulaville, they did not have a car, so they hired a friend to bring them to our house to spend their honeymoon. Alma and I let them use our bedroom and we slept on our feather beds on the floor in Mother's and Daddy's bedroom. The young couple fitted in with our family really well. They helped with all the chores and seemed to have a wonderful honeymoon. The friend who brought them to our house returned to pick them up at the end of the week.

This was typical of the way young people had to make do with less than ideal honeymoons during the Depression years.

In the lean years there were many people without jobs. Harry Whaley, around twenty years old, the son of Daddy's brother, Bob, who had moved to Georgia, was unemployed and came to our house in 1928 and spent the summer with us, helping on the farm.

Going to the Circus with Daddy

Daddy once took all four of us to see the circus when it came to Warsaw on the railroad. The high tents trapped the above-ninety degree late August heat and humidity, but in eastern North Carolina summer weather has never been a deterrent when working or playing, and this was the tops in real playing. We had just finished harvesting tobacco and this was our very special treat before school started.

The thick, soft sawdust covering the dirt inside the tent, the hard boards we sat on to view the wonders of the trapeze artists, the horses with gold (surely it was gold!) ropes and capes around their necks, and the skimpy costumes of the women trapeze performers made the circus the most exciting place for us to be. We all knew taking us to the circus was a real financial sacrifice for Daddy. In our childlike way, we also knew he was enjoying this as much as we were. The mixed odors of popcorn, animals and the sweating people could not lessen the euphoria we experienced. We could hardly wait to get home and relate our tales to Mother about what we had seen and heard.

Washing Clothes at the Hines Farm

Our hand pitcher water pump was in our front yard, about fifteen feet from what used to be the house's back porch. When the house had been built back in 1910, the Kenansville-Warsaw Road ran between the front porch and the railroad. Now, this porch where the water pump was located had to be used as our front porch, because it was next to the new Kenansville-Warsaw Highway. Our water pump had a little wooden table built around it, about four feet square. On this table we always left a half gallon glass Mason jar filled with water to be used in priming our water pump the next time we used it.

Our big, black iron wash pot stood about thirty feet beyond the water pump. This pot was such an unattractive sight. It always had a pile of ashes and partially charred bits of wood around it, left from fires built on weekly wash days. The wind sometimes blew these ashes and wood bits over our yard. So, we couldn't have the pot any closer to our pump and porch where our friends and family entered our house.

Before we built a fire around the wash pot, we had to pump cold water into our ten-quart galvanized pail and carry it the thirty feet from the pump to fill our wash pot. It took twelve trips from the pump to the wash pot to fill it. Then we put some of Mother's handmade soap into the pot.

Before we had put our clothes into the black wash pot of hot water, we had wet them at our water pump table and rubbed the dirty spots on our galvanized washboard. If we weren't very careful, the galvanized ridges on our washboard would scrape and bruise our knuckles.

Once the clothes were in the pot of hot, soapy water, we punched them continuously with a long handled wood paddle that Daddy had whittled. The paddle looked exactly like the ones used for rowing wooden boats. We punched the clothes until we thought they were clean.

We used the same pot of hot water for three washings. First, we washed the bed linens, towels, white shirts, and other white items. Then came the colorfast shirts, tie aprons, et cetera. The last washing was Daddy's bib overalls, dark socks, and any dark pants that were in the wash. All clothes were rinsed in cold water in our two wooden washtubs at the water pump table.

We heated water on the wooden cookstove to wash our dresses, lingerie, hose, et cetera. These, too, were rinsed in cold water in our wooden washtubs at the table around the water pump, and hung on a line on the back porch.

We couldn't do our main family wash on rainy days, because the clothes had to be hung on our outside clotheslines.

We used store-bought clothes pins which were about five inches long and five-eighths inch in diameter with the center cut from the bottom about two-thirds the way up the clothes pin. The pins were placed at two points on the edges of each article that had to be hung on the outside clothesline.

As we took the dry articles off the clothesline, we folded the bed sheets, towels, and any other pieces that we didn't plan to iron with our solid metal smoothing iron. We heated our smooth iron either on our wood-burning cookstove or in front of the fire in our one fireplace that warmed Mother's and Daddy's bedroom that we used for a sitting room.

Nothing seemed to trigger inflammation of Mother's bronchiectasis like putting her hands in cold water in winter to rinse our clothes and hang them on the clothesline. So, until I became old enough to rinse and hang out the clothes, Daddy went the two miles to the edge of Kenansville to get a woman to do the main family washing.

On one blustery day in March, this woman had sorted out the usual three piles of clothes near the wash pot. She was boiling the first bed linens group when a sudden gust of wind blew into the fire around the wash pot, scattering the blazes into the second and third piles of our clothes and damaging most of them beyond use. What a loss! The woman cried her heart out, but Mother could always look ahead to a solution, so she tried to comfort the woman.

No more clothes were piled too near our wash pot.

The Kenansville Post Office

We had no rural free delivery of mail by our house until I was in high school. On the way home from elementary classes, we always walked by the Kenansville Post Office where Mrs. Laura Gavin, Postmistress, had the foyer of the post office plastered with powerfully printed signs which read:

"Do nothing that you would not like to be doing when Jesus comes."

"Say nothing that you would not like to be saying when Jesus comes."

"Think nothing that you would not like to be thinking when Jesus comes."

"Go no place that you would not like to be found when Jesus comes."

There was also a sign which quoted John 3:16: "For God so loved the world that He gave His only begotten Son that whosoever believeth on Him should not perish, but have everlasting life."

The margins of these poster board signs were so bold and prominent that they must have impressed many people. They really impressed us.

Of course, there was also the poster of the FBI's wanted persons.

In 1972, the stately little post office building was purchased by attorney Robert L. West and moved seven miles to Warsaw where it has served as his law office. It is just as beautiful and well kept as the first day I went in it in 1922.

Funds for a New Kenansville Consolidated School

During the 1920s, the public school system in North Carolina experienced the greatest growth since the beginning of public education. During this time the state adopted a uniform teacher's salary schedule and established a building loan fund from which counties could borrow money, through the use of county bonds, to construct school buildings. From these funds came the money for the construction of the new consolidated Kenansville school and several other Duplin County schools.

1927

Attending the New Kenansville Consolidated School—My Grades Sixth through Eleventh

When the long awaited day arrived to enter the new Kenansville Consolidated School in September 1927, we couldn't believe our eyes when we first saw this new red brick building. We were accustomed to the yellow brick courthouse but we had never been in a red brick building before.

There were massive, white columns in front of our new school that went almost to the top of the second story. The columns were each as big around as a full sized barrel! They were almost as big as the columns we had seen as we had walked past the yellow brick county courthouse on our way to the new school.

We were astounded when we saw the heavy, burgundy velvet stage curtains with the monogram, KHS, in huge letters, woven into the fabric. These must surely be as beautiful and luxurious as the ones we'd heard about on the theater stages in New York.

The desks were new and had a shelf for books! The chalkboards were shiny and black all over, not cracked or broken as we had been accustomed to at the old James Sprunt School. There was a coat closet in every room. And the school had a real school library, next to the principal's office. We didn't have a lunchroom, but that was all right, because we always brought our lunches from home anyway. Of course, there was no gymnasium, but we had not really expected one. We could play basketball on the clay court outside. We just couldn't play out there in bad weather.

When we entered the sixth grade room, there was our pretty, eighteen-year-old teacher, Miss Katherine McKenzie, seated at her desk. She was from Wilmington, had finished high school at age sixteen, and completed two years of college.

We had never heard anyone read like Miss McKenzie. She had her own, very special style which held us spellbound. We would just beg and beg her to read. She always promised that if we would work hard and get our regular work completed, she would read to us. This was worth the special effort. She soon married a young Kenansville man, Joe Wallace. She taught at the Kenansville school until her retirement.

Milton was a grade ahead of me. Alma had entered the first grade while we were at the old James Sprunt School. Rdell would be entering the new Kenansville school in the fall of 1928, so all of us would enjoy a few years together in our fine new school.

While the sixth grade at our new school proved to be so delightful and rewarding, our family had a very difficult year at home. Mother had her worst pneumonia bout of all during this year. There were no antibiotics in those days to curb such infections. Kenansville's Dr. Reid could not get her fever down. He told us there was a young doctor, J. W. Straughan, at Warsaw, whom he wanted to see Mother. Dr. Straughan came to our house, examined Mother, and could think of no solution. Both doctors left and gave us little hope. Hattie Belle Burch, a registered nurse in Kenansville, had been with Mother two days and, though she was an expert at caring for critically ill patients, Mother had been growing worse.

A neighbor of ours had heard of a Reverend Ezzell in Magnolia who believed in the power of prayer and asked Mother if she would like to have Reverend Ezzell come and offer prayer for her. Mother agreed and Reverend Ezzell arrived with his worn Bible. He had long white hair, very penetrating eyes, and stood very erect. All of us were around Mother's bed, hoping to catch a glimmer of hope. As Reverend Ezzell prayed aloud it seemed to us that he was mighty good friends with God and we had a feeling that God was understanding our whole situation. While Reverend Ezzell was there Mother seemed to start breathing better and as he left, her temperature started coming down. She slept better that night and all of us breathed easier, too.

The next morning when Dr. Reid came and took Mother's temperature, he asked her, "Have you been holding ice in your mouth?"

Mother's reply was, "No."

"Well, your temperature is normal," said Dr. Reid. "What has happened?"

Mother related Reverend Ezzell's visit and Dr. Reid remarked, "Well, nothing but God could have done it."

Following this recovery, Mother developed an infection around her fingernails that lasted several months. Again, there were no antibiotics. Mother soaked her fingers in a medicated solution prescribed by the doctor. The infection cured slowly. She was not able to put her hands in food or water during this time and Daddy and I had to take over the food preparation until her hands healed. This is when I learned to make buttermilk biscuits. Mother carefully watched as we cooked and gave the pointers we needed.

This was the year I remember as my most memorable Christmas.

Following is a copy of the article I wrote for *The Wallace Enterprise* newspaper many years ago when that newspaper invited a few people to write about the Christmas they remembered most.

The Christmas I Remember Most

There never was much money for Santa Claus at our house. But, the love and concern our parents showed to us always seemed to make up for the things money could buy. We never doubted that they did the best they could for us in every situation.

The year of 1927 when I was turning twelve years old had been our family's hardest year ever. Mother had been her very sickest with her bronchiectasis and her very worst of all bouts with pneumonia. Then had come the lasting infection around her fingernails. That year, our money from the one half of the crop sales had been smaller than usual and Mother's medical bills had been much larger.

But as Daddy had set his steel traps in the woods by the streams and visited them to take out the trapped animals so he could sell their dried hides, he had searched as usual to find the prettiest Christmas tree to brighten our house for the holidays.

We had never had a tree like this one! It was a perfectly shaped holly tree, just loaded with sparkling red berries. We located it in Mother and Daddy's bedroom where our one fireplace was because we used this room as a family room during winter.

Our fireplace room looked like Santa's workshop as we strung popcorn we had grown in our garden and made white paper snowflake ornaments for our tree.

Of course, we had no electric lights on our tree because we had no electricity yet. But, the light from our fireplace shined on it and the rays from our kerosene lamp seemed to give the red berries a special glow. We decided it must be the most beautiful tree in the whole world.

We believed our stockings would have the usual apple, orange, stick candy, and raisins with seeds that crackled but we really did not expect anything else because we were aware our financial situation was not even as good as it had usually been at Christmastime.

Mother was not strong enough to ride with Daddy in to town in our open buggy to get our Christmas supplies which always included a fresh coconut for that once-a-year mouthwatering cake we thought no one could make like Mother. So, Daddy had to go alone.

That night before Christmas was especially meaningful to all of us because there had been one time during the year when we did not think Mother would be with us any longer. After supper, Mother read the Christmas story from Luke and played her pump organ while Daddy played his harp for us to sing "Joy To The World" and "Silent Night." I had difficulty getting to sleep that night for thinking back over the events since last Christmas and reflecting on how fortunate we really were to be able to be together as a family at Christmastime.

Imagine our gleeful surprise on Christmas morning when my sister and I each found a pretty "store-wrapped" box under our tree. We gazed at the box wrappings, then squeezed the boxes to our chests before opening them to find brightly colored birthday party invitations for which we would never have a use.

You see, Daddy couldn't read what was on the outside of the pretty box. He thought he was buying some lovely stationery for us. He had heard us say how we liked to write to our cousins at Beulaville and Magnolia.

We never let him know our stationery he had been so proud to buy was birthday party invitations because we knew our gifts marked twenty-nine cents each were truly gifts of love.

The Impact of the Charles Lindbergh Saga

The year of 1927 when I had been in Miss McKenzie's room in the sixth grade at our new red brick school had been a landmark year for another great exciting reason.

It was on 20-21 May 1927, when at twenty-five, Charles A. Lindbergh made a solo flight in his tiny single engine plane, *Spirit of St. Louis* from Roosevelt Field near New York City to LeBourget Field near Paris in just thirty-three hours and twenty-nine minutes.

This world news gripped school students and people of all ages all over the world for the next nine years as the continuing saga of the Lindbergh family unfolded. It was discussed in every school classroom as well as in every family.

He was a world hero, just the kind children and young people needed during those hard times when finances and morale were sinking to an all-time low. Other Atlantic flights had been made, but no pilot had made it alone. And he had made it in such a tiny, tiny plane. He became affectionately known in every household as Lucky Lindy or the Lone Eagle. He was an idol.

In 1929, Charles Lindbergh married Ann Morrow, whose father was our country's ambassador to Mexico. President Coolidge had awarded Lindbergh the Congressional Medal of Honor and the first Distinguished Flying Cross in American history.

The bubbles of all Americans were burst 1 March 1932 when Lindbergh's twenty-month-old son was kidnapped from their home and found ten weeks later—murdered.

On the night the Lindbergh baby was found, Alma and I had gone with friends to Clinton, twenty miles away, to see the movie *The Light of a Western Star*. All was quiet when we entered the theater, but as we came out when the movie was over, news boys were on the streets yelling, "Extra, extra. Read all about it. Lindbergh baby found dead!"

From the time of the kidnapping, all Americans had lived and breathed every bit of information on the investigation as it was released by radio and newspapers. Our family had anxiously awaited every news report on our battery radio hoping for some good news. When the dead child was found, children everywhere had been deeply affected and felt a close kinship with the Lindbergh family. The next day at school, there was a lot of weeping. It was hard to hold back the tears.

It would not be until 1934 that Bruno Richard Hauptman would be found guilty of the kidnapping and murder of the Lindbergh child. By that time, most Americans had a pretty good idea of what the shoe box full of ransom money looked like that was found in his garage. It was not until 1936 that Hauptman was executed for the crime.

The whole affair was so overpowering to the Lindberghs that in 1935 they took their three-year-old son and moved to Europe seeking privacy and safety. Their move left a sinking feeling in the hearts of most Americans who felt a great void with their absence.

Lindbergh's plane, *The Spirit of St. Louis*, hung in the Smithsonian Institute in Washington, D.C. for many years until it was moved to the National Air and Space Museum.

Though I have personally viewed this airplane many times, I still stand in awe each time I assess this little plane which took him across the Atlantic Ocean alone, and made him the hero of boys and girls, men and women, all over the world.

I took an eight-year-old great-grandson to see the airplane in 1995. It was hard for him to realize that a plane so small could fly one man alone over the Atlantic Ocean.

High School—Grades Eight through Eleven

After we had our wonderfully exciting first year in our new red brick school in Miss McKenzie's sixth grade, we spent our seventh grade in Miss Elizabeth Hobb's room where she prepared us to enter our four years of high school.

Our high school math teacher was Miss Laura V. Cox, a retired missionary to Mexico. She was a very capable math teacher. She required her students to recite the multiplication tables up to fifteen times fifteen. Most of the students feared her, because she would sometimes pull our ears if we gave wrong or dumb answers and she treated all of us like heathens to be ministered to according to the Biblical gospels. She seemed to assume none of us were familiar with any Bible teachings. About two-thirds of us were regular churchgoers. She often had us sing religious hymns and taught us to sing "Wonderful Words of Life" in Spanish. All of her students complained about her strictness. Once she saw Nannie Gray Stephens and Ralph Brown holding hands in the school hallway. She required them to stay in at recess and gave them a lecture because they were holding hands. They had been sweethearts all of their school years. After high school they married, had a beautiful life, and made great contributions to their families and the community.

As time has gone by and Miss Cox's students have reminisced about high school days, without exception they agree Miss Cox made a more lasting impression on them than any other teacher. We sometimes had mighty heavy doses of religion and discipline, but we also received a math foundation that allowed us to quickly call up our mental faculties and solve diverse problems not only in math, but in reasoning for solutions in every day living problems.

We walked two miles to school every day until I was in the eighth grade as we never had a school bus serve our road before that time. J.D. West, who lived a mile beyond us, Billy and Durwood Murray, who lived between us and Kenansville at the now famous Murray House, and Milton, Alma, Rdell, and I, walked together. The memories that we shared and the sound friendships we made have never diminished in importance to us. Sometimes Mr. Clay McCullen, an oil dealer from Warsaw, would pick us up and let us pile into the cab of his big oil delivery truck and take us on to school. Later, when Mr. Faison McGowen came to work as an office deputy sheriff and our county accountant, he offered all of us a ride in his wine-colored Chevrolet sedan and took us to school. If the weather was too bad, Daddy would take us to school in our buggy.

We learned in the first grade that we were expected to go to school every school day. The cold wind or pelting sleet and snow were not excuses. Excuses such as too cold, too rainy, or too snowy did not change our parents' intention that we were to go to school regardless of the weather conditions. Bundled up in our heavy wool coats that we had ordered from the Sears and Roebuck catalog, with wool scarves wrapped around our faces, exposing only our eyes, I'm sure we sometimes looked like young robbers.

We mostly had perfect attendance. There were only a few times we were too sick to be in class. My perfect attendance record lasted until the tenth grade when I was absent a week with the flu.

When there were threats of ice and snow, we had the benefit of long underwear camouflaged beneath long black or brown stockings that Mother had knitted. I can still feel myself weighed down with the heavy clothing and coats.

I especially remember heavy wine-colored long coats with little bits of cheap fur around the collars that Mother had ordered from Sears for Alma and me. We had wine-colored wool bonnets to match and when we wore them we felt like princesses. Milton and Rdell also had warm winter coats, long underwear, and long socks. In rainy or snowy weather all four of us had four-buckle black overshoes covering our black high top shoes that Daddy kept soled for us.

Since we started to school, Milton had been responsible for the most important part of our school paraphernalia—our family lunch bucket.

All grades ate lunch at the same time, so our family lunch packing worked fine. Eating lunch together seemed to contribute to our family closeness. We could swap tales of the morning happenings.

Our lunch bucket was always filled with good things to eat. To us, buttered biscuits with homemade cane syrup or Mother's jelly, or baked sweet potatoes were real treats. Mother frequently surprised us with leftover fried chicken, country sausage, either fried or canned, or a slice of cured, mouthwatering ham from our own smokehouse. Sometimes a homemade tea cake or piece of bread pudding finished out a delightful lunch that we ate in the auditorium in cold weather. In warm weather we seated ourselves outside on the steps, on the grass, or on the old dried logs at the edge of the woods.

One day we caught a ride to school with a farmer on his wagon. Milton hung our lunch bucket on the wagon tongue sticking out of the back of the wagon. When we got out of the wagon at school, Milton forgot to get our lunch bucket until the farmer had gone on about two hundred feet. The farmer picked up his speed after we got off his wagon. Milton chased after the farmer, retrieved the lunch bucket, and was out of breath when he returned to the three of us waiting for him. We knew Milton would not let us all go without lunch, no matter how far he might have had to run.

The old school lunch pails may be empty of food today, but they are chockfull of some of the most precious memories of our childhood.

Classes were dismissed each day at three o'clock. When the bell rang, students scrambled noisily for coats, caps, and scarves. Milton retrieved that all-important, now empty lunch pail, which hung from a nail or peg in the cloakroom.

We would start the two mile walk home. After being cooped up in a schoolroom all day, we were eager to get out in the fresh air. Quite often we played catch with Milton and Rdell's baseball as we meandered along the way. Sometimes the road would be too wet and muddy to play. Until our road was paved in 1930, we had to pick our way along the ruts, stepping from one firm plot of ground to another in an effort to keep our feet dry. One time in winter we fought our way through a blinding snowstorm that had blown in during the school day. We had no television in those days to warn us that a blizzard was bearing down upon us. On such an occasion and on all cold damp days Mother had hot chocolate waiting for us, plus a supply of warm, dry clothing. A roaring fire in the old fireplace soon thawed us out.

We nearly always received perfect school attendance certificates at the end of every school year. Only my absence due to having the flu marred my record. I never had any of the childhood diseases, like measles, mumps, or chicken pox, whereas Milton, Alma, and Rdell had most of these. Our main medical attention came from the four big jars of Vick's VapoRub that the Vick's company from Greensboro sent to Daddy every August for looking after a big Vick's VapoRub billboard that was near the highway on the Hines farm. Mother also made mustard plasters for chest colds and sinus infections. She used white cloverine salve, bought from a Watkins Products peddler, for our chapped lips.

Our road was first on a school bus route when I was in the eighth grade. Robust Perry Smith, a high school student, was the driver. The first day he drove the bus he told us if we would just be good for him, he would celebrate his first four dollar monthly paycheck by buying each of the twelve of us a penny Baby Ruth candy bar, and good we were! And he kept his promise!

Will Rogers Never Met a Man He Didn't Like

During our high school days, Will Rogers was a famous cowhand, circus and vaudeville performer, author of six books, actor in fifty silent movies and twenty-one talking films. He helped the American people get through the Great Depression with his easygoing chatter and his humorous lecturing on current events. He wrote a daily column that appeared in 350 newspapers. His column was the first item I, as well as many others, read every day.

His two favorite sayings were: "All I know is what I read in the newspapers" and "I never met a man I didn't like." His saying that I like best is, "If you think you don't like somebody, it may be just because you don't know them."

Will Rogers delighted his audiences, depositing goodwill as the champion trick rough rider and lasso thrower in the world.

He made five presidents—Wilson, Harding, Coolidge, Hoover, and Roosevelt—the butt of his observations, but not one of them disliked him. Woodrow Wilson once said, "Will Rogers' remarks are not only humorous, but illuminating."

When Will Rogers and his good friend, Wiley Post, died in a plane crash in March 1935 on a trip to Alaska, our whole country grieved. President Roosevelt made a radio speech and said, "He helped the nation smile."

I felt that one of my best friends had died. The daily words he had said through his column were inspiring to me and gave me something to ponder.

I have been to New York twice to enjoy *The Will Rogers Follies* and relive the humor, good sense, and entertainment that he brought to us during the tough Depression years.

Characteristics of Our High School Days

In those days, we entered high school in the eighth grade and finished in the eleventh. We were fortunate that our parents never required us to stay out of school to work on the farm. Many of the rural high school students took extra years to finish school because they had to work on the farm so much in the fall and spring. Those students would be held over another year by their teachers. Many students just gave up on their quest for a diploma.

The prosperity of the early '20s vanished and tax collections plummeted. At one point there wasn't enough money on hand in our county treasury to pay the teachers. F. W. McGowen was by that time county tax supervisor and county accountant. He called some well-off taxpayers and asked them to please pay their taxes immediately after tax listing and before notices of amounts due were mailed, so the teachers could be paid. In 1929, sixteen special school tax districts were established in Duplin County in an effort to try to help tax collections.

Some of the county school bond money, borrowed to build the new Kenansville consolidated brick school and other new brick schools, started coming due. The county did not have the tax collections to meet the school bond payments for several years and had to refinance the payments as they came due.

Times were so tough during 1929 to 1932 that most families could not afford the niceties enjoyed by just a few fortunate students. When it came time for a class ring, we selected the cheapest one available. For the junior-senior banquet, the parents prepared fried chicken, potato salad, home canned string beans, and lemon pie. We had no lunchroom so we had our banquet in the downstairs hall of the school building. All girls in my graduating class in 1932 got one new homemade dress and wore it to both the class sermon and graduation exercises.

None of the dresses were alike. The boys wore their Sunday clothes, white shirts and dark trousers.

The high school principal, Willard V. Nix, took the seniors on one of the county school buses to his mother's home near Hendersonville in the mountains of the western part of our state for their senior class trip. That was the year I finished the eighth grade. Every year our high school's Parent Teacher Association gave a free trip to the student with the top scholastic standing to go with the seniors on their class trip. That year I was awarded the trip.

The first night on the road was spent at the Esmeralda Inn at Chimney Rock. There is where I tasted my first corn flakes with milk and bananas. A picture of this delicacy had hung for years in our kitchen/dining room. At home, Mother cooked pork meat, eggs, rice, and gravy with biscuits every morning for breakfast. But I had looked at that picture and wondered if I would ever taste corn flakes with bananas and milk! Mother had cut out a colored ad for corn flakes and mounted it on a piece of cardboard to brighten the wall it hung on.

The year I finished the ninth grade, the PTA awarded a prize for the student with the highest grades in high school. It was a trip with Mr. Fleming, the principal, when he took the seniors on their class trip to Washington, D.C. I received this prize, too.

When I returned to our house from working in the fields the day before this bus trip, I found a package between our front door and the screen door. The box contained a solid gold-looking powder compact, a gift from Mrs. Henry L. Stevens, Jr., my history teacher. What a thrill to leave on this trip with a real gold-looking compact, containing a cake of powder and a puff! A real feeling of luxury!

Our busload of seniors and I stopped in Richmond, Virginia to eat lunch at a spaghetti house. I had never eaten spaghetti. As I attacked the strings of spaghetti with tomato sauce, I had the feeling I was eating white worms covered with blood and I really had difficulty swallowing it, but managed not to get sick and not to tell anyone the struggle I was having.

When we went to the dining room for dinner at the hotel in Washington where we were staying that night, we frankly did not know how to order a meal from a complicated menu which contained several foods we never heard of. Some of the boys and girls began to giggle and Mr. Fleming, who was so prim and precise in his demands for proper behavior, announced that he would place the same order for all of us.

The first course served was a saucer with a cup that did not have a handle and it contained a dark liquid which we agreed had to be thin coffee. We were certainly not familiar with any other such appearing liquid. There were crackers on the table and we thought that was pretty dumb, to eat crackers with coffee! But we decided that we should use cream and sugar in our cups of apparent coffee. When we tasted the concoction the giggling really took off. Mr. Fleming was so embarrassed at our behavior and seemed perturbed with himself that he had not explained to us anything about what he had ordered, realizing none of us had ever heard of French consommé before. He then explained what our main entree would be and we completed the meal without further incident.

That night after dinner several of the boys invaded a nearby tobacco store and made their first purchases of cigars. Several got really sick and received lectures from Mr. Fleming.

As the Depression became worse, the senior trips were discontinued and the PTA changed its policy and awarded medals for academic achievements.

Because of my early start in school which created a special incentive in learning and because our parents gave us time for getting lessons and encouraged us to achieve, I was able to receive the academic medals in the tenth and eleventh grades. Then I became valedictorian of our senior class.

Private Elmer Whaley, U. S. Army

One of our classmates who dropped out of school and joined the U. S. Army in 1931 was from a different Whaley family than ours. His name was Elmer Whaley. He was a handsome and friendly young man and very popular with both boys and girls. He soon wrote a long letter to our class telling us how happy he was to be in the army earning his own money.

None of us knew anything at all about the army but all of us understood that only the very top people in any big organization had private offices. We had even seen "PRIVATE" lettered in gold looking metal on some office doors, and we knew that the top people in big organizations were accorded "PRIVATE" privileges.

We knew the U. S. Army was a whopper of an organization and when we noticed that Elmer's return mailing address was Private Elmer Whaley, we just knew he had gone straight to the top post in the army. Of course, we had heard of generals, but we decided that private must surely be higher in rank than just a general.

My brother Milton went in the navy at the same time Elmer joined the army, but Milton only had the rank of seaman apprentice and here was classmate Elmer a private already!

So, we wrote Elmer a letter with several of us writing portions of it telling him how proud we were of him for getting top rank so soon after entering the army.

Making Furniture

When we were growing up, Alma was the creative one. She begged for a coping saw to use in cutting out little animals from some plywood that had been left over from a house repair project.

Then she got the bright idea of making a combination magazine rack and night stand, using the measurements from our Sears and Roebuck catalog. I took the measurements from a catalog description and drew a picture of each of the five pieces of wood that we would need to cut. She and I made three magazine rack/end tables, one for each of us to keep for our hope chests and one for Mother and Daddy. The racks were sanded and stained with mahogany varnish and looked quite good to us. I kept mine for about sixty years, using it for the night stand in my bedroom.

When I was fourteen, Alma and I decided we would make a two-seater swing on a frame like the one pictured in the Sears catalog. I wrote down the measurements for the frame and the seats, then we started looking for wood around the farm. We used some scrap wood for the frame and some "tobacco sticks" to build the two swing seats. We finally finished the project by hanging the seats facing each other on the frame.

As Alma and I labored over this project for several weeks, Milton taunted us and called our project *Fulton's Folly*, from the story of Robert Fulton building his first steamboat. Milton was not interested in carpentry. Even Mother had not been optimistic that our swing would ever really swing. But the whole family was surprised when the project was finished. We had to use the swing seats carefully, but to our amazement the whole swing set lasted two years and afforded us many happy swingings while enjoying our handmade project. Alma and I set as one of our goals in life to have a "bought" double swing someday.

Alma's Imagination

Alma made up names for everything. I remember one day she said to Mother. "I feel sick." Mother said, "Well, what do you think is wrong?" Whereupon Alma answered, "I'm sure I've got the 'breakings.'"

Little wild marigolds grew at the edge of our yard. One day Alma broke a bouquet of these, took them to Mother and said, "I brought you some marigold 'blantons.'"

Alma's Artistic Abilities

When Alma was forty-five, she was grieving over the loss of her only child, Austin, who had died of cancer. She joined an art class in Mt. Olive sponsored by the Wayne Community College. Her real talents showed through her sorrow. Now, my home as well as hers is made beautiful by her oil paintings that range from red and blue birds enjoying a feeder in the snow, to butterflies and flowers.

Nine elegant pieces of ceramics fired and delicately painted by Alma grace my home. Among these are berry pickers, a magnolia blossom, a Grecian girl, vases, and praying hands. A tea kettle painted by Alma showing birds sitting on tree boughs enlivens my living room hearth.

I consider all of Alma's handiwork among my greatest treasures.

Our Parents' Participation in Political Affairs

Both our parents always voted. Mother wrote letters to our county commissioners, our state legislators, United States congressional representatives and senators. Even in Mother's last days she was receiving letters from lawmakers and government officials. I would see replies on her lamp table and ask about them. She would say, "Oh, I wrote to him (or her) about so and so." Once I saw a letter from Lerlean Wallace, bearing her blazing red, white, and blue insignia: "Lerlean Wallace, Governor of Alabama." I asked Mother why she was hearing from Lerlean. She said, "Oh, I just wrote my congratulations upon her being elected governor, succeeding her husband, and this is her reply."

Our Civic and Political Affairs—Old Soldiers Reunion

Our parents encouraged us to attend and take part in civic and political affairs at Kenansville. Every year until the last Civil War veteran in the county died, there was an Old Soldiers Reunion in August at the Duplin County Courthouse. This was the grandest of the county civic events. We never missed one. There would always be an outstanding speaker, band music, and a picnic lunch at the ever-flowing water spring adjacent to the courthouse. There would be a baseball game in the afternoon and lemonade stands with five cent lemonade poured over ice shaved from a big block. The old soldiers wore their gray uniforms and they were indeed "generals for a day."

Yellow Brick Courthouse

The present day Duplin County Courthouse with its yellow brick, pinkish mortar, and copper top was erected in 1911-12, replacing the three-story wooden courthouse which had stood nearby since 1784 when Duplin and Sampson counties were divided into their present boundaries. It is reputed to be one of the most beautiful courthouses in North Carolina. It stands as a great source of pride for Duplin County citizens who have, since 1912, used it as a county center for many types of events.

The Boneyard

Across from the courthouse, next to the Kenansville Baptist Church, there was a section of tall pines called the Boneyard. Here, in earlier days, horses and mules were tied to the trees and hitching posts while their owners attended court and looked after other business. The Boneyard had also been used as the location for buying and selling horses and mules, thus the name of the lot.

One of my most beautiful childhood memories is the May Day celebration in 1930 when our county 4-H clubs used pink and blue crepe paper streamers and danced around the May pole erected on the Boneyard.

The song we sang that day taught me a lifelong lesson. I have found the words useful many times.

> Come, let us be joyful
> While life is bright and gay,
> Come, gather the rose buds
> E'er they fade away.
>
> Oh, don't you worry
> And don't you fret,
> There's lots of love
> In this old world yet.
>
> So take a rose,
> The thorns forget,
> And go on your way
> Rejoicing

Life's Ambitions

The Hines farm was located next door to the Murray farm where our friends, Billy and Durwood, grew up. Mr. Murray's sister, Miss Katie Murray, was a Baptist missionary to China until the communists took over in 1949 and all the missionaries had to go home. During her assignment in China she came home every two years on furlough. We were intrigued by her spellbinding stories about the Chinese children and how hungry they were to hear the Bible stories she told them. It was her visits home that let me know my goal in life was to be a missionary, at least for a while, with the hope I would be sent to China.

We understood that China was on the other side of the world. So, once after Miss Katie had returned to China, Alma, Rdell, and I decided to dig down to China to see her. We found one of Daddy's shovels and started digging in the side yard. However, we were soon too deep to manage the shovel handle and could go no further. We filled the hole with the dirt we'd taken from it, quite disillusioned.

1929
Our First Family Automobile

In 1929 Daddy fulfilled one of our most recurring dreams. We had not only dreamed of getting a family automobile, but we talked about it incessantly among ourselves morning, noon, and night.

How tired we were of having to depend on Mr. Early Carr Newton to take us to church activities, though he was always gracious. How much we would like to have an automobile to take us to movies, parties at our friends' houses, and many other places. Though the Trailways buses ran several times a day by our house, we knew that Daddy and Mother also needed their own transportation.

That fall, Daddy had told us he had been looking for a used family car that he could afford. We could not contain our exuberance on Friday, 18 October 1929 when we arrived home from school and saw a used black Studebaker touring car in our yard. That was the same year the first school bus came our way.

All four of us jumped off the bus and scrambled to see which one could first push hard on the black horn button we knew would be in the middle of the big wooden steering wheel. Rdell outran all of us and pushed the button as hard as he could to get, "Ah-ooo-gah! Ah-ooo-gah! Ah-ooo-gah!" These were the sweetest sounds we had ever heard. We knew the wonderful changes that this car would bring to our family.

Being a touring car meant its sides were open to the weather. In fair weather this was nice, but when it rained we had to pull over the edge of the road and snap on the side curtains. They were in a pocket on the back of the front seat along with steel rod which fitted into sockets on the top edges of the doors. The curtains were waterproof and had transparent windows in them. What an improvement over our buggy which didn't have any curtains to snap on!

The windshield was composed of two horizontal sections and the windshield wipers were hand operated. If it rained hard, we pulled off the road and waited for it to stop.

Our car did not come with a spare tire, but that was all right with us, because Daddy and Milton knew how to patch a tire inner tube and put it back inside the tire. Daddy had bought some patches and glue. The car did not have a starter. There was a loose starting crank that we had to insert through a hole below the radiator. The ignition was turned on, then the crank would have to be turned by hand until the engine started.

On each side of our automobile were running boards which were about ten inches wide and eighteen inches from the ground and extended the length of both the front and back seats. We stepped up on the running board to get into the seats.

Our automobile had no luggage compartment. Some folks had folding luggage racks they fastened onto their running boards. But we really didn't need luggage racks because we never stayed anywhere overnight.

There were no laws requiring drivers licenses, so Daddy and Milton started driving at once. We were all so happy and proud. I carefully watched Daddy and Milton drive and they explained every detail to me.

One day soon after when the whole family was going to Warsaw I tried my driving skills. We were about four hundred feet from our house and I was picking up speed to about forty miles an hour when the right front tire burst making the car very hard for me to control. Every family member screamed different instructions! "Mash the brake!" "Take your foot off of the gas!" "Get on the shoulder!" "Watch out!" "Don't hit that car coming!"

The ditch on the right side of the road where the tire blew out was very shallow, hardly a ditch at all. I guided the car to the right and the right front wheel with the flat tire was almost in the ditch, but not quite. Daddy and Milton patched the inner tube and put it back in the tire. I was not ready to try driving again right away.

Soon I asked Ivey Cooke to teach me all the points I needed to know about driving, including how to change gears to go through mud holes or sandy places and how to parallel park on a street. In his kind and gentle way of teaching, I gained all the expertise I needed and soon enjoyed trying again. I never had another flat tire on that car.

The family had a lot of fun laughing about my first attempt with driving. We had many other lasting memories regarding our automobile. These memories are constant reminders of how good it is to own a car with all of today's improvements. Now we just turn the key and the engine starts without having to use a crank. We turn a button and get heat, air conditioning, cruise control, or listen to stereo music. All of this is good, except that I would still love to hear a horn that sounds like the one on our old black used Studebaker touring car.

A Child's Pain at Losing Earthly Possessions

All people seemed totally sympathetic with grown folks who lost their all during the Great Depression. Their "all" included their possessions, their spirit, their belief in their families and in themselves. People generally seemed to forget that the children were hurting, too.

In 1997, a friend related to me as clearly as if it were yesterday how, when she was six years old in August of 1929, she rode with her father on their farm cart from their home near Warsaw to Chinquapin. They went to deliver to G. B. D. Parker their cart, the chestnut colored horse pulling the cart, and the two chestnut colored horses being led by ropes behind the cart.

Mr. Parker had a mortgage on these and her father couldn't pay. Now he had been asked to bring them in to Chinquapin. They would be sold at one of Mr. Parker's frequent auctions and she wondered who would be the new owners. Would they care for the horses as her family had?

Her throat seemed to be full of lumps on the way to and from Chinquapin that day. There was little conversation. She and her father were sad. Their horses seemed to be slowly walking to a funeral. She had learned to love the beautiful chestnut horses with their snowy white spots and trimmed manes. She would miss helping to feed and water the horses and sitting in front of her father as they rode on a horse's back. The horses had been an important part of her life.

Her mother drove their farm truck to Chinquapin that day to take her mournful daughter and her sad husband back home after they made their delivery to Mr. Parker.

My friend remembers how she had a miserable sinking feeling, because in her suffering mind she believed her hard working father felt like a failure and she felt she and her whole family were failures, too.

In 1928, crops had not brought enough money to pay Mr. Parker for his crop lien and mortgage on the cart and horses or to make the payments to the bank on the mortgage on their home and farm.

At the beginning of the previous winter, her father had built a little house on his two-ton, flat-bodied farm truck. He then loaded up his family, taking along a tent, some bedding, and cooking utensils and had gone off to a hurricane damaged area of Florida. His goal had been to make money as a carpenter to help with their finances.

The family had spent the winter in their truck-house and their tent in a Red Cross village set up for hurricane victims and construction workers. Her father worked all winter on replacement homes for those the hurricane had destroyed.

As spring came on, they had returned to the farm at Warsaw, North Carolina, hoping for good 1929 crops which would be mostly market vegetables but the weather and prices that year were a disaster. There was yet no such thing as contract growing or assured prices. Now, there was no alternative but to give up the cart, the horses, the farm, and farming. It seemed like the end of the whole world to let their farm, including their nice home they had built, be repossessed and sold at auction. They would have to move to town and rent a small house, which would be a poor substitute for their comfortable farm home.

Her family had not experienced a death, but she had seen grieving families at funerals and felt sorry for them. As her family moved out of their beloved home, she felt all of them looked like they were grieving, because they had lost one of the dearest of all family members: their home.

Her father got settled in a public job and she entered the first grade at school that year. But her mind and thoughts were not on reading, learning to write, and working with numbers. Her thoughts were consumed by her belief that her whole family was a failure, that she was a failure and would never be anything else! Her entire childhood was clouded by her memories of 1929 and the changes her family endured.

To this traumatized six-year-old, being told that other families by the hundreds and thousands were enduring the same tragedies never eased her pain or diminished the hurt of the sad expressions she saw continually in her parents' eyes as they tried to adjust to their losses.

1930—Traveling Free Medicine Man Shows

After the Civil War, traveling medicine man shows were born in the South. These popular, free, one-night affairs featured homespun folk entertainment and attracted great crowds in small towns and villages once a year in the fall, after crops had been harvested and most people had dollar bills in their pockets.

The music varied from jug bands to fiddles, banjos, guitars, combs, reeds, and portable pianos. Sometimes there was a ventriloquist with a dummy or a minstrel show or a clogger or comics, and perhaps even magic tricks. The country music star, Roy Acuff, and Red Skelton, the famous sad-looking comedian, as well as some other budding stars, performed in these shows.

UNC public television in Chapel Hill recently produced an entertaining one-hour video depicting the history of medicine shows. This video describes how the last known show was held in Bailey, North Carolina. Efforts were made to use actors at this one last show who had participated in medicine shows during the days of their popularity. In the video, a performer, named Bob, and his wife tell about how, when their makeup supply ran out at a show in Kenansville, the county seat of Duplin County, they improvised by using burnt cork for Bob's black face makeup which they made from the inside corks of metal Coca-Cola bottle caps.

This video mentioned that after the Food and Drug Act of 1906 which permitted medicine to use forty percent alcohol, the medicine shows sold medicines containing the maximum of forty percent.

I recall when Daddy took us to a free medicine show in 1930, held on the courthouse square in Kenansville. My main memory is that the medicine was described as a sure cure for every known ailment.

After the show it was difficult for the medicine man and his assistant to accommodate all of the purchasers quickly. He announced the supply was running short. The audience stampeded the stage, waving their dollar bills in the air. Then, suddenly, a show worker appeared with a new supply "just received." Two hundred to three hundred bottles were usually sold at each performance, for one dollar each. That was a fortune back then.

This medicine man drove a shackly model T Ford pickup with a big, red hand-built wooden cab on the back. His cab held a small stage and posts, musical instruments, clothes, and his medicine supply. He and his helper cuddled up and slept in the red cab at night.

The medicine shows left everybody feeling good. Those who hadn't felt good when they came had not only been well entertained but they had bought medicine for one dollar a bottle, which would surely cure whatever ailments they had. And all who could, had purchased several bottles, because these shows didn't come often.

By 1940, the medicine shows were dead. They had been replaced by radio shows such as "Amos and Andy" and later by television shows.

1931

The County Stockade Fire

Saturday, 7 March 1931

The Hines farm where we lived was less than a mile through the fields and cart paths to the wood frame county prison, which was called the county stockade. It was next door to the Duplin County Home, which housed the homeless elderly folks, where we visited often. We had to walk past the stockade on our way to the county home and the sight of the stockade made me sad. These men worked either on the county roads or in the county garden used to feed the prisoners and the residents of the county home. At night the prisoners were locked in their iron cells. So, we assumed the prisoners just sat in their iron cells when they were not working.

In early morning of Saturday, 7 March 1931, when I was a junior in high school, the Jim Henry Miller family came to our house. They lived between us and the stockade. They were very upset. The stockade was burning and several prisoners were trapped inside. We just couldn't resist walking to the stockade and standing helpless with a lot of other people, smelling the strange and strong odor of burning human flesh. There must be no other smell like it. I hope there is none other akin to it, because this odor is still fresh in my nostrils and mind after sixty-six years. It never leaves.

I never saw an official report on the cause of the stockade fire. But the explanation that I always heard was that when the fire broke out at 3 A.M. on 7 March 1931, there was no employee on duty who had keys to the locked cells. The Duplin County recorded death certificates include data on eleven men who died during the fire, with cause of death shown as "stockade fire." All eleven death certificates show place of birth as Duplin County and the ages of the dead ranged from sixteen to fifty-two with nine being listed as twenty-two or younger. The death certificates all reflect their remains were buried in the Duplin County Cemetery, except for one, whose family claimed his remains and buried them at Hallsville in eastern Duplin County.

I searched the minutes of the Duplin County commissioners for this period of time in 1931 and could find no mention of this fire.

Duplin County Cemetery—
County Home and Stockade Fire Burials

The Duplin County elderly homeless lived at what was called the Duplin County Home until the era of U. S. Government old-age pensions provided funds that enabled them to live elsewhere. Later Social Security helped the elderly and the county home was closed.

The county home was located on property next to the county prison and the county unit of the state highway department.

The Duplin County death certificate records show that twenty-nine homeless persons, mostly those who died at the county home between 31 August 1914 and 27 June 1968, were buried in the Duplin County Cemetery. Records also show that ten male prisoners who died in the county stockade fire of 7 March 1931 and three other homeless persons were buried in the county cemetery.

During my years of service as county Register of Deeds and custodian of other records, some of the descendants of the forty-two persons buried in the abandoned county cemetery for whom we found death certificates recorded have sought information on their ancestors from the Duplin death records. Some asked for directions to the county cemetery where their relatives were buried. It was always difficult for me to tell them that the county cemetery was abandoned, the temporary grave markers gone, and that full grown trees were lifting their branches skyward over the graves of the folks buried there.

In 1988 before I retired, I compiled data from the death certificates for persons buried in our county cemetery and presented it to our county board of commissioners, as recorded in County Minutes Book 66 at pages 9-14, hoping the commissioners would consider erecting a monument of some sort at the cemetery containing names and dates for all of the persons buried there. No action was taken at that time.

I continued to keep in touch with Judy Brown, assistant county manager and clerk to the board of county commissioners, who continued to have a concerned heart and listening ear regarding our county cemetery as did Millie Brown, director of social services, and L.H. Sikes, our County tourism director, who serves as unofficial county historian. The four of us had informal discussions and then met, visited the cemetery site, and decided to present a proposal at the commissioner's first September 1997 meeting to appropriate funds to install a fence around the one acre county cemetery and erect a single monument bearing the names and data regarding all of the persons buried in the cemetery for whom records are available.

The board approved the proposal and appointed the four of us and county commissioner Zettie Williams to serve on a new County Cemetery Committee to monitor the restoration and maintenance of the cemetery. The county commissioners appropriated two thousand dollars to a Cemetery Restoration Fund.

Residents of the nearby State Department of Correction cut down the tall trees which had grown up in the cemetery during the thirty years since there had been burials.

Alas, not just forty-two sunken graves became visible, but there were sixty-eight. There could have been some burials before 1913 when death certificates were first filed and there could have been some County Home burials with no certificates filed.

A news reporter from the *Wilmington Star News* took a picture of stakes marking the sixty-eight graves showing some members of the Cemetery Committee and distributed it across the state through the Associated Press.

Dr. Mott Blair, of Siler City, and others who had lived in Duplin County and who saw the burned bodies of the young prisoners on 7 March 1931, had their tragic memories rekindled and sent a total of fourteen hundred dollars in contributions.

The North Carolina Department of Cultural Resources awarded a Historical Grant of seven thousand dollars, making a total of $10,400 available to at last restore the cemetery in a creditable manner, give the sixty-eight persons buried there the recognition they have so richly deserved for so long, and provide an adequate burial place for future homeless.

A dedication ceremony will be held when restoration is completed.

Milton Joins The Navy—His Family

Our financial situation prohibited Milton from going to college when he graduated from high school in 1931, so he studied the options available to him in our military branches and settled for the navy. His first paycheck was twenty-one dollars a month. He sent home ten dollars each month for our family's use. It was unbelievable how far that ten dollars would stretch. How much we appreciated his generosity and loyalty to his family! We realized that he had only eleven dollars a month left to spend for himself and that he could not participate in many activities with his shipmates when they went in to a port for a few days where there were movies, sightseeing, and restaurant meals available for them to enjoy.

On Milton's first trip home, when he and a Navy friend stepped off the bus, his friend said he came to see Milton's hometown of Kenansville, "Where Milton says you have to back out of Main Street." This was true. Later a vacant store building on Main Street was purchased by the Town and Main Street became the one-way street that it is today.

After I had gone to work in our county farm office, Milton's ship came into the Philadelphia harbor for only one weekend. At that time, he had not been able to come home in a full year. I boarded the Pullman train in Warsaw, seven miles away, and rode to Philadelphia where Milton met me at the big train station. I was able to spend the weekend with him. When our visit came to an end, he went to the station with me and made sure I was settled in my Pullman seat to return to Warsaw, then he waved me off.

Milton's leaving home to join the navy had been a big adjustment for me, because we were born just eighteen months apart and had been true soul mates all our lives.

When his first enlistment was up he reenlisted. By the spring of 1937 Milton had decided to muster out, come home, and marry his high school sweetheart, Ella Taylor from Warsaw. He arrived home just a week before Rdell's death in April 1937.

Milton and Ella were married and had Thomas on 29 August 1938, and Betty, on 1 September 1940. Betty was the only girl among the grandchildren in our family and she has always had a special place. She now lives in Hertford, North Carolina, so I do get to see her fairly often. She has a husband and two sons. The sons live in Chesapeake, Virginia. Betty has been like the daughter I never had.

When World War II came on, Milton rejoined the navy and later transferred to the air force. He retired a chief warrant officer after a total of twenty-four years military service.

Ella died in her forties, with a brain tumor and was buried in Portsmouth, Virginia.

After retiring, Milton took a job with our government in Turkey and lived there ten years, teaching diesel engineering to the Turkish people working on our military base there.

While in Turkey he married a Turkish lady, Senel, and a fair headed son, Senol, was born to their family circle. Senol graduated from Iowa State University with a degree in rural and city planning. He has been such a great joy to all our family. He joined the army reserve after college and while serving in this capacity drew the plans for the army base the United States built in Guatemala and spent six months there while it was being constructed. Senol is now serving our regular army in Germany and writes to our family regularly. His mother is living in the country of Turkey.

Thomas and his wife and only daughter, Michelle, were living in South Korea where he was supervising the maintenance of our military bases when he came down with terminal leukemia and moved to Satellite Beach, Florida in March 1986 to die. Thomas's only son, Thomas, Jr., his wife and two daughters live in Vancouver, Washington.

From March until he died in October 1986, I visited Thomas and his family four times at Satellite Beach. This is where I saw Home Care and Hospice functioning at its best. His family was assisted by two volunteers in addition to four paid professional workers.

It was during Thomas's illness that I made a decision to become a Hospice Volunteer when I retired. I saw the inside picture of how the burden of watching a loved one die can be lightened by regular visits and assistance of Hospice volunteers who have no monetary responsibility to perform services for the family of the terminally ill, but do so from seeing a need and activating the Christian spirit of filling the need. The Hospice Volunteers get abundantly paid through the joy that comes from their service.

I have now served as a Hospice Volunteer nine years and performed services varying from just listening, to keeping the patients provided with fresh flowers from my yard, to making flower casket blankets for two patients. I have found no other relationship like the one that develops from helping a family care for a dying member.

Through the years, whenever Milton has been in the States, the Norfolk-Portsmouth area of Virginia was his home and he visited us frequently. He usually made the drive to my house by one o'clock in the afternoon.

It was always a ritual that on the afternoon of his arrival, we visited our family cemetery at Beulaville on the farm Grandpa Thomas once owned. We always walked among the grave stones and relived childhood memories of our visits to our relatives at Beulaville. Driving by Mother's little house she built in Beulaville after Daddy died in 1948 was our next stop. We paused by the side of the street and discussed her twenty years there.

Then we drove over to the Hines farm near Kenansville and turned into the driveway to the long abandoned house where we had lived from 1922 until we left home. If the weather permitted, we walked around the house in the deep layers of oak leaves that had accumulated from long years of no one living there.

Sometimes we ventured the distance of about a city block down the hill from the house toward the lonely abandoned railroad bed, where we used to watch the train go by. Every visit to the Hines farm brought back healing memories of our childhood and helped us to relive our years there which so shaped our future.

Milton had never been sick and was never in a hospital until July 1994, when all of his internal organs began to fail at one time. He died 7 January 1995 and was buried beneath five inches of snow beside Ella in the Chesapeake, Virginia cemetery.

1932

The Most Fantastic Wage Around—People Leave Magnolia to Search for Better Lives

In 1931, standard farm wages and most other laboring wages in Duplin County were still five cents an hour for a ten hour day. Mr. John Croom's flower bulb industry at Magnolia was at its height of production and worldwide fame.

People were shocked in 1932 when Mr. Croom hired Edd Dudley Monk as the first black supervisor in the surrounding area for $9.50 a week to supervise fifty flower bulb workers for six ten-hour days a week. This was almost sixteen cents an hour. Not only was it unheard of to pay this great salary, but there was trauma at him hiring a black to supervise his mixed group of field and bulb-house workers.

Edd Dudley Monk and his family had been swapping work with our family in harvesting tobacco and we would miss him. He made good at his new position, learned a lot from Mr. Croom, and bought a total of nearly one thousand acres of land, mostly from foreclosures. He used a lot of his resources to educate his family. At his ninety-eighth birthday dinner in 1996, James Sprunt Community College awarded him an honorary doctorate degree in appreciation for his long years of service on the James Sprunt Board and for his contributions to education.

At his ninety-eighth dinner, he recalled the poverty that existed in Duplin County in 1910, the '20s and '30s. He also recalled the resentment against his 1932 salary and position.

I was delighted that his family invited me to be one of the speakers at his big birthday dinner. He looked forward to his one hundredth birthday celebration in July 1998 and I was there to help him celebrate and to present him a big bouquet of flowers from my yard.

Edd Dudley and I often talk about how so many folks moved away from the Magnolia area to try to find better jobs and how hard it was for some of them to endure the Great Depression foreclosures on their homes, sometimes for very small debts, and how the ownership of the land became concentrated in fewer owners, and the population of the town dwindled at one time to as low as three hundred.

Mother's niece from Magnolia, Lillian Matthews, had assembled wooden quart cups for strawberry crates in her home during the years she gave birth and cared for nine children and her husband, Clifton Matthews, a barber. Six of their unmarried children, three married children and their families, together with Lillian and Clifton, all packed up and moved to Miami, Florida to seek better livelihoods. Most of them prospered in the building trades, but some followed other professions, including one grandson and one great-grandson who became Southern Baptist ministers. The Matthews' descendants now live in many parts of Florida where they still prosper. They get together once a year for a Matthews Dynasty reunion, which is a most professionally organized and delightfully executed family affair. They could write a book titled *Up From The Poverty Of Magnolia To The Good Life In Florida.*

After High School—College
Out of Sight—I Must Study
at Home

During my high school years, I received all of the parent teacher association awards for academic excellence. My goal had been to go to Flora McDonald Presbyterian College at Red Springs, North Carolina. I had lived this dream since I was in elementary school and heard so much about Flora McDonald at my church. But when I graduated valedictorian of my high school class in 1932 the country was at the height of the Great Depression. Tobacco prices dropped to ten cents a pound that year. The Hines pack house, where we had always stored our cured tobacco, was leaking. We had to use the vacant tenant house for storage. It was the distance of about four city blocks from our house. There was no other building near it. Half of our cured tobacco was stolen at night from the tenant house.

Our tobacco was stolen just before Franklin Roosevelt became president and influenced Congress to enact the law requiring tobacco quotas and warehouse selling cards. So the thieves had no problem in selling the tobacco they stole from us.

I received scholarships and could have gone to Flora McDonald or one other college for one hundred twenty-five dollars a year. Several people offered to lend the money. But Daddy and Mother looked around at the few fortunate young people who had graduated from college during the past few years of the Great Depression. They were all sitting at home, jobless. My parents had a fear of agreeing for me to borrow five hundred dollars for a college education.

During this time, Reverend Frank L. Goodman, my minister at Grove Presbyterian Church, preached a sermon on "Making Good At Your Second Choices." He enumerated an array of great men and women who, through the ages, have made good at their second choices of careers and marriages by working hard and keeping their faith in the goodness of God and faith in themselves.

This sermon gave me hope to believe I would be able to fulfill my goal of getting into a field of endeavor where I could serve people one-on-one even if I couldn't go to college.

Later on, this sermon would be the inspiration to help me to believe if I kept my faith and worked hard at it, I could endure and make good at the marriage of my second choice when fate kept me from marrying the one true love of my life.

So, I checked out all of the information I could find on home study courses because I had no other option. Finally, I made a fifteen dollar down payment on a home study bookkeeping, business, and secretarial course from Southeastern University at Rock Hill, South Carolina.

The down payment had been earned by working on the Taylor farm for fifty cents a day when Daddy didn't need me to help him.

I ordered a four dollar used typewriter from a Raleigh newspaper ad. It was truly an ancient machine, but it worked, even if slowly. We called it "Noah's Ark," though we knew Noah didn't have any typewriters on board his ark.

My completed lessons were mailed to the university with a two cent stamp. I had to enclose a self addressed stamped envelope for the return of my graded lessons.

I continued working enough for other people on their farms for fifty cents a day to pay for the postage, textbooks, and fifteen dollars quarterly tuition.

1933

Years at the Duplin County Agricultural Adjustment Administration Office

Beginning December 1933

In December 1933, I had almost finished my home-study course when Mr. L. L. McLendon, our county farm extension agent came out to our house to see me. He wanted to know if I could help him sign up the farmers with tobacco acreage reduction contracts. I would be paid the unheard of sum of $1.85 per day. I was literally jumping up and down inside of myself.

Under President Roosevelt's leadership, Congress had gone to work and enacted the 1933 Agricultural Adjustment Act providing for payments to farmers to reduce their tobacco acreage. Later cotton, wheat, corn, and hogs were included in these reduction payments.

I soon became the office manager and stayed eight years and four months. The regular staff soon became six. Later on as more farm reduction programs were added. the staff increased to as many as twenty during summer compliance checks.

We sometimes employed as many as fifty men in summer after crop plantings were completed. At first, they measured all farm fields in the county using chains and links that we had to calculate into acres to determine if farmers had planted their allotted acreage of crops. Later came aerial photographs of all farms and we could use rotometers to make calculations of compliance with acreage allotments. More technical improvements followed for streamlining operations.

The first man from the state agricultural office who came to Duplin County as a traveling supervisor for the State office was Howard Stamey, originally from Haywood County, North Carolina. Each time he visited us his first statement was: "Let's 'git' organized before we start." Mr. Stamey had the only comptometer I had ever seen. He would get that machine, as well as every other item we would be using, perfectly positioned on our work table and then start to work. "Let's 'git' organized" still rings in my ears when I begin every task.

A Whole Hoop of Cheese

Mr. L. L. McLendon was an interesting, efficient and hard driving man and he was a good teacher.

One day he told the staff how he loved cheese. He said he never had enough of it when he was a boy and vowed that when he got his first job and his first paycheck, he'd buy a whole twenty-two pound traditional hoop of cheese. He graduated from North Carolina State University in 1923 and true to his word, when his first paycheck came in, he bought a whole hoop. It was about a foot and a half in diameter and all of six inches thick. During that day, storekeepers kept a whole cheese on a round, wooden platter on their store counters. A heavy steel slicer was attached to the cheese so wedges of different sizes could be cut. But Mr. McLendon's goal was to feel the exuberance of owning a whole cheese and doing his own slicing with his own butcher knife.

The favorite snack food at country stores was this typical southern hoop cheese eaten with "johnny cakes." Johnny cakes were large oblong cookies with the word "Johnny" indented on top before they were baked. They were ever so lightly sweetened and were just perfect with a slice of hoop cheese and a carbonated drink. Country stores kept them loose in glass or wooden bins.

Maw, It's Your Turn

One of my first experiences when I went to work for Mr. McLendon in 1933 was regarding chewing gum. We were signing up farmers at the agricultural office for the first tobacco acreage reduction contracts. A woman and her teenage son came in and I offered to help them. While I was getting the necessary crop data from the woman, the son took a big wad of chewing gum out of his mouth and handing it to his mother, said, "Here, Maw, it's your turn."

This incident reminds me now how tight times had been during the Depression and how lucky our family had been to have had our personal supply of chewing gum from the Hines Farm sweet gum trees.

Farm Programs Growing, Growing, Growing

In 1933, when the Federal Crop Reduction Programs started, the county farm agent had one small office in the county courthouse which did not accommodate the influx of workers who came with the Programs. The county farm agent moved his office to the large upstairs, unfinished room of the Dail Building adjacent to the courthouse. We operated the Agriculture Office in that location until a Federal grant and the Works Progress Administration (WPA) in 1936 built the handsome yellow brick Agricultural Building, which matched the county courthouse, with its pink mortar. This new building provided adequate offices for the county extension agent, a private office for me, and a large work room for the staff.

I must have been a mature looking woman for a long time. One day soon after we moved to the new Agricultural Building, when I had turned twenty one, I was in my private office when I overheard a farmer at our service counter say: "I want to speak with that middle-aged lady I talked to last week." The middle-aged lady who worked in the main office offered to help him. But he said she wasn't the one he was looking for. At that moment I had to go into the main office to speak with an office assistant. When the farmer spied me, he said: "There she is."

During my years in the Agricultural Office about a fourth of our farmers could neither read nor write. Helping the mass of non-reading farmers understand and interpret for their own use the complicated rules and regulations of the Federal Crop Reduction Programs that would benefit them, seemed a great mission to me. I adopted a policy in our office that every farmer would receive the same care and attention, except that the non-readers would be given special attention and help to understand the programs.

Most of our county residents, even those who lived in the nine little towns in Duplin County, owned some interest in farming and were entitled to some benefits under the Federal programs during the Roosevelt presidency from 1932 until his death on 12 April 1945. There was probably no one else in our county who was as close as I to the struggles of our diligent, hard working, non-reading farmers during the deep Depression years. My Daddy was one of them and I had breathed his breaths with him as he had struggled. So, I was always truly on the same wavelength as the farmers when we worked together in participating in the Federal programs and the farmers' financial recovery.

In order to accommodate the farmers when I was working with them, once a year we would take the Government papers for them to sign out to a central point in the various communities where they could come in and sign, with little travel and time loss. I found great satisfaction in getting to personally know and work with all of them. The farmers were so appreciative.

Many farmers had already lost their farms through foreclosure and many more were on the brink of foreclosure when the Federal programs came along in 1933 and later.

Some of the saddest scenes I had ever witnessed was observing six men in different locations in the county foreclosing on valuable farms and purchasing them for small debts, such as a one to two hundred acre farm for eight hundred to a thousand dollars. This was still going on after I went to work in December 1933.

There was one wealthy man in our county who hired an out-of-state farm manager to handle his farm foreclosures. I dreaded to see him come, hurrying into the Agricultural Office because I always knew he had just supervised some poor farmer's foreclosure at public sale at the courthouse door across the street and he was coming in to transfer the unfortunate farmer's tobacco acreage allotment to that of his employer.

This went on for three to four years after 1933. It took that long for the farmers to get back on their feet after the Federal programs were implemented. Many didn't make it in time to avoid foreclosure.

An uplifting side to this story is that of a representative of the United Life and Accident Insurance Company, Ely J. Perry, from Kinston, North Carolina. His company held Depression-made mortgages on many Duplin County farms. This kindly gentleman with a great heart would hold off foreclosures as long as he could and give the farmers time to refinance after they began to recover. One such case was the family of Ruth Spell, my best friend, and the second young woman who was hired to work in the Agricultural Office after I was employed.

Her family owed the United Life and Accident Insurance Company nine hundred dollars on their farm and they could not pay. Mr. Perry supervised her monthly payment of twenty-five dollars at first when she was making $1.85 a day and then fifty dollars a month after her salary grew. She completed payment of the mortgage and saved the farm for her aged parents. This young woman would bum a ride to and from work with a man who worked in the county seat. She could not buy a car as long as she was paying off the debt on the family farm.

The Federal government began lending money to tenant farmers for farm purchases in 1933, but my daddy had always been terrified at the thoughts of debt. Too, he had so recently seen many of the farmers he knew so well lose their farms under foreclosure for small debts they couldn't pay because of the Great Depression.

So, we lived on in the tenant house that never had an indoor toilet or running water. He seemed to make up for our lack of having a better house by bragging on us for working hard and helping us to take advantage of every opportunity available.

1934
Can You Help
with David's Funeral?

In March of 1934, a man, his wife, and their twenty-seven-year-old unmarried son, David, moved from Greene County to a small, frame house next door to the Hines property. The family had come because the father had a job with a sawmill which had relocated next door to the Hines farm. Son David was in the last stages of tuberculosis.

They were not only poor people, but they were unchurched, so they did not have the comfort of a church family. Folks in our neighborhood were afraid to go in a house where there was a tuberculosis patient.

I saw this family as lonely, deserted, desolate, and isolated in their new and strange surroundings. No one except the local physician found the way to their door. I immediately started visiting them and taking a sweet potato pie, bread pudding, or a few vegetables. Their son loved to read, so I shared devotional materials, newspapers, and magazines. He and his parents seemed delighted to have a visitor. I felt gratified at the great amount of joy they expressed at my visits.

The parents had said when David died they would take him back to Greene County for burial in their old family cemetery. The father came to our house when David died and told me the undertaker said they needed to ask someone to lead the funeral.

"Can you help us with David's funeral?" the father asked me.

A sense within me seemed to say, "How can I refuse? They don't have anyone else." My answer was, "I've never done this, but I'll try."

So, on a cold, blustery day in March with only twelve people gathered at the graveside, I did the best I could. David's parents were so appreciative of my feeble efforts at trying to help them feel rewarded for their love and tenderness in their unfailing care of David.

I tried to assure them that they had not been alone in their frustrations during his illness and that they would not be alone now in their sorrow and emptiness.

1935

Agricultural Adjustment Act Declared Unconstitutional

As I look back on the happy eight years and four months at the Duplin County Agricultural Adjustment Administration Office, I like to just skip over the memory of the trauma we endured one day, two years into the program. It is one of the "thorns" I've tried to forget.

Mr. L. L. McLendon, the county farm extension agent, under whose umbrella the office functioned at that time, received a telegram from Henry A. Wallace, United States Secretary of Agriculture, which read: "SUPREME COURT DECLARED AGRICULTURAL ADJUSTMENT ADMINISTRATION ACT UNCONSTITUTIONAL. STOP ALL ACTIVITY THIS DAY. NO PAYROLL FOR SERVICES RENDERED FOLLOWING THIS DAY WILL BE HONORED."

We were in the midst of completing the year's compliance records. All farmers would not get the devastating news immediately and would be coming into the office. Mr. McLendon called a meeting of the six full-time staff members and read the telegram to us. He asked me and Ruth Spell if we would stay on and operate the office while the Congress enacted a revised Agricultural Adjustment Act which would, hopefully, be Constitutional.

Ruth and I were the only staff members who lived with our parents near Kenansville. Mr. McLendon said he had no means of guaranteeing pay for our services, but if no means could be developed, he would give us a little expense money from his salary.

The pay wasn't as important to us as the fact that we just couldn't desert Mr. McLendon and the farmers who would be shattered. They had just begun to feel a sense of continuing hope. So we stayed on and worked our hearts out for two and a half months, trying to comfort the farmers until Congress enacted a revised Agricultural Adjustment program, and the entire staff could return to work.

We were delightfully surprised when Mr. McLendon was able to make arrangements for us to get paid for the two and a half months we thought we had willingly donated.

The main thing that helped me to smile during the time when everything had gone wrong was a cheap wooden plaque that had hung near the fireplace in Mother's and Daddy's bedroom ever since I could remember and I read it hundreds of times. It said:

It's easy enough to be pleasant
When life flows along like a song
But the one worthwhile
Is the one who can smile
When everything goes dead wrong!

One Time I Couldn't See the Joke of Little Henry in the Funny Paper

Back in the thirties when we were measuring acreage allotments under the agricultural programs, a young man, Randy Munn, the school principal at nearby Deep Run, worked in summers as a district supervisor spot-checking the men who were measuring the crop acreage. He loved to laugh over anything funny, but his favorite excuse to laugh was Little Henry.

Every time he came to Duplin County he always came in to my office with his Raleigh *News & Observer* funny paper, just chuckling over the antics of Little Henry.

Showing me Little Henry and letting me shake with laughter with him was his first order of business. Little Henry was always a scream back then. In fact, it was the first thing I daily searched for in the newspaper myself.

But, one day Randy came in holding the funny paper. He was laughing so hard, he was literally screaming. He put the comic section on my desk in front of me and try as I could, I did not catch the joke. I stared and stared, but still couldn't get it.

Finally, as he was still almost hysterical, I hated to admit I couldn't catch on, so I just joined in his laughter and never did tell him I hadn't caught Little Henry's joke.

Alma's Marriage and Leaving Home

During the four years after Milton joined the navy and left home, Alma and I had become very close, sharing all our experiences. We always double-dated together. When Alma was fourteen she had started dating Norman Anderson from Warsaw. This had continued for three years until she dropped out of school on her seventeenth birthday in 1935 to marry Norman.

For two years they had been begging Daddy and Mother to give them permission to marry. Our parents had finally promised that they could marry when Alma reached seventeen. Norman was five years older than Alma and he was a fine young man in every way. He had been the youngest child and the only boy in a family of eight sisters. His father had died when he was a small boy. His mother had kept all of the children at home with her, except Norman and the youngest girl, who were sent to the Odd Fellows Orphanage in Goldsboro because she could not provide for all of her children. She knew they would get good care at the orphanage. Norman had played the saxophone in the orphanage high school band and developed his talents in art.

Norman worked at night at the Warsaw Theater operating the projector and did carpentry jobs during the day. Building kitchen cabinets was his specialty.

Soon after marriage they moved to Mt. Olive where they spent fifty-nine inseparable years of marriage until Norman died 1 October 1994.

In Mt. Olive they purchased a modest home, making payments of twelve dollars a month. Norman continued to operate the projector at the theater until it closed, then he expanded his carpentry and went into wallpapering. He gained a great reputation for his expertise in workmanship. A baby boy, Austin, was born to them when they had been married a year and a day, on 3 March 1936.

This son was a complete joy to them, except that as a child he had frequent illnesses of varying kinds. Upon graduation from high school he spent four years in the air force. Upon returning home after his time in the service, he attended North Carolina State University and graduated with a degree in furniture design.

Austin married his longtime sweetheart, Josephine Waters, after he had been in college two years. Upon his graduation from the university, they moved to Lenoir, North Carolina, where he went to work in June of 1962 designing furniture for the Barnhardt Furniture Company. Josephine taught home economics in Lenoir.

They came home for Christmas that year, arriving with presents for each member of the family, excited that they could at last afford to buy gifts for all. On the day after Christmas, Austin came down with an illness. They immediately returned to Lenoir where he spent a month in the local hospital. He then stayed either in Duke Hospital or the Veterans Hospital in Durham until he died on 7 April 1963, of cancer of the liver.

For Austin and all of us, there was never a girl like his Josephine. Every day since his death, she has called his parents. In the meantime, four years after Austin died. Josephine married another only son. He died of cancer of the lungs. He and Josephine had no children. Josephine's second husband seemed as interested as she was in her daily telephone calls to the Andersons and was always concerned about their welfare. Nineteen ninety-seven makes thirty-four years since Austin died. Josephine continues her daily calls.

Rdell's Illness

In August of 1935, after Alma had married and left home in March of that year, we noticed a loss of energy and appetite in Rdell, now thirteen years old. At this time we also noticed a lump, which we did not understand, in his neck area. We took him to Dr. Gooding, our Kenansville family physician. Dr. Gooding did not place any significance on the lump in Rdell's neck and suggested that this might be just a temporary situation.

The first week of that December when our young county health physician, Dr. White, was making an annual check of the Kenansville schoolchildren, he noticed the lump in Rdell's neck. Dr. White wrote a letter to Mother and Daddy, suggesting that Rdell be taken to Duke Hospital in Durham as soon as possible for examination to determine if the lump could be caused by Hodgkin's disease, a terminal form of cancer of the lymph glands.

Daddy and Mother immediately went in to talk to Dr. White, because they had continued to be very concerned. An appointment was set up at Duke Hospital for Rdell on Thursday, 26 December 1935, to remove the suspicious lump, have it studied, and a diagnosis made. The answer from Duke Hospital came in the mail in about a week. Rdell had incurable Hodgkin's disease and would not live more than two years, possibly not that long.

The Duke physicians recommended X-ray and radium treatments. These were available at the office of Drs. Howard and Ivey in Goldsboro, thirty-five miles away. Daddy and Mother were devastated with uncontrollable grief at the thought of their youngest child suffering and dying within two years.

My food stopped digesting well in my stomach. I realized that I was simply overcome with shock and premature grief. Rdell was all that I had left at home to love and enjoy. Brother Milton had reenlisted in the navy. Since Alma married and moved away, Rdell had been going with me and my dates to the movies. We had become so close and depended on each other. He was so sweet and such a joy to Mother and Daddy, too.

The previous year I had been bothered for some time with chronic appendicitis. I had ridden on the bus to Wilmington where Dr. Henry Bullock, a surgeon about sixty years old, had removed my appendix. I stayed in his hospital a week, which was the usual stay at that time. Daddy and Mother had driven the fifty-five miles to bring me home. I had been very impressed with Dr. Bullock's kind and concerned manner. I needed to talk with someone about how facing the illness and death of my little brother was affecting my digestion. I went to see Dr. Bullock.

His advice helped me to understand that I was not responsible for Rdell's sickness and that it could not be changed. So, I had to learn to live with it. Dr. Bullock helped me to see that I could do more to make Rdell happy during his illness if I accepted his fate rather than rebelling at the situation. His counsel not only helped me then, but it also helped me to face and live with other tragedies and disappointments later in life.

Rdell's Last Days

We took Rdell to Goldsboro many times during the next two years and four months before he died in April of 1937 at the age of fifteen. The treatments kept him from swelling or living in pain and discomfort. He continued to attend school in the ninth grade on days he felt up to going until November of 1936, when he had to start resting at home.

Rdell's main problem seemed to be a lack of appetite and energy. We had begun to think he had accepted dying and that he was aware of the approaching of his last days. But a week before he died, it was so heartbreaking for us when a neighbor brought him a bag containing about a pound of raw peanuts. Rdell handed the bag to me and asked me to put them up where no one would eat them, because he wanted to plant them when he got better.

Since the time Rdell died, I worked for two years on a study commission with Dr. Rachel Davis of Kinston. She told me she never had a cancer patient who, as they faced dying, didn't express expectations about doing certain things in the future. But, her heart patients were usually afraid their heart would suddenly stop any minute. Then I realized Rdell's hope of planting the peanuts was typical.

After Rdell discontinued going outside, his faithful collie dog, Rover, insisted on coming in his bedroom, spreading out on the floor with his chin toward Rdell's bed, keeping watch, and spending his nights there.

When Rdell died and was brought back home in his casket to await the funeral, Rover stayed by the casket until it was moved out. After that, for a long time, his dog remained by the door through which the casket had been removed from the room. Six months later, Rover died. Mother, Daddy, and I diagnosed his disease as grief.

After Rdell died, we were glad we had tried to go on living as we helped him to reach for whatever joy he could find in each day. We had tried to focus on what was most important to strengthen him for whatever was to come. This was our first experience in helping to usher a fragile young life into eternity, but we found there was a sweet reward in feeling we had made his journey through the shadows comfortable and caring.

There was a calm in the realization that we had given him our reassuring hands with the promise to walk with him.

1936

A Good State Job Offer

It was soon after Rdell's terminal illness diagnosis that Mr. Frank Parker, statistician for the North Carolina Department of Agriculture in Raleigh, asked Mr. McLendon, our county extension agent, to get someone to compile a report for him on certain Duplin County statistics regarding crop acreages, yields, and tax data.

Mr. McLendon asked me if I would consider doing this in my spare time and keep a record of hours spent, because I would be paid what sounded to me to be the highest hourly fee I had ever heard of: three dollars.

I prepared the report on big, ruled, stiff sheets of paper, about 24" x 30". After about a month, I submitted the report to Mr. Parker, along with my carefully kept time sheet. In about two weeks, Mr. Parker called me by telephone saying he had a vacancy in his office and wanted me to come to Raleigh for an interview. Mr. McLendon encouraged me to go, saying the pay was so good.

I don't think Mr. Parker ever did believe that the time sheet I had submitted reflected all the time I had spent in compiling his report. I understood his disbelief, because he had no way of grasping the impact of Miss Cox's high school math classes, the thoroughness of the bookkeeping segment of my home study business course, nor the work habits taught by my parents.

When lunch time came the day I visited Mr. Parker in Raleigh, he took me to a little restaurant near his office. I ordered fried bananas as one of my vegetables. I had never heard of fried bananas, but enjoyed such an exotic taste! Once I tried preparing some, but mine were a disappointment.

Mr. Parker had to be in his fifties, a kind and gentle, graying man. Just the fatherly type to enjoy working for. The salary was excellent.

But, I explained to him that I could not leave home at this time and why.

Reaching Out to Other County Offices

The Duplin County AAA Office had formulated an efficient operation which had caught the attention of state and national U.S. Department of Agriculture officials. Throughout our country many counties had experienced difficulties in coping with the ever increasing demands and the ever changing regulations of the expanding Federal farm programs.

J. L. Kelton, USDA efficiency expert, was sent to Duplin County to study our operation. I assisted him in writing a handbook entitled *How to Organize and Operate a County Agriculture Adjustment Administration Office* which was distributed to all counties in the United States having farm operations. The cover read "Written by J. L. Kelton, U. S. Department of Agriculture, and Christine W. Williams, Office Manager of Duplin County, North Carolina Agricultural Adjustment Administration Office."

Several nearby county offices had experienced problems in organization and productivity. I had been invited to take some of our staff and go to adjoining Pender County and supervise the reorganization of that office to ensure greater efficiency. One office assistant and I drove to Burgaw daily for a week and brought that office up to date. Later, one of the Duplin County AAA staff members went to Jacksonville in Onslow County where she boarded and roomed during the week and returned to her Duplin County home weekends for several months, helping to reorganize and supervise the Onslow office. She then returned to the Duplin office and after I left she became the office manager for a short while.

1937

Eleanor Roosevelt, First Lady, Visits Wallace, North Carolina

Beginning in the early 1900s and continuing into the 1940s, peaking in the 1920s and 1930s, the area around Wallace, Teachey, and Rose Hill produced and shipped more strawberries than any other section in North Carolina. Wallace was said to be the single biggest strawberry market in the world.

The Wallace Strawberry Festival in 1937

Dedicated and flamboyant Wallace Mayor Aubrey Harrell was a great promoter of the town of Wallace and its fame as the greatest of the strawberry markets. The Wallace Strawberry Festival had become known throughout the United States.

The best festival ever staged in Wallace was said to be the one to close on Saturday night, 12 June 1937 following six spectacular days of entertainment which had reached its climax on Friday of that week when Mrs. Franklin Delano Roosevelt, the First Lady, was the guest of honor.

Opening on Monday to a capacity crowd, the festival management, led by Mayor Harrell, had left no stone unturned in this event to furnish the crowds the very best in entertainment at the biggest Wallace tobacco warehouse every night during the entire week. The large number of people who were on hand each night was evidence that the management had been highly successful. With some added attractions on each night's program, anyone attending could hardly find room to complain of a dull moment.

The dances which were held each night on the street, following the main program in the warehouse, were usually clean and orderly as was the warehouse floor show sent to Wallace by the celebrated showman of that time, George Hamid, of New York.

Pretty girls from throughout eastern North Carolina competed for the coveted title of "Queen of the 1937 Strawberry Festival." The queen's contest and coronation was always held on Friday night, but no queen's contest or coronation had ever been witnessed by the First Lady. This Friday night would be very special! The queen's ball held following the coronation on this Friday was the most impressive and the most crowded ever!

The entire festival of 1937 was agreed by all to be the best ever staged in Wallace and Mayor Harrell and his large corps of assistants were heaped with many words of praise for the excellent manner in which the festival was handled.

Wallace Mayor Harrell had invited Mrs. Franklin D. Roosevelt, First Lady, to attend the 1937 Wallace Strawberry Festival. Bringing a message of hope and cheer at every public appearance in Wallace and vicinity, Mrs. Roosevelt returned to Washington on the night of 12 June, leaving behind thousands of thrilled and delighted North Carolinians.

Arriving in Wallace on the early morning train, Mrs. Roosevelt was escorted to the palatial home of Dr. and Mrs. John D. Robinson for a brief stop before proceeding to the Coastal Plains Agricultural Extension Station at Willard, a small settlement two miles from Wallace. Mrs. Roosevelt and a hundred others were the guests of the director in charge, Dr. Charles Deering, at an old fashioned North Carolina breakfast served on small tables on the lawn. Here Mrs. Roosevelt received the honor of having a new variety of strawberry named for her. This variety, formerly known as No. 337, was renamed "The Eleanor Roosevelt."

From the Coastal Plains station the party was driven to the Penderlea Homesteads where a very interesting pageant entitled "From Settlement to Resettlement," was presented by the Homesteaders under the direction of Miss Margaret Valiant and Nick Ray of the U. S. Resettlement Administration. Here, too, the First Lady showed her mettle when she participated in an old fashioned square dance which was put on by the Homesteaders for her enjoyment. In a brief talk to the several thousands who braved the stifling heat and swirling dust to witness the pageant and catch a glimpse of the First Lady, she impressed her audience with her simple dignity and radiant personality as she preached the doctrine of cooperative effort.

Returning to Wallace following an inspection tour of the Homestead project, Mrs. Roosevelt and party were guests of Dr. and Mrs. Robinson at lunch, following which the First Lady made her appearance at the street festival, to be greeted by a crowd estimated to be more than ten thousand. Here Mrs. Roosevelt held her vast audience spellbound as they endured the blazing sun as she stood on a temporary platform in the heat and revealed her intimate knowledge of agricultural conditions. Here, too, she again proclaimed the doctrine of cooperative effort and lauded the work being carried on to rehabilitate farm families who sank to the depths of despair during the Depression, losing all. She was given a thunderous ovation following her address, which was broadcast over nationwide radio hookup.

My Participation

I was probably one of the most excited citizens in our county at Mrs. Roosevelt's visit.

At five o'clock on Friday afternoon, 11 June 1937, when she was in Wallace, the Kenansville Junior Women's Club assisted other women's clubs in Duplin County in entertaining at a reception for Mrs. Roosevelt at the Robinson home. At this time I was twenty-two years old and serving as president of the Kenasville Junior Women's Club. What a thrill this was to work with other women in being a vital part of this momentous occasion in the life of our Duplin County people.

The Robinson home and grounds were replete in all their splendor and graciousness, with arrangements of local flowers beautifying the interior of the home and arranged in big, white wicker baskets on the lawn. Mrs. Robinson was a most beautiful and charming hostess and genuine in her Southern hospitality. After Mrs. Roosevelt's visit, the Robinson home in Wallace was lovingly called "The Little White House" by local residents.

The First Lady's visit had very special meaning to me because I had keenly watched farmers losing seventy percent of their income, forty percent of farm and home mortgages in default with many heartbreaking foreclosures, every bank closed, and my own hopes of college education dashed.

And then came Mr. Roosevelt with his useless legs dragging. But, I had watched his actions inspire the hearts of our Duplin County people like no other leader before or since. His beaming optimism, his never-say-die trust that we were greater than our plight, and his bursting self-confidence had given our people their first glimmer of hope.

Mrs. Roosevelt exerted moral influence in her own way, encouraging and inspiring us. She would continue her far-reaching influence and activities for another eight years and become one of the most admired of all American First Ladies.

In 1997, it seemed to be the perfect culmination of the Roosevelt era when the four-room Franklin Delano Roosevelt presidential monument was finally dedicated in Washington, D.C. with one of the rooms containing a life-size statue of Eleanor. She became the only First Lady in the history of our country to be honored as a part of her husband's presidential monument.

Death Knoll for the Annual Strawberry Festival

Had it not been for the North Carolina child labor laws and the coming of the red spider plague, Wallace might have continued as the world's biggest strawberry market. Children in the strawberry growing area had been often absent from school during parts of April and May because they were in the strawberry fields. Hand picking was then, and still is, the only known method of harvesting the delectable fruit known as the strawberry.

The North Carolina child labor laws prohibited children under age sixteen from picking strawberries during regular school hours. This was the day before the era of migrant labor in eastern North Carolina and there were not enough adults available to do this seasonal work.

Then came the hard to control red spider, draining strength from the leaves of the strawberry plants. These two events together dealt a death knoll to the famous Wallace strawberry market and the festival that had caught the imagination of the world.

Think Chrysthine Will Be an Old Maid?

Nineteen thirty-seven proved to be the most momentous year of my life! Not only was it the year of my dear young brother's death in April, and Mrs. Roosevelt's visit in June, but it was the year that I turned twenty-two years old and was feeling pressured to get married.

Mother's sister, Ella, had nine children. Her marriage license shows she was married at fifteen. All of Mother's and Daddy's families had married young. Sister Alma had followed this family tradition by marrying on her seventeenth birthday.

When I had reached the ripe old age of eighteen, I had begun to hear Mother's sisters, Ella and Nora, whisper such concerns to Mother: "Don't you think Chrysthine is going to be an old maid?" As if this were the worst thing on earth that could happen to a girl! If it did happen, the girl felt disgraced.

These whispers began to escalate after Rdell's death in April of 1937.

Aunt Nora's husband had died soon after her sixth child was born. She was left to rear the children by herself on sharecrop farms. She never married a second time. Her eldest son became head of the household.

Aunt Ella's husband had abandoned her after their eighth child was born, stayed away for more than year, then returned home for a short while. She became pregnant with her ninth child and he left again and started another family in a different location. She had to rear her children on various sharecrop farms, working hard all those years. Her eldest son, also, became head of the household.

Aunt Nora's oldest son and Aunt Ella's oldest son, both at around age twenty, had each fallen deeply in love and wanted to marry. But both mothers seemed to believe that their sons' main mission in life was to substitute for the children's absent fathers. Each of these mothers seemed to make it clear that her eldest son was to manage the sharecrop farms they lived on, supervise the younger children and teach them how to work.

They taught all of the children how to work and all of them have made good livings. Both of these young men stood by their families.

One of the jilted girls and I were good friends. We often visited and shared our heartbreak at the way family responsibilities had affected our romances.

Later on, both men finally married but there never seemed to be the same romance and excitement they had known with their first loves. One of them and the woman he chose to marry, after most of his brothers and sisters were grown and settled, were too old to have children.

The two young men and I developed a bond and comradeship that could only be understood by one who had walked in our shoes! We often talked in confidence about our loves and our frustrations in being drawn from unfulfilled romances by three sisters who depended on us to be the pillars of our families and who honestly thought they couldn't do without us.

Left: The Hines House after long years of being empty.

Daddy in his typical farm clothes.

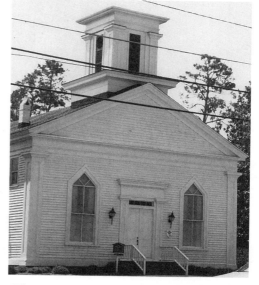

The Kenansville Grove Presbyterian Church where I attended for fifteen wonderful years—1922-1937.

Right: The Murray House on the farm next to the Hines Farm. Now used as a Bed, Breakfast and Gift Shop.

A hog dripping on the gallows on hog-killing day.

1927—Our sixth grade at the new Kenansville School grades one through eleven, Katherine McKenzie, teacher. I am in the middle row, third from left. Only six of us are living in 1997.

Left: 1936—We took three days at our County Agriculture Agent's cottage at the ocean. L to R: Mother (holding Austin), Daddy, Alma, Norman. Seated: Chrysthine and Rdell. We had learned of Rdell's illness eight months earlier.

Daddy, Milton and Mother

Cyrysthine, Alma, Milton and Rdell

Right: Home of Laurie and Carol Jackson in Smith township. Used as a tenant house by my Aunt Nora Smith and her six children in the 1920s and 1930s. Built by Jule Thomas, Laurie's great grandfather in 1893.

1934—Staff and L. L. McLendon, County Agriculture Agent. I am second from left, back row. This office was upstairs in the Dail Building.

1936—New county Agricultural Building erected with WPA labor.

Left:
Agricultural
office staff on
back steps of the
new building
after an increase
to nineteen.

Right: Rdell at fourteen
and a half years old,
about six months before
he died.

Left: A 1924 touring car
like the five-year-old car
Daddy bought in 1929.

Part Four

1929

1929

Ivey Cooke—The Beginning
of a Friendship and
an Unfulfilled Romance

In 1929, when I was turning fourteen and a freshman in high school, romance came into my life when I met Ivey Cooke from Warsaw. Milton's girlfriend and future wife, Ella Taylor, introduced us. The spark that ignited that summer day never diminished in spite of distance and circumstances.

Ivey was four years older than I, having just completed high school. Good jobs and opportunities in Warsaw were not to be found in 1929. Ivey took a job with the Warsaw ice plant, delivering big ice blocks to the stores in Warsaw and Kenansville and to the homes of people who were fortunate enough to have an icebox. His wages were low, as were all area wages at that time, but Ivey was a good money manager and always had a good, secondhand car. He was living at home with his parents, sister, and three brothers. Ivey, his sister, Essie, and I became good friends along with Milton and Ella.

Ivey came to see me often. Being with him always brought a warm, safe, and comfortable feeling that I knew would never change. Our love was based on a deep sense of mutual admiration and respect. We understood and adored each other with the kind of understanding that never grows dim but grows more enduring.

Ivey was dependable and reliable. Being lovable was just a part of his general character. He was affectionate with no desire to show or prove anything. He was always kind and sentimental but reserved and never gushy. Our love was always steady with no lows or highs that ever needed explaining.

Above all, our love was innocent and wholesome, the kind that breeds no regrets and provides eternal memories of times shared together, memories that always seem freshly stored and can be called upon anytime when needed.

The Bouquet of Red Cannas

It was in August of 1929 after I had started dating Ivey Cooke that we had our sudden and only lesson in honesty.

At that time young people loved to ride to Magnolia on Sunday afternoons to gaze at the radiant beauty of the far reaching fields of blazing flower blossoms. One could sometimes not see to the edge of some of these immense fields on the John Croom farms. Not only did the summer flower fields beckon to me but there had always been a strong attraction to draw me back to Magnolia since I was old enough to learn that it was my birthplace.

As sightseers approached the tuberose fields, the sweet smell of their white funnel-shaped blossoms wafted through the air and seemed to remind the viewer of Heaven. This was a favorite outing for Ivey and me.

Sometimes there would be fields of twenty to thirty acres in one color of canna flowers of brilliant red, yellow, or purple. The caladiums were either green and white or green and pink, their massive leaves soaking up the sun. There would be small fields of giant green elephant ears and I wondered how their stems held up under the weight of such heavy leaves. They really looked as big as the ears of elephants I had seen in the circus at Warsaw.

On this particular Sunday as we drove slowly by a field of red cannas, Ivey said to me, "Wouldn't you like me to pick you a bouquet of red ones?"

We had discussed how Mr. Croom never used the flowers and what a shame that all the beautiful blossoms just dried up. Surely he would not care if we picked a bunch from among the millions of blossoms. So, Ivey got out of the car, stepped onto the hot, dry, and dusty field and carefully picked a big bouquet of red cannas. I was so proud of this gesture and carefully held the bouquet on our way home.

Upon arrival, Mother asked, "Where did you all get those flowers?" We told her about our procurement. She spoke in the kind and gentle way she had of dealing with us about what she considered unacceptable behavior. She explained that while Mr. Croom did not have a use for the flowers and they would dry up when they matured, we really did not have his permission to pick the flowers and we should not keep them.

Both of us just stood there before Mother, stunned by the reality that she was right. We really did know better. Above all, we observed Mother's face reflecting disappointment. She then kindly suggested we should drive back to the field where we picked the flowers and leave them there. We accepted her decision because we never doubted that she was trying to teach lessons for then and for the future.

We never needed another lesson in honesty. But, the memory of that beautiful bouquet of red cannas and Ivey's tenderness in picking them provided happy memories later on when I urgently needed them.

Ivey Moves Out of the Area

In 1931, Ivey moved to Rocky Mount, more than one hundred miles away, where he had found a job in the maintenance department of a big cotton mill. We wrote to each other about once a week and he came to visit his parents and me at least once a month.

After Ivey moved to Rocky Mount, my lifelong best friend, Ruth Spell, and I took the popular and much traveled train at Warsaw several times to Rocky Mount where Ivey joined us for the train ride to Norfolk, Virginia. There we took the street car to Ocean View Beach for the weekend.

Ruth looked forward to these jaunts, as well as Ivey and I did. It was at Ocean View that my most beautiful and lasting memories were etched in my mind and heart: Memories of Ivey, Ruth, and I walking on the boardwalk, eating hot dogs, riding the roller coaster, Ferris wheel, and hobby horses. Memories of sitting on the beach in the moonlight watching the lights of the off-shore boats go by, and thinking of the popular song, "Harbor Lights."

We planned these trips as close to full moons as we could. The three of us agreed there was no other place in the world where the moon could reflect the same romantic light as at the Ocean View Beach with the soft sounds of the waves lapping on the coarse sand and washing bits of the sand back into the ocean as they receded.

"Love Letters In The Sand" was the most popular summer song during this period. The coin music boxes played this song more than all others. It seemed to give the invitation to sit in the moonlight on the sandy beach and use shells for pencils to write our feelings in the sand which seemed perfect for recording our messages.

As we wrote, we knew that whatever came in the future, the memories we created there would never fade. I could feel that they would always be real and present to lift me up when I needed to be raised above circumstances I couldn't change. I knew then that they would always make me glad that I had known real love that would never diminish in my memories in spite of distance or situations.

That was the day we sang:

> When your hair has turned to silver
> I will love you just the same
> I will always call you sweetheart
> That will always be your name.

And I knew this was a never dying promise Ivey and I were making to each other. We also sang:

> I am dreaming dear of you
> Day by day
> Dreaming when the skies are blue
> When they're gray
> Let me call you sweetheart
> I'm in love with you
> Let me hear you whisper
> That you love me, too.
> Keep the lovelight glowing
> In your eyes so true
> Let me call you sweetheart
> I'm—in—love—with—you.

Through the years as I have gone about the daily chores of living while humming or singing these tunes, they have renewed happy memories and have given me strength to face the future.

At the time, Ruth Spell was dating her future husband, Jasper Herring. He was a swine and tobacco farmer and never went with us on our jaunts with Ivey. There are few true lifetime friendships like mine and Ruth's. We would eventually work together in two county offices for a total of more than forty years, share our innermost thoughts, and comfort one another in all our concerns of life. The fact that we had been together all week did not keep us from enjoying Sunday luncheons and family visits every third Sunday while our children were growing up.

Only Ruth Spell and Ivey's sister, Essie, knew and understood how the endearing and enduring love that Ivey Cooke and I shared affected our lives and how I chose to stand by my parents instead of marrying him.

Ivey and I continued to write letters. If he was not coming home at my birthday, he always mailed a gift. We seemed to have a perfect understanding on all matters.

After Ivey moved to Rocky Mount, Mother began to say to me in different ways: "You can never marry Ivey. Milton is gone. Alma is married and gone. We just can't have you marry Ivey and move to Rocky Mount. You're the only one we'll have to depend on." So, I tried to keep marriage to Ivey out of our plans.

A New Man Comes into the Picture

Later, when Rdell came down with Hodgkin's disease in 1935, my parents' dependence on me increased. Soon after Rdell developed this incurable disease, a young man, Lehman Williams, who was working part-time in summers helping to measure croplands in the county for compliance with the Federal farm programs, started coming to see me. He lived in the B. F. Grady community of Duplin County, about sixteen miles from our home.

Lehman was very attentive to all of us and continued his visits several times a week throughout Rdell's illness and death. He was so kind and caring and regularly took Rdell with us to the movies at Warsaw or Clinton and to visit Alma and Norman and their baby in Mount Olive, twenty miles away. We often attended the movies with Alma and her little boy in Mount Olive, where Norman worked at the theater.

Lehman always had a good car and plenty of spending money. He wore expensive clothes. He was an excellent dancer, smooth and graceful. We attended square dances at both Marvin Simmons farm pack house and at the old Pink Hill tobacco warehouse. We also enjoyed round dancing. There was no way of knowing that after he married, he would never dance another step. There was no way of knowing how he pressured his aging mother for money.

Toward the last of Rdell's illness he sat with Mother, Daddy, and me late at night when Rdell would be so sick. He was so compassionate and understanding towards all of us and seemed to share our grieving. During this time, Alma couldn't visit much and Milton was often on ships in faraway ports. I could not have been aware that there were other sides to Lehman that we were not seeing because we were so blinded by our deep concern at Rdell's deteriorating health and Lehman's continued kindness. Following our utterly devastating grief at Rdell's death in April 1937, we were not able to see anything except the compassion he continued to show during our sorrow.

Lehman had one sister and three brothers. He had been born after the deaths of two young brothers. They had died of childhood diseases around four and five years of age. Lehman's only sister had already married and left the home when he was born. His brothers were much older than he. We were not aware that his parents had apparently felt that Lehman was an unexpected gift when they had thought they would have no more children to replace their losses of the two little sons. We later understood that they had treated Lehman differently than the other children, always letting him have whatever he wanted to have, regardless of the cost or the wisdom of his wants.

Lehman's persistence for us to marry began to escalate after Rdell's death. Deciding to marry was a great, great struggle for me. Lehman had been a comfort and help during Rdell's two years and four months of illness and death. He seemed to always be there. But there was total absence of the love, romance, adoration, respect, deep and ardent affection, and devotion that Ivey and I had felt since the beginning of our acquaintance.

Every aspect of knowing Lehman had seemed good except I had some serious concerns that he did not seem to feel close to either of his parents or his siblings.

He admitted that since his sister was married and gone from home when he was born, he hardly knew her. Also, his three brothers were so much older than he. There seemed to be nothing in common with them. I was concerned that there were no family gatherings, no closeness, no invitations to visit or eat a meal with any of them, though they all seemed to like me very much. But, I was already five years older than Alma was when she married. And Mother's two sisters kept saying I was becoming an old maid.

Above all, there were Mother's continued admonitions that I could never marry Ivey Cooke and move away from her and Daddy because I was all they had left and they needed me.

I had been at the Agricultural Office four years, loved my work, and my salary had greatly increased. It appeared that we would always have Federal crop programs. I could marry Lehman and still work there and keep in close contact with Mother and Daddy.

I realized later that Lehman had always had what he wanted from his parents. He wanted to marry me and he didn't give up. He got the commitment he wanted and we announced our engagement in October to be married in December 1937, in my beloved Kenansville Grove Presbyterian Church.

As soon as our engagement was announced I wrote to Ivey to tell him. Ivey wrote that he was very disappointed, after eight years of our friendship and romance. He had always expected that when he was properly situated financially we would get married. But he said that whatever happened in his future, he would always treasure our eight good years. He said the color picture I had given him two years previously would always be kept on the mantle of his home where he could see it and feel that I was near. It would always be a source of happy memories. Ivey moved to Norfolk, Virginia, where he became the director of the maintenance department at Leigh Memorial Hospital, and held that position until he retired July 1976, after thirty years of service at age sixty-five.

In 1941, four years after I married, Ivey married devoted Emily and she bore him two daughters, Carolyn and Virginia Lou. Ivey died in July of 1977 after only one year into his retirement. Upon his death his wife collected my picture that Ivey had cherished, a laminated copy of his newspaper obituary bearing his picture, and a half page feature article on Ivey's service at Leigh Memorial Hospital, which appeared in the hospital newspaper the month after his retirement. She gave these to his sister, Essie, to give to me.

Through the years when Ivey and his family visited Warsaw relatives in the summer, he always came to the Agricultural Office and later, to the courthouse in Kenansville where I was working and paid a visit during office hours. The occasion of these visits were the only times we saw each other after I married. His sister tells me that he always told his family when he was going to drive over to Kenansville to pay me a visit.

During each of Ivey's annual visits, he would say to me "How are things going with you?" I always told him about the good aspects of the life I had created, the enjoyment of my two sons and my work. I never discussed the disappointments in my marriage. But, after each of Ivey's annual visits I realized anew that while I had pleased Mother by always being nearby to help her and Daddy as long as they lived and while I had been able to reap great rewards in enjoying my children and in serving others in my profession, I had missed the boat to have a happy marriage.

Once when Mother and Alma visited Milton and his family in Norfolk, they went to visit Ivey's family nearby. My beautiful colored picture on Ivey's mantle looked down at Mother, Alma, Milton's, and Ivey's families as they visited. Tears came to Mother's eyes as she related to me the emptiness she felt as she realized her mistake in telling me I couldn't marry Ivey. She observed the tranquillity in the home he was providing for Emily and their children and compared it to the raging turmoil and impossible financial situation of the home I was enduring with Lehman.

Following are excerpts from the half page article that appeared in the July 1976 issue of *Medical Center Highlights*, Norfolk General Leigh Memorial Service Center, on the occasion of Ivey Cooke's retirement. The article was captioned "Conversation with Ivey Cooke" and displayed a 3" x 5" picture of him at his office desk, with framed certificates on the office walls. These excerpts reflect the kind of man he really was:

"A conversation with Ivey Cooke, LMH Director of Maintenance, is sure to hold you spellbound. Besides being a fascinating man, his thirty years of service to Leigh have given him a wealth of knowledge about the hospital.

"On his office walls hang many pictures and certificates.

"Another experience Ivey Cooke will never forget was when a physician called him to the Emergency Room to help him take a little girl's hand out of a meat grinder. Mr. Cooke skillfully manipulated her hand out of the machine with a minimum of injury to the little girl. The situation sums up the kind of man Ivey Cooke is.

"Hospitals are unusual places to work, and perhaps that explains why many unusually dedicated people can be found within them. However, Ivey Cooke is unique among hospital workers. His face shines with kindness and his hands reflect years of hard labor. Though his occupation is not directly involved with patient contact, he knows what patient care is all about. And though he is experienced, he knows what learning is all about.

"If you just want to talk with someone who can fascinate you for hours, seek out Mr. Ivey Cooke, Leigh Memorial's historian, handyman and storyteller. You'll not soon forget him."

While my hopes and dreams of a life of romance and love in wedded bliss with Ivey Cooke were never realized, the knowledge that I have experienced true and enduring love has always been a great source of happiness and contentment during my times of anxieties, impoverishment, and loneliness and caused me to deepen my dependence on God.

The picture of me made when I was twenty years old that I gave to Ivey Cooke and he kept it on his living room mantle as long as he lived.

Part Five

1937-1952

1937

My Wedding

After my engagement to Lehman Williams, plans were announced for us to be married at eleven o'clock, the morning of 23 December 1937.

Kind and practical Mrs. N. B. Boney was the advisor and director of the weddings held in the Grove Presbyterian Church. She asked me two weeks prior to the ceremony for details of our wedding because the local newspapers liked to write up the weddings a week before the event. I had never seen Lehman upset until I told him about preparing the wedding information for Mrs. Boney. But he soon cooled down.

I would wear my new burgundy and gray wool tailored suit with a small gray fur collar which I had purchased at the fashionable Weil's Department Store in Goldsboro. Sister Alma would be my only attendant. She planned to purchase a green silk dress but she had not had an opportunity to go to Goldsboro shopping yet. So, I told Mrs. Boney Alma would be wearing a green dress. Unfortunately, when she was finally able to go shopping there was not a green dress to be found! She had to settle for a beautiful mustard colored dress which complimented her blonde hair and blue eyes and made a lovely contrast with the church decorations.

When Lehman heard Alma relate her shopping experience to me during the wedding rehearsal party at my employer's home, he was transformed into a lunatic, a raving maniac. He verbally abused me in a loud voice because I had told Mrs. Boney that Alma would wear a green dress and shouted at Alma for not buying a green dress. Mother, Daddy, and I couldn't sleep that night for trying to analyze how Lehman, on the eve of his wedding, could change from the kind, considerate, understanding, and compassionate young man he had been to all of us for two whole years and become an insane madman having no respect for any of us including my nice friends who were hosting the rehearsal party.

Little did we know that such exhibitions of temper tantrums over matters of little importance as well as important ones would be the rule from then on instead of the exception. Neither did we know such displays had been his trademark with his family, especially when badgering his mother for money, nor could we envision that the badgering of his mother for money would escalate after his father would die the following June. But the one strong reputation our whole family had was that of sticking to our word. This was no time to ruin that reputation, so the wedding went on.

And so, at eleven o'clock on 23 December 1937, we were married by the Reverend Frank L. Goodman in the Kenansville Grove Presbyterian Church where couples had pledged their vows for almost two hundred years.

Daddy had cut fifteen stately pine trees, each about six feet high and secured them with nails on wood board cross pieces to grace the front of the Church. We had entwined southern smilax vines around three standing candelabra holding white candles. Two tall baskets of calla lilies from the Warsaw Florist added to the beauty of the antique sanctuary.

Evelyn Reynolds, wife of our county agricultural agent, played "I Love You Truly" and "At Dawning" accompanying the engaging and talented Erma Williams. Her sweet voice sounded more like that of an early morning songbird than the voice of a young schoolteacher.

Daddy and I entered to the tune of the traditional wedding march from *Lohengrin*. I held to Daddy's arm as we walked down the aisle. Alma was standing in front of the pines and calla lilies, just as pretty as a picture in her mustard colored silk dress, waiting to take my bridal bouquet and supply the groom's ring. I was trembling, but I was all right until I let go of Daddy's arm and handed my flowers to Alma. Suddenly, I had the feeling that I had no knees and that I was going to slump to the floor in front of the altar in the crowded church! I closed my eyes and started praying silently: "Lord, I need your help. Please give me the strength I need." Strength did come to keep me standing. I don't remember repeating the vows nor saying, "I do." But, I am sure I did.

Lehman and I stood in the vestibule and greeted the guests as they came out from the sanctuary. We had chosen a morning wedding service because at that time receptions were not usually held following an eleven o'clock wedding. The reason was simple—the expense of a reception was a cost few families could afford.

When Lehman and I ran from the church to our car, a freezing rain had started peppering down and continued for twenty-four hours. The temperature of the rain matched the temperature of my spirit as we set out for our destination, a hotel in Fayetteville, fifty miles away. There we would spend the night and return to my parents' home the next afternoon, Christmas Eve, so we could be with them this first Christmas after Rdell's death. Alma, Norman, and their little boy would be there but Milton and his family would be absent.

I felt guilty for leaving Mother and Daddy to face the new year without being there to continue to comfort them. The least I felt I could do was be with them most of Christmas Day. Then I would go on to begin a lifetime of comparing every temper tantrum and disappointment with Lehman to the calm, loving, and courtly manner of Ivey. Every day and every night I would regret marrying Lehman, but there would always be the shadow of my obligations to my wedding vows and my reluctance to admit my marriage was a disastrous failure.

I would go to bed every night mulling over what would happen if I should call the marriage quits. I would relive all of the happy memories of my eight years of totally satisfying association with Ivey Cooke and the knowledge that he still loved me. But the reality that would always overshadow my deliberations would be that the law then required two years of separation for divorce and Lehman would give me two years of torture that I would not be able to endure and keep my sanity. And, above all, Mother would never agree to let go because she so depended on me.

1938
Our First Year on
a Farm Near Warsaw
and the Fire

Before we were married, Lehman's father had made a down payment on a one hundred acre farm near Warsaw with sixty acres of cropland and two small dwellings. Lehman and I had painted the inside of one of the two four-room farmhouses and installed a small bathroom with running water in one corner of a bedroom.

When it came time to purchase furniture and appliances, to my surprise, Lehman said I would have to buy them because he would not have any income until the next fall when crops were sold.

I had been the office manager at the Duplin County Agricultural Adjustment Office now for four years and my salary had steadily increased. So I bought our furniture and appliances, but I did not get a hot water heater. It seemed that could wait.

Four dollars a week at that time covered our groceries and household supplies. Preparing menus a week in advance and buying groceries at the Great Atlantic and Pacific Food Store in Warsaw helped my budgeting. When I learned it would be up to me to pay all other living expenses including electric, phone, taxes, and fire insurance, I was shocked. Lehman just wouldn't have any income until the next fall.

Every morning before going to work, I prepared Lehman's lunch and left it ready to eat. During that first year of marriage, my lunch was eaten with Mother and Daddy which gave us daily contact. This pleased them and we could still enjoy our close family ties.

During 1938, a sharecropper named Walter Rouse and his family lived in the other house on the farm. Mr. Rouse had a grown son, a wife, and a daughter. They tended the crops, a garden, hogs, and cows. They frequently gave me fresh vegetables.

All county offices worked from eight until five o'clock weekdays and from eight to one o'clock on Saturdays. On Saturday morning, 7 August 1938, at about ten o'clock, I arose from my desk to offer to help Mr. George Bennett, a farmer who lived near us at Warsaw. He was later the chairman of our board of county commissioners. Mr. Bennett walked past the gate at the counter where we served the farmers, and met me as I was approaching him. He lovingly put his arms around me and said, "Mrs. Williams, I'm so sorry about your house burning down." I said, "Mr. Bennett, what are you talking about?" He replied, "I just passed your house and a crowd was standing around the ashes of your home."

My first sensation was that he had to be mistaken, but upon his insistence that he was correct, I quickly drove home to find Lehman and about twenty people standing around looking at the debris, twisted frames of appliances and ashes that had been our house. Suddenly I realized that I was wearing a washable summer dress and canvas shoes. These, plus my car, were the only earthly possessions I had left. I would have nothing to wear while I laundered the dress I wore. I had no gown to sleep in, no toothbrush, no paste.

Then more substantial losses occurred to me. We had no place to sleep, no place to awaken in. Nothing to eat for supper. How would we start over so suddenly? I had spent nearly all my savings in getting us set up to live in the house that had gone up in smoke. Gone were all of our expensive wedding presents, the photographs, and scrapbooks that I cherished and the furniture, fixtures, and appliances I had used most of my savings to purchase.

Lehman explained that the stream of water in the woods where Mr. Rouse's hogs had been drinking water had dried up and he had gone to the edge of the swamp to dig a hole for them to get water. Before leaving the house he had placed a kettle of water on our oil cookstove and lit a burner under it, because he knew he would need a bath when he finished digging the hole and returned to the house. He theorized the water must have boiled over, causing the flame from the burner to leap toward the ceiling, igniting the house fire. He told how as he came out of the swamp he saw the flames leaping skyward. It never occurred to him he should let me know about the fire or ask someone else to tell me about it. Later, he said if I had put in a hot water heater, the house wouldn't have burned.

Mrs. Myra Carlton, an elderly neighbor, invited us to spend the night after the fire with her. She had a big house and subsequently let us spend a week with her to give us time to collect our thoughts and make arrangements for a place to live. When we left her house she gave us a beautiful handmade quilt to help out.

While we were spending the next week with Mrs. Carlton, we set about renting a two-room apartment from Miss Martha Southerland, about a block from the Agriculture Building in Kenansville where I worked. On Sunday night following the fire, I washed my one dress and underwear and wore the same gown of Mrs. Carlton's that I had worn the previous night.

I went back to work on Monday to make arrangements to take Tuesday off to go shopping to purchase clothes and the bare necessities we needed to keep house.

While most of our staff were at lunch on Monday, I spent a little time feeling sorry for myself, because I had lost so much, until I went to our service counter to help a very elderly man, a Mr. Jones. Before he told me how I could help him, he related how he and his wife were too old to work and their house had burned down on Saturday. They were away from home at the time of the fire. Everything they owned was lost. They had no fire insurance. They would have to live around among their five married children.

I was suddenly ashamed for feeling sorry for myself. Since that day, when I have been prone to feel sorry for myself, I have always been able to quickly find someone who is worse off than I am.

On Tuesday following the fire, Lehman and I went shopping. He proposed that I pay for his clothes, as well as mine, and for the furniture and other things we would need until the fire insurance settlement check came. He would see that I would be repaid then.

For about three months I continued to ask if the insurance payment check had been received. He said he was still waiting for it. This was my first experience with an insurance settlement and I insisted that he try to expedite the payment, but he said it would just take time.

One Saturday night in November of the same year, after our August fire, I rode with Lehman over to the farm. It was dark, but I could see in the path of the headlight beams of my car that there was a monstrous piece of equipment of some sort covered up with a canvas tarpaulin under the shelter of the pack barn next to the spot on which our house had burned. I asked him, "What is that equipment under cover?" To which he replied, "Oh, that's a neighbor's combine. You shouldn't be concerned about it."

On the next Monday morning, I called Mr. D. H. Carlton, our insurance agent. He told me our fire insurance claim check had been paid the week following the fire. Then I learned the entire amount of the insurance check covering our house, our furniture, our fixtures, our expensive wedding presents, and memorabilia had been used as a down payment on an expensive new combine. It was hard to believe.

Combines are used by big farmers to harvest corn, wheat, soy beans, oats, barley, and other grains. Lehman's farm had only forty acres of corn. I learned he was planning to harvest for hire to other farmers with his shiny new combine. When the first installment payment on the combine was due, it was repossessed.

I was in a state of absolute trauma. Lehman was being totally dishonest, deceitful, and concealing every bit of truth from me in all of our financial dealings and relationships. His behavior was so bad I couldn't tell anyone except my family.

Never had I seen my Daddy cry except over Rdell's illness and death but now his tears flowed when he realized the situation I was in. Mother was visibly shaken too. This was the total death of any last bit of respect I and all my family had for Lehman.

In my heart, I knew this should be the last straw of our marriage. But in 1938, no nice girls gave up on a marriage in such a short time. People wouldn't understand. They felt sorry for Lehman, too. He had lost a house and his clothes. No one would understand if I deserted him now.

When the time came for Lehman to make the first annual installment on the Warsaw farm, he did not have the money to pay it, so we deeded the farm back to the original owner who had now lost the value of the house that burned down, because Lehman had not replaced the house with the insurance money. He chose to surrender the farm rather than go through foreclosure procedure.

I seriously considered giving up on our marriage and going back home with my parents, but in 1938 I knew of no one in public life who had separated and divorced. I believed, in honest humility, that I was probably the best loved and respected person in our county because for five years now I had worked with and for our farmers, many of whom could not read nor write.

I had helped them to understand and interpret the many complicated and changing Federal rules and regulations of the farm programs which were helping the farmers to receive Federal payments, reduce crops, get better market prices on their crops, and get back on their feet. I was one of them and spoke their language.

I loved them and they loved me. At that time most of the people who lived in our rural areas and the nine little towns in Duplin County had some farming interest. So, I really knew most of the residents in Duplin County well. I knew they respected me in every way for my kindness while I had been helping them to get the most benefits from our farm programs, and for my personal behavior in what they knew of my private life. I did not want them to know my sorry marital situation.

I believed that with the standards of the day regarding marriage, any suggestion of upheaval or divorce might cause them to regard me in an entirely different, and perhaps unflattering, light. I was afraid I could easily lose their complete approval and confidence in me which seemed to be the main compensation I was receiving for the trauma I was enduring in my marriage. I was trying to hide my unhappiness and utterly disappointing marriage. I tried to constantly put on a face of living above and beyond all the devastating happenings that were going on in my marriage.

While I knew my marriage had truly fallen apart and was void of any satisfaction, I simply was not ready to admit to the people of our county that it was a disastrous failure. So, I stayed on in the two-room apartment in Miss Martha's house for a few months longer while I continued my work in the Agricultural Office.

Lehman stayed at the apartment some of the time and with his mother some. He was not working, but doing what the local people called "just piddling around."

1939
An Unsettled Time

A Ride to Work with Uncle Mortimer

When Lehman's father had died in June of 1938 after we had married in December of 1937, his farm had been divided between his four sons and one daughter. Lehman's mother was not allotted a share in the division of his father's estate.

Lehman's three brothers and his sister had engineered the division. Because they disliked Lehman so much, they had not consulted him or their mother about the division of his father's land. They had apparently begrudged the many monetary handouts their mother had made to Lehman in answer to his badgering through the years. I had seen this badgering of her since we had married and I had shuddered many times. There were times when I went outside her house to avoid hearing him.

In the division, each of his siblings received valuable crop lands, but Lehman was allotted the eight acre piece of land on which the Williams family home rested, regardless of the fact that they knew their mother had expected to continue living alone in the family home. She had lived there since it was built in 1928. This was the first brick farmhouse built in the area and the finest house around.

Lehman negotiated with his mother to deed the eight acre homestead to her so she could continue to enjoy living there, if she would deed to him the 140 acre farm with fifty-five acres cleared, which she had received in settlement of her parent's estate. This property was a mile from the Williams place and had no buildings on it.

Since I was still loathe to admit to the public that my marriage was such a failure, I moved with Lehman to his mother's house for a few months while I built a modest, white wood frame house which still stands on the 140-acre farm Lehman had acquired from her. I paid all of the bills for construction and materials for this new house. It was fifteen miles from the county Agricultural Office where I continued to work and my salary continued to increase. At this new house I continued to leave Lehman's noon meal prepared every morning before I left for work. I paid all of our household bills and other living expenses while Lehman continued his "piddling around."

Lehman's family seemed to have a natural suspicion of their in-laws, accusing all of them except one daughter-in-law of philandering. My mother had taught me well and I was very careful how I conducted myself. I knew how to get along in working with both men and women and never had any problems with either.

I recall so well the first time I went to Lehman's mother's home after our marriage. She had said to me then, "I want to get something straight with you. Two of my daughters-in-law have run after my daughter's husband and I don't want to hear of you doing the same." Fortunately for me, her daughter separated from her husband very soon after our marriage and I never did get to meet him.

One day while we were still at Lehman's mother's home waiting for the little new house I was building to be completed, I was having repairs made to my car at a Pink Hill garage. I was standing out by the highway at her house waiting to catch the Trailways bus which came by at exactly the right time for me to ride into Kenansville to my work at the Agricultural Office.

While I was waiting for the bus, Mrs. Williams' oldest brother, who lived in Raleigh, had spent the night with a sister in Pink Hill. He was returning to Raleigh in the early morning and saw me standing by the side of the road waiting for the bus. I was just delighted that he gave me a ride into my work in his shiny new car.

About thirty minutes after I arrived at work I was in a staff meeting. Lehman came stomping and raging into the office. I heard him demand to know if I was at work. Then he opened the door to the room I was in and demanded to know who brought me to work that morning. He threw one of his terrible temper fits like the one he had thrown the night of our wedding rehearsal and many times since.

I tried to explain that I had ridden in to work with his Uncle Mortimer, but he said he didn't believe me and continued to rage for several minutes. He approached his uncle on his next visit to Pink Hill and Uncle Mortimer verified my explanation.

I learned later that Lehman had been in the field near his mother's house on that morning, using a new piece of farm equipment that he had made a down payment on, and had not seen me getting into the car with his Uncle Mortimer. His mother had run out into the field to tell Lehman that I did not get on the bus, but that she saw me get into a fine car driven by a man.

The fact that I was her favorite daughter-in-law, because I paid her a lot of attention, had nothing to do with her decision to tell Lehman about my ride. She just simply thought it was her duty to tell him I rode to work in a fine car with a man instead of riding the bus.

A decade later when she was dying from cancer which started at one ear and spread over one side of her face, I was the one she asked to sit by her and read the Bible, especially Psalm 91. She especially liked me to repeat verse eleven of this Psalm: "For He shall give His angels charge over thee, to keep thee in all thy ways."

A Convict Visits Our New House

One day in September of 1939 while I was at work in Kenansville and Lehman was not at home, a convict, wearing the traditional stripes, had escaped from a road gang about a mile from our house. He had walked through the woods and entered our house where he took a bath in our tub and left the dirty water in it. He dressed in Lehman's best clothes, including his white suede shoes. In his haste, he slung out every article of clothing and everything else in the drawers of our chest and dresser and left everything on the floor, obviously looking for money. He found no money, but he took Lehman's shotgun. Upon leaving our house, he stuffed his striped outfit in our woodpile in the backyard, then took off through the woods, gun in hand, to the sharecrop home of widowed Lettie Pate next door.

Mrs. Pate and her three sons were sitting under the shelter of their tobacco curing barn, sorting and tying cured tobacco leaves for market. The convict pointed Lehman's shotgun at Mrs. Pate and her boys while he demanded that one of the boys give him the keys to the family car, an old Plymouth sedan, parked in the yard of the farmhouse the Pates occupied. One of the boys gave the convict the car keys. He jumped into the car and took off speeding. State patrolmen had been called and were chasing him when he failed to make a curve just before he reached Kinston, twenty miles away, wrecking the car. However, he fled the car, jumped a barbed wire fence, tearing Lehman's Sunday trousers, and ran into the woods.

This man had been convicted of armed robbery in Asheboro, North Carolina. He was later caught, prosecuted for escaping, and eight years were added to his original ten year sentence.

When I arrived home that day and saw the ransacked house and the dirty bathroom I was overwhelmed. It took me a while to overcome the trauma of having the convict visit our house.

1940
War Clouds Gathering— World War II

In 1941 while I was still manager of our Duplin County Agricultural Adjustment Administration Office, the United States Selective Service System required all young men to register for possible military duty. When the first group of Duplin County draftees were selected, Lehman's name was called. He was not working and he had no dependents to exempt him.

When he received his draft notice, he was furious and blamed me for not having had children during our four years of marriage so he could escape the draft. His mother gave me an unkindly piece of her mind, saying, "You are to blame for Lehman's draft problems. If you had been home where you should have been, having children, he would not have been called up."

I had never discussed Lehman's financial situation with his mother, because I was aware that he had continued to badger her, for considerable sums of money, just as he badgered me. I had never told his mother that he had never contributed to our living expenses since we had been married nor that he had not paid one dime on the little white frame house I had built. I could see she lived under a terrible strain as a result of Lehman's monetary demands, so I didn't attempt to explain that I had to continue working if we were to have a roof over our heads and food on the table.

All my life I had looked forward to being a mother, but Lehman had shown no interest in our having a child. He was most always in a bad mood, because someone was always after him about the debts he made.

Once Mr. E. C. Thompson, highly respected manager of Branch Bank in Warsaw, called me at work and said, "Mrs. Williams, your one thousand dollar note is past due and I must ask that you pay it at once, plus the interest." Whereupon I said, "Mr. Thompson, I don't know what you're talking about, because I have never borrowed from your bank." He related that Lehman had been to his bank and said I wanted to borrow one thousand dollars on an open note and that he gave Lehman a note to take to me for my signature. Lehman had returned with the note purportedly signed by me, and witnessed, and had received the one thousand dollars. I told Mr. Thompson that I was totally unaware of any such transaction. He then contacted Lehman and threatened indictment for forgery, whereupon Lehman produced the money. His mother paid it for him.

Lehman negotiated with the county selective service and received permission to take a defense job in lieu of being drafted.

The North Carolina Shipbuilding Company had been established in Wilmington, seventy miles away, and had been awarded contracts for the building of Liberty freighters. Lehman went to work there and for three months lived in a small mobile home until Federal housing became available.

The war was going on in Europe and our country had declared war against Japan after the Pearl Harbor attack on 7 December 1941.

I continued my job in Kenansville as office manger of the county Agricultural Adjustment Administration Office until February 1942, when I took leave of absence and joined Lehman in Wilmington. We occupied one of the neat little two bedroom prefab government housing units at beautiful Greenfield Lake.

Young Dr. Pritchard, who had just come to engage in family practice in the little town of Pink Hill, rented the small white house I had built on the farm Lehman had acquired from his mother.

In evaluating, my situation, I had reached the conclusion that our country would most likely be engaged in this war for quite some time and that Lehman would probably be gainfully employed at the shipyard for an extended period. It appeared that if I ever expected to have children, this might be the only opportunity I would ever have. It would be the first time Lehman had a steady income to support a family.

After I left my job and arrived in Wilmington, I felt considerable guilt about Lehman not serving in the armed forces. There was also my own guilt for not helping out with the war effort. I just simply had to do a little bit toward the war effort. So, I volunteered three nights a week from 11 P.M. until 1 A.M. at the Secret Army Filter and Information Center in the basement of the Wilmington post office. At that time, there were German submarines based off our North Carolina coast and there were fears of an attack. At the information center, we channeled calls from the several listening posts along the eastern United States. Secret clearance was required for this duty. This volunteer service gave me just a little bit of satisfaction that I was making some contribution to our country's war effort.

The U. S. Women's Army Corps was established during this period. One of the first volunteers was Lehman's sister-in-law, Mary who had been married for twenty years to one of his brothers, with no children. She had been a dear friend to me, doing my sewing and cooking delicious food for me when I was having guests. She took the army's lab technician's course and when the war was over, found a job with a Goldsboro, North Carolina hospital where she met and married a fine man. They had a beautiful daughter who became the joy of their lives, giving them the added joy of grandchildren.

From Facing Motherhood to the Peace

From the beginning of our marriage, I had faced the reality of missing my fulfillment of having children, because there had been no evidence of any stability in Lehman's financial plans. Giving up on our marriage did not seem to be a part of my make-up or beliefs. When Lehman took the shipyard job, I thought I could and should have children while he was gainfully employed for the first time. I honestly believed I could teach the children the same integrity and strong character traits my parents had given me enabling them to live good and productive lives. I also hoped there was a possibility that Lehman might see the advantages of full-time employment with a steady income and he might be different in the future. It was with these thoughts, hopes, and aspirations that I entered into motherhood, not realizing bringing children into Lehman's presence could be detrimental to their happiness and well-being and make life hard for them and me. It just seemed to me that if I gave motherhood my all that I could make up to the children what might be lacking in Lehman's parenting. It was impossible at that time for me to see that what I had become was the result of both a father and a mother giving their all to me at all times in spite of times and circumstances. It was impossible for me to envision what it would be like to rear children with no monetary help—only interference—from a father.

After I moved to Wilmington I went back to the Duplin County Agricultural Office a couple of times to give some requested assistance, then settled down to expectant motherhood and the study of rearing children. Until the baby was born, I boarded and roomed a young man from our neighborhood, Lehman's cousin, who worked at the shipyard.

Sundays, I attended the Fifth Avenue Methodist Church in Wilmington. Soldiers stationed at the nearby army installation, Camp Davis, who desired to attend a church service, were bused in to town to this church. Many Sundays the soldiers who were being shipped overseas knelt at the expansive altar and prayed before their departure. I could not resist praying at the altar with them. I prayed not only for their safety as they went off to battle, but also for my own situation as I ventured into motherhood. It was at this altar, as I prayed with the young men who were shipping out to the war zone, that I recommitted my own life to being a good mother and to continuing my path of service to others in whatever way might be available to me. I would try my best to be the kind of parent that I had known during my childhood.

On 30 November 1942, healthy, eight pounds, six ounce Melvin was born.

Lehman had taken me to the hospital the day before, then returned home. He called the hospital a couple of times during the night to ask if the baby had been born. He went to work the day of delivery and came by the hospital after work. When he saw Melvin his only comment was, "He's ugly to me." It seemed to me that Melvin was born mature. He was so easy to deal with in every respect and a pure joy to me.

We lived about two blocks from one of the points on Greenfield Lake and that was a perfect spot, the following spring, for mothers to stroll babies through the azaleas and other flowering plants. A group of us mothers pushed our babies in carriages to the Easter sunrise service on the banks of the lake. An angelic looking children's choir, dressed in white robes with red bow ties, sang "Fairest Lord Jesus." The minister, in a white robe, declared, "He is risen from the dead." Suddenly the sun's rays penetrated the air that was heavy with the cool morning dew. We were reminded once more of the empty tomb on that first Easter morning!

Lehman paid little attention to our baby and showed scarce interest in him. A neighbor took turns with me keeping our babies when we went to our own doctor's appointments or had to run errands.

Lehman never kept Melvin but once. When he was a year old there was a baby shower for a neighbor. I had been at the shower for about fifteen minutes when he called and said the baby was crying. Melvin so seldom cried that I hurried home only to find him sitting in the middle of the floor, happily playing with toys. I questioned that he had cried at all. This just seemed to be Lehman's way of saying, "This is your baby. It's your job to stay at home and look after him."

Melvin had been such a joy that about the time he was eighteen months old I began to feel it would not be fair to him to grow up alone. I had enjoyed life with my own siblings so much because they had been such an important part of my every day life. This would probably be my only chance to have another baby because I might have to go back to work when the war was over.

Lehman was clearly not interested in more children. His theory was "I won't be drafted now, so why go to all that trouble?" But he finally agreed.

About the time I became pregnant with the second child, Lehman grew very tired of his shipyard job. Everyone on the job irritated him and he began to despise going to work. There appeared to be no chance of him leaving the job anytime soon. The war was escalating and he was trapped!

Our second and last son, Glenn, was born 9 April 1945 in Wilmington at New Hanover Memorial Hospital. V-Day had come in Europe, ending the war there. But the Pacific war was still raging and President Roosevelt had begun his unprecedented fourth term. He was showing signs of physical and mental strain because of the terrible complications of the long war.

Our next-door neighbor kept Melvin while I was in the hospital giving birth to Glenn. My customary fourth day of hospital care would be up on Thursday, 12 April and Lehman was scheduled to pick up baby Glenn and me at five o'clock after he ended his work day at four o'clock.

At 4:45, a nurse came to my room and said, "Mrs. Williams, I was preparing to dress your baby to go home when I found he has a high temperature. Hospital policy will not permit you to take him home until his pediatrician checks him. Dr. Kosruba doesn't usually make his rounds until about eleven o'clock at night. So, we'll just have to wait."

Lehman appeared at exactly five o'clock and was mortally upset that we could not go home, whereas, my concern was the reason for the baby's temperature. Though I gently questioned the nurse, she told me she was not allowed to discuss my baby's condition with me. I would just have to wait for Dr. Kosruba. The thought occurred to me that my baby could even have died and she had to wait for his doctor to tell me the sad news. I began to pray silently for strength to accept whatever the news might be and for patience to wait.

In a few minutes after the nurse left my room, another nurse came in crying her heart out! News had just come over the radio that President Roosevelt had died in Warm Springs, Georgia. Lehman's tirade, baby Glenn's temperature, and the president's sudden death with the Pacific War still going on, provided me with six sad ensuing hours. Tears began to quietly flow as I prayed not only for us to have the strength we needed, but for the whole world in the loss of its number one citizen.

Lehman moved constantly in and out of my room and to the nurses' station cursing the hospital and the nurses. He was just plainly upset that he couldn't take us home. He never commented on the baby's temperature, or the dilemma the world faced in losing Mr. Roosevelt who had guided the whole world since 1932.

When Dr. Kosruba finally came at eleven o'clock he pronounced Glenn had a severe case of hepatitis, but we could take him home.

When we arrived home at 11:30, our next-door neighbor was there with Melvin, who was standing in his crib anxiously waiting to see his baby brother. Glenn's problem cleared up in a few days and all was well.

My neighbors and I continued our pleasant practice of pushing our babies along the paths among the azaleas and other flowers around Greenfield Lake. But after President Roosevelt's death, our topics of conversation changed from tidbits about our babies to how would

President Truman bring peace to the Pacific War and when would the men and women in the military forces start coming home?

On 6 August 1945, President Truman ordered the first atomic bomb dropped on Hiroshima and another one on 9 August dropped on Nagasaki. Japan surrendered and peace was declared on Wednesday, 14 August, five days after the second bomb was dropped.

On the morning following the declaration of peace, Lehman rode in his usual carpool to the shipyard. The pickup truck he had last owned before he went to the shipyard had been repossessed. We had used my 1940 Chevrolet sedan during our stay in Wilmington. After Lehman reported in to work on 15 August, he turned in his time and walked off the job. He caught a ride back to our house, collected his clothes, got in my car and headed for his mother's home near Pink Hill. This left two little boys and me in the edge of bustling wartime Wilmington without transportation except for the city bus and streetcars.

The existing laws required all persons employed on defense contracts to continue in their employment following the peace treaty until all existing contracts were completed. The Wilmington shipyard still had contracts for a considerable number of Liberty freighters. Shipyard and government officials came to our house several times and inquired as to Lehman's whereabouts. I gave them his mother's address so they could contact him there. They did contact him but Lehman did not return to work as ordered. The shipyard continued production for several months, until all contracts were completed.

The house I had built near Pink Hill was rented when Lehman quit work at the shipyard. It was two months before the boys and I could move back. These were trying times for me to be alone in a big city with two small boys, having to ride on the city buses and street trolleys to take them for medical checkups, to buy groceries and get the things we needed.

Melvin has said that one of his first vivid memories is the day I took them to Dr. Sidbury, their pediatrician. The whole city was crowded and the trolleys were running in every direction. With my pocketbook and diaper bag in hand and two little boys, I made the mistake of getting on the city bus headed for Wrightsville Beach instead of the one going to our home at Greenfield Lake. As we approached the outer city limits of Wilmington, I realized my mistake. We dismounted the bus at the next stop. Melvin remembers the three of us running across the busy four-lane street in the blistering summer heat to catch the next bus back to Dr. Sidbury's office and waiting to get on a bus back to our house at Greenfield Lake.

The boys and I finally moved back to Pink Hill in the fall of 1945.

1945
The Four Sweet Potato Pies

Milton, his wife, Ella, and children, Betty and Tom, from Norfolk, came to Mother's and Daddy's for a long weekend soon after we moved back to Pink Hill from Wilmington in 1945.

As far as Milton and his family were concerned, there was no food like sweet potato meringue pie. They would be staying for three days, so I offered to make four deep dish sweet potato meringue pies to take to Mother's and Daddy's house. The finished pies were carefully lined up on the back seat of my car. Melvin and Glenn rode on the front seat with me.

When we arrived at Mother's and Daddy's, Milton's family was already there and rushed out to greet us. Amid the hugs, kisses, and excitement, I went on in the house with baby Glenn and forgot all about the sweet potato pies.

It was a warm, sunny day. The children were so glad to be reunited and stayed outside to play. That was the fall Melvin would be turning three. Betty was five, and Tom, seven.

Ella and I began helping Mother finish up the chores, cooking collards, backbone, butter beans, sweet potatoes, and cornbread.

Soon Betty came running in the kitchen yelling, "Aunt Christine, Melvin has stepped right in the middle of every one of those sweet potato pies!"

I ran out to see Melvin running down the driveway in his blue corduroy overalls, white shirt and what had been his white shoes, now covered in sweet potato meringue pie.

I opened the car door and sure enough, he had made one little shoe print right in the middle of each pie, just exactly like Epaminondus had done in the story I had told him.

All the family chimed in, "He needs a good spanking!"

The family did not know how many times I had told Melvin the story of Epaminondus. They did not know that he once asked me if Epaminondus' mother had spanked him and I had answered that Epaminondus didn't get spanked.

Melvin had been two years and four months old when Glenn had been born in April of that spring. The time I could spend reading to Melvin was cut short after Glenn came. So, while I cared for Glenn, I resorted to telling Melvin stories.

When we moved from Wilmington back to Pink Hill, Melvin missed all the Wilmington children who had come to play in our fenced-in yard. He had no Pink Hill playmates. So, I had to tell him more and more stories.

One day I was low on story supply and told him the story of Epaminondus.

Epaminondus was a little boy who loved to walk the path through the woods to visit his granny.

Granny most always gave him something to take home and he almost never followed her instructions.

She gave him a doggie and a big string telling him to tie the string around the doggie's neck and lead him gently home.

She gave him a pone of freshly baked bread and told him to put it on top of his head to take it home.

She gave him a mold of freshly churned butter and told him to stop at the little stream on the way home and cool it in the water.

Instead of following Granny's instructions, Epaminondus stopped at the cool stream and doused the doggie in the cool water and nearly drowned it.

He tied the string to the pone of freshly baked bread and gently drug it home through the dirt.

He placed the mold of butter carefully on the top of his head. As he slowly walked home, the hot summer sun melted the butter and by the time he arrived home, all of the butter had formed little rivers down the sides of his head, face and neck.

Each time he reached home with his near disasters, his mother would say: "Epaminondus, you ain't got the sense that you wuz borned with."

One day his mother said to him: "Epaminondus, now you be careful around those pies I have cooling on the porch."

Epaminondus was careful. He stepped very carefully right in the middle of each of those pies cooling on the porch.

This was the very best story Melvin had ever heard. He asked to hear it over and over again.

One day, he asked me: "Did his mother spank him for stepping in the pies?" And I made the great mistake of answering: "No, but she told him again, 'You ain't got the sense you wuz borned with'."

What a dilemma I was in now! My family thought I should spank Melvin for stepping in the pies and I had told him Epaminondus' mother hadn't spanked him! It was hard for my family to understand that day why I couldn't be worse than Epaminondus' mother, but they have always understood that Melvin's imagination in acting out the story of the pies gave them an unforgetable memory.

While my siblings and I had loved this book, I was glad, a few years later, when it was banned from further publication.

1946

Lehman's Mother Dies

In April of 1946 Lehman's mother died, leaving a will, providing that the home and eight acres of land Lehman had deeded to her as part of his father's estate would go half to him and half to his only sister, Eva. Eva decided to sell her half interest to Lehman. On 14 May 1946, we borrowed money from Mrs. Leo H. Harvey of Kinston to pay Eva for her half interest in the house and eight acres. We moved into the Williams home. Lehman built a tin farm machinery repair shop on one corner of the eight acres. Several times he told me that he had paid off the mortgage to Mrs. Leo H. Harvey, but in 1948 Mr. Sam Waller, a respectable money lender from near Mt. Olive, called me and said that at Lehman's request he had paid Mrs. Leo H. Harvey for the total amount of the mortgage and interest on our home and that the mortgage had been transferred to him. Mr. Waller said he could not wait any longer for payment and that he had contacted Lehman many times, but Lehman had failed to make a payment. Mr. Waller offered to set the payments up on a monthly basis provided I would agree to make regular monthly installments until the entire amount was settled.

I agreed to do this because in the meantime Lehman had borrowed four thousand dollars from the local bank on the 140 acres his mother had deeded to him, on which I had built our little white house. I could see that there was little possibility that Lehman was going to pay off the four thousand dollar mortgage to the bank.

Subsequently, the mortgage to the bank on the 140 acres came due and Lehman sold that farm to a neighbor for just enough money to pay the bank off. So I lost the dear little white house I had built when I had worked in the Agricultural Office before the war.

1947

Mr. White Comes to See Me

One hot August Saturday morning a year after we moved in the Williams home, a Mr. White was scheduled to come see me on business.

Six-year-old Jennie Johnson from Elizabethtown had spent the week with us. Her folks had lived next door in Wilmington and we had been good friends. Her parents and two sisters were coming to spend Sunday and take her home. I was cooking and getting the house ready for their visit.

The boys had a new unpainted birdhouse and begged to paint it that morning. Melvin was four and Glenn, two. I helped the three children get settled in the yard at a little table with some brushes, a can of white paint and the unpainted birdhouse. They were wearing only their underwear and were to call me when they finished or when Mr. White came.

It took quite a while. Finally, Melvin opened the front door and called: "Mama, Mr. White is here."

At the front door stood Melvin and Jennie, giggling, and Glenn still happily contributing to the project by stroking his chest with his paintbrush. They had used the leftover paint on Glenn's arms, legs, top of his head, and chest.

Removing the white paint was no fun.

When they still get together, they giggle about the day they used their creative talents to paint the new bird house and Glenn.

My Cup Runneth Over

When Melvin was four, we were celebrating "No Silent Pulpit" at our church, because we did not have regular worship services every Sunday.

The lay speaker for this Sunday was William Sullivan from near Mount Olive. His wife, Gay, and two little daughters would be coming with him. So I invited them to have lunch with us after the service.

That morning, during Sunday school assembly, prior to the morning worship service, a young girl in the church, named Hilda Grace Stroud, had recited the Twenty-third Psalm in a most dramatic and meaningful manner. One of the parts of the psalm which had seemed especially dramatic was the sentence, "My cup runneth over."

After lunch that day we moved to our big front porch to chat and enjoy the cool breeze. When we had been on the porch just a little while, Melvin came running to the porch yelling, "Come see, come see, my cup runneth over."

He had placed a china coffee cup right in the middle of the kitchen table and carefully poured water in it until the water was just barely standing above the rim of the cup and a little had run over on the table.

1948

I Struggle with Odd Jobs and Daddy Dies

From the day of my agreement to pay fifty dollars a month to Mr. Waller on the mortgage he held on the eight acres of land, I faced the reality that I must find a full-time job, so I could make the mortgage payments, support the boys, care for them, and feed Lehman.

In the meantime, I fixed an upstairs furnished apartment at our house for a young married couple of teachers. Using porch furniture and secondhands, it brought in enough rent to pay our family utilities bills.

Until I could find regular employment, the boys and I tended two hundred laying chickens and sold the eggs. There were no modern methods for caring for poultry. There were no automatic feeders or waterers. They had to be caught and held by hand to vaccinate against Newcastle disease. The eggs had to be gathered, cleaned, and put in cartons for sale.

The superintendent of the construction of a Pink Hill school addition and the supervisor of road repaving in our area boarded and roomed with us during the week. They paid well.

Being the substitute mail carrier on our long rural route helped to bring in extra cash.

Setting up home demonstrations and selling Stanley Home Products worked well because the boys could go with me.

The odd job the boys and I enjoyed the most involved performing survey work for the North Carolina Department of Agriculture and the University of North Carolina School of Public Health at Chapel Hill. We had good times on these jaunts. Sometimes a neighbor came to our house and stayed with the boys and cooked if I needed to be away for a whole long day.

Back then, I kept a supply of boxed greeting cards in my car and sold them at every opportunity.

It was during this period when I was trying to avoid taking a full-time job until the boys were bigger, that I really appreciated my childhood experience in selling *Blade and Ledger* newspapers.

These were very trying times and Lehman was getting deeper into debt with his farm machinery repair shop.

He actually complained about customers bringing work to him. He was making debts that he wasn't even thinking about paying. He finally had the lot on which his shop was located surveyed separately from our house lot, and made a mortgage on the shop lot to pay off some of his accumulated shop debts.

In the meantime, Daddy had been suffering for several years with continuing high blood pressure problems. He and Mother had sold their farm animals and tools and moved off the Hines farm to near Mt. Olive where Alma lived. On 5 February 1948, he fell during one of his dizzy spells. Just the freak way he happened to fall caused his spinal cord to be severed in his neck and he died six hours later.

Daddy died without a will, so brother, sister and I signed over our rights to his cash in the bank to Mother. She went to Beulaville and built a neat, two bedroom house a block from the center of the place of her birth where she had lived until her parents moved to Magnolia when she was sixteen. Three of her sisters, two brothers, and their families still lived there.

Mother's new home in Beulaville would be just nine miles from my home.

Teaching Melvin and Glenn

When school started in the fall of 1948, we did not have public kindergarten. Melvin could not enter the first grade, because his sixth birthday would not come until 30 November. North Carolina then had a strict law providing that he could not enter first grade unless he would be six before 15 October. Melvin was a very large and mature boy. His friends were going to school that year and he was ready to enter the first grade, too.

I ordered a complete first grade home study course from the Calvert Home Study School and taught him at home. This course came with several first grade reading books, math books, work and activity books, and all needed materials for an excellent first grade education. He took the standard second grade academic test in the fall of 1949 and entered the second grade.

He graduated from high school as valedictorian of his class and received an Angier B. Duke Scholarship to attend Duke University in Durham, North Carolina. He graduated from Duke after four years.

The same year I taught Melvin first grade at home, I ordered a complete kindergarten home study course from Calvert and taught Glenn kindergarten skills at home.

During this year when I was doing several kinds of odd jobs and teaching the boys, we found their trips with me provided excellent times for them to do their school work at their own pace. We really had good times combining my work with their school work. A few times when I left the boys home with a neighbor, Melvin would say: "I read a new book while you were gone." I once asked: "What did you do about the new words you didn't know?" His answer was: "Oh, I just guessed at the new words or skipped them and went on to the ones I knew."

1949

The Duplin Story—
A Historical Play with
Two Hundred Years of History:
1749-1949

Duplin County, North Carolina, was cut off from New Hanover County in 1749 and at that time Duplin County covered the areas that are now both Duplin and Sampson counties.

As the two hundredth anniversary of the founding of Duplin County approached, the County board of commissioners, on 1 November 1948, appointed a committee to organize a County Historical Association to make plans for the two hundredth anniversary celebration in 1949.

The county historical society employed Sam Byrd, a Broadway playwright, who grew up near Mt. Olive, North Carolina, to write and produce a new and highly entertaining, modernized treatment of an historical drama, *The Duplin Story*.

It was presented 22-24 September 1949, in a scenic outdoor amphitheater constructed near the Kenan Auditorium in Kenansville, the Duplin County seat. The wooden benches in the amphitheater could accommodate 5,145 persons to enjoy the play at one time.

The Duplin Story depicted a fictionalized history of the county with actual characters called by name, and true events in actual places in Duplin County. There was a cast of five hundred taking part in the seventeen scenes with eight very realistically painted backdrops, 20' x 30' in size. An orchestra, several choruses, and a one hundred voice choir made up of residents from all over the county, furnished the music.

One scene was assigned to each of the eight county schools. The other nine scenes were performed by residents throughout the county with a few professional actors employed.

The B. F. Grady School, which our boys attended, was assigned the Sarecta Scene. This portrayed an early, one-room elementary schoolteacher and her students performing a minuet for Dr. William Houston, an English stampmaster visiting Sarecta on the Northeast Cape Fear River. At that time all shipping of lumber, tar, pitch, turpentine, and other products from Duplin County was done on barges floated down the river from Sarecta to Wilmington. This continued until the era of the railroad when Magnolia became the shipping center.

Our son Melvin, seven years old, danced the minuet with the schoolchildren in the Sarecta Scene and recited a simple poem about a plowman working "from early dawn to dawning gray." His was the only child speaking part in the drama.

All seventeen scenes were highly acclaimed by the overflowing crowds which came from many parts of North Carolina and several other states.

But, the reenactment of the Battle of Rockfish, which had been fought in Duplin County near Wallace on 2 August 1781, during the Revolutionary War, took the prize as the most realistic scene of all. It was supervised by Colon Holland, Kenansville postmaster, who was a former naval engineer and construction expert. He had experience as a demolition supervisor at Guadalcanal during World War II.

This scene portrayed the firing at Colonel James Kenan's command post during the Rockfish battle. It was staged in the field adjacent to the amphitheater. Colon Holland's expertise in creating the battle scene was so perfect and precise that the audience believed all of Colonel Kenan's soldiers were being killed. Gunfire from the exploding scene appeared to be leaping out into the crowd of spectators where people shuddered and shook. Little children screamed. When the gunfire died down, tunnels of smoke filled the air, and all of us breathed a sigh of relief that we were still alive.

Spectators declared "this scene was as awe-inspiring as any similar scene that had ever been viewed on any stage or in any movie."

The area used for the amphitheater had been a cornfield. *The Wilmington Star* called *The Duplin Story* "a miracle in a cornfield."

It was also in 1781 that General Cornwallis' troops marched through Duplin County on their way to Virginia and defeat. They encamped at the first Duplin County Courthouse, which at that time was on Turkey Branch near Warsaw. They burned and plundered as they stalked their way through the county, leaving behind a path of destruction of farm pack houses, crops, store buildings, and whatever else was in their view.

The Combine that Broke Down on New Year's Eve

At 1 A.M. on 1 January 1950, after 1949's New Year's Eve had passed, our phone rang. I was awakened and answered it.

A deep male voice said, "I need to speak to Mr. Williams."

"He's asleep and he's hard to wake up. Is it an emergency?" I asked.

"Yes, it's an emergency. Please call him."

"Is it a dire emergency?—because he gets upset if he is awakened after he goes to sleep."

"Yes, this is a dire emergency."

The voice was so sincere. I could visualize a bad highway accident nearby and Lehman's help was needed.

When Lehman finally got to the phone, he soon slammed the receiver down and shouted: "Somebody's damn combine is broke down at this time of night!"

Then he cursed, shouted, ranted, raved and paced the floor for an hour, blaming me for calling him to the phone. He finally went back to sleep, but I did not.

The next day Lehman learned that some young people were having a New Year's Eve party. As the New Year dawned, they decided to make some phone calls.

Bright, young Russell Bostic knew of Lehman's temper and decided to play a prank on him.

Russell was in my Sunday school class and often refers to the good times we had. He was a model student in Sunday school and public school. He became a pharmacist and owned a drug store in Beulaville until his defective heart caused his early retirement.

Through the years when I have seen him, he still laughs about the night "his combine broke down."

At age sixty, in 1997, he received a transplanted heart from a thirty-nine-year-old man and looked to many more years to laugh about "the night his combine broke down" and other teenage antics.

Russell and his adorable retired schoolteacher wife, Doris, who helped steer him through heart operations and a successful transplant, enjoyed their three children, grandchildren and traveling until his body finally rejected the new heart and he was honored with a joyful funeral celebrating his life of community service.

I Must Begin Full-Time Work

Lehman's financial situation was growing worse and he was talking of closing his farm machinery repair shop and stopping work altogether. He would lease the shop and accompanying gas tanks for one cent per gallon on gasoline sold by the renter.

The several part-time jobs I was performing did not bring in adequate income to make the monthly mortgage payment to Mr. Waller and support the family. I knew I must begin full-time work.

On 1 January 1950, when the ten year U. S. census began, I worked as full-time supervisor for Duplin County. My first assignment was to go to the congressional district census office, thirty miles away in Goldsboro, to take a three-day course of instruction on how to train and supervise census enumerators for the county.

Then I had to conduct a three-day training course at our county seat in Kenansville for Duplin County enumerators. When I was in the process of this course, Lehman had leased out his shop and quit work, but had not yet received a monthly check from the gasoline company which had leased his shop. He came home one night driving a brand new Chevrolet from Hatcher Smith Motor Company in Mt. Olive, where Alma lived. Lehman's car had been recently repossessed and I still had the car I had bought in 1941 before I left the Agricultural Office.

Lehman had never allowed me to use his cars, but on this day he insisted that I drive his new car to the training course. It really was a nice car. But as I was conducting the training course at the Kenansville Masonic building on the day I drove his brand new car, two gentlemen knocked on the door of the classroom. I stopped my lecture and went outside to talk to them. They had come to get the car. Lehman purchased the car after bank closing time. The next morning the motor company had taken the check, which was for the full purchase price of the car, to the bank and found it was worthless. The president of the motor company had called my sister, Alma, for advice regarding this and she had suggested they get the car. The two men took the car and left me in Kenansville without a ride home. I had to ask one of the census enumerator trainees to take me home when the day's session was over.

Lehman had been writing worthless checks ever since we had been married. But laws making worthless checks a crime had not been passed in North Carolina at that time, so the people he gave worthless checks to had to either get their goods back or lose them to Lehman.

When the 1950 U. S. census enumeration was completed in Duplin County, I drove to the District Office in Goldsboro and helped compile the 1950 census statistics for the Third Congressional District.

As I was completing my census work in October of 1950, Turner and Turner Insurance agency in Pink Hill, two miles from our home, was looking for an office manager. I began working full-time at the insurance agency. This position worked out well for me, because I could come home at lunch time and the boys could call me on the phone any time. Melvin was now eight years old and Glenn was five.

While my salary at the Turner's was not great, I was earning enough to meet the fifty dollar monthly mortgage payment to Mr. Waller and pay for food and other necessary family expenses. And the Turner partners, T. J. and Lynwood, were great employers.

Following this page is a copy of a portion of the back of the note which accompanied the deed of trust to Mrs. Leo H. Harvey for the money we borrowed to pay Lehman's sister for her one-half interest in the eight-acre Williams home place.

After I went to work at Turner's Insurance Agency in the fall of 1950, I paid fifty dollars a month because that was all I could pay and still support the family.

Later, when I became register of deeds, in December 1952, I paid as much as I could to Mr. Waller each month and made the last payment on 6 December 1956, thus finishing paying off Lehman's sister's one-half interest in less than eight years while supporting the family.

Following is a photo copy of my check for the final payment:

FOR VALUE RECEIVED I HEREBY TRANSFER AND ASSIGN THIS NOTE TO
S. J. WALLER WITHOUT RECOURSE ON ME.

THIS THE ___4th___ DAY OF NOVEMBER, 1948.

Mrs Leo H Harvey
Mrs. Leo H. Harvey

Interest paid up to Nov. 4, 1948. S.J.W.
Paid on within note $50.00 This Jan. 15, 1951
Paid on within note $50.00 This Feb. 15, 1951
Paid on within note $50.00 " March 15, 1951
Paid on within note $50.00 This April 19, 1951
Paid on within note $50.00 This June 1, 1951
Paid on within note $50.00 This June 18, 1951
Paid on within note $50.00 This July 13, 1951
Paid on within note $50.00 This Aug. 20, 1951
Paid on within note $50.00 This Sept 14, 1951
Paid on within note $131.31 This Oct 20, 1951

1950

The Stuffed Pocketbook

Up until the past few years, sister Alma felt like cooking for a crowd, so our family had Thanksgiving at Alma's and Norman's house, twenty-two miles away in Mt. Olive, and Christmas at our house.

On Thanksgiving Day in 1950, our family was returning from Alma's and Norman's lunch time feast. We were driving on the rural road between our house near Pink Hill and Mt. Olive. Glenn, Melvin, Milton and Ella's children, Thomas and Betty, were all riding with us.

There were small trees and underbrush along the road and a deep, dry ditch on either side. The shoulders of the road had not been mowed recently. The grasses and weeds had grown tall and seeded out.

Lehman was driving along about fifty-five miles per hour on a straight stretch of the road. He suddenly slammed on the brakes and started backing up rather fast. He shouted at us, "There's a woman's pocketbook back there on the shoulder just stuffed full of money!"

He came to a quick backing stop, opened the car door, jumped out and was attempting to reach for the pocketbook when it was suddenly jerked through the high grass on the shoulder, through the dry ditch, to be rescued by three ten-to twelve-year-old boys who had tied a rope to the stuffed pocketbook. They had been crouched quietly in a patch of tall weeds near the shoulder of the road.

As soon as one of the boys had his hands tightly holding the pocketbook, they started giggling and running for their lives through a thicket of small pine trees and underbrush where they quickly disappeared. No doubt, they were still giggling.

Lehman searched quickly in vain for a stick or stone to throw at the boys. But, too bad— neither was in sight! He started shouting all sorts of obscenities but the boys had run with the speed of a deer so they hadn't heard his comments. No doubt, they laughed a long time at their success.

All the way home we were entertained by Lehman's anger. He shouted and screamed and broke the speed limit. Our boys, Betty, and Thomas, never spoke a word all the way home. Then, they scampered off together to giggle, too.

Thomas no longer lives, but Betty seldom visits without retelling "The Stuffed Pocketbook" incident.

1951

The Boys' Savings Accounts and Some Growing Up Activities

In 1951, the boys and I suffered probably the most devastating blow of all.

I had been determined from the time I considered having children that I would try to help each of them at birth to start a savings account for their college education. When my family and friends asked me what would be appropriate to give the boys when they were born, on their birthdays, at Christmas, et cetera, I would always suggest money for their college savings accounts.

One account was captioned in the bank savings records: "Melvin Williams or Christine W. Williams." The other read: "Glenn Williams or Christine W. Williams."

From the time the boys were big enough to sit on the counter at the local bank, I would jump them up on top of the counter where they would hand their savings books with the deposits to the cashier and watch him make the entries. By the time Melvin was nine years old and Glenn was seven, they understood the significance of making their own deposits as we talked about how the bank would pay them for allowing the bank to keep their money until they were ready for college. One year the boys and I had one-half acre of tobacco and put the profit into these accounts.

Their savings books were kept in the glass-doored bookcase in our living room. The boys sometimes took them out and looked at them.

After they received their Christmas money gifts in 1950, we looked for their savings books to take to the bank to make deposits. The books were not there! We asked Lehman if he knew where they were and he said he didn't know. The boys and I took their money to the bank and told the head cashier we could not locate the books, but the boys had Christmas money to deposit.

The head cashier said, "I thought you all would have found out before now that Lehman came out here and said he needed to borrow the boys' money and I let him have all of each account, except for twenty-five dollars. Lehman promised to repay it right away, but I have not been able to get him to do it."

After a sleepless night, I determined that this could not be ignored. Lehman had been doing this sort of thing to me since our marriage, but for him to destroy the faith of the boys seemed like the last straw. The next morning the boys and I dressed in our best clothes to go to the bank headquarters in Smithfield, sixty miles away, to report this to the bank president. But consideration of the consequence began to surface. I never wanted to be branded a troublemaker and I knew when the bank took action our whole community would know the boys' father had stolen their savings and the head cashier had broken the law. To expose the boys and me to yet another crisis would be hard to endure. We did not go to Smithfield.

The very next day the news broke that this head cashier had allowed one bank customer to borrow a large amount from the savings account of another customer, without the knowledge or permission of the innocent person whose money was taken. A bank examiner was in the bank when the wronged person attempted to make a savings withdrawal. The account was almost emptied. The head cashier was arrested, tried, and served time in the Federal prison in Atlanta, Georgia.

Melvin had set his sights on attending Duke University from the time he started watching Duke play basketball on television. Later he was fascinated with Duke when he attended Methodist Youth Fellowship meetings there. With the savings account incident, Melvin's faith in his father was visibly shaken. Lehman never said he was sorry or replaced any of the money. From that time on, Melvin never trusted his father again. Glenn did not seem to understand as much about all this as Melvin did.

Lehman never gave the boys spending money, bought their clothes, or paid household expenses after he quit work at the shipyard.

Glenn developed a fondness for spending time at Lehman's farm machinery repair shop. Lehman allowed Glenn to start welding and driving farm tractors at age eight. This made Glenn feel really grown up and induced him to spend a lot of time in the repair shop. When I'd call for Glenn to come to the house to get lessons and eat supper, Lehman would tell him he could wait and come with him later. So Glenn's lessons were poorly prepared. I sent Glenn to expensive summer schools two times during grade school to get him away from Lehman's influence during the summer and to try to improve his poor grades. I also sent him to summer school after he graduated from high school to try to get help with his poor English grades before he entered North Carolina State University.

I had daily struggled with Lehman's insistence that Glenn spend all of his spare time at the repair shop where he had to observe Lehman continually trying to avoid paying his bills and hear his tirades against education. It really bothered me that he insisted Glenn stay at the shop until it was too late to get lessons. Usually, Lehman wasn't working in his shop at night. He was just hanging around and letting Glenn develop poor study habits.

Melvin was in the third grade when Lehman wiped out their savings accounts. Soon thereafter Melvin said he wanted to take piano lessons at school. Dollars were so scarce, but I wondered if it could be possible that Melvin had inherited his Whaley grandparents' music genes when neither of their own four children could scarcely carry a tune? The next week Lehman's aunt called to ask if we would keep her piano because she was moving to a small apartment and had no place for it. This was the answer to Melvin's desire to take piano lessons.

For the remainder of his public school days he took one piano lesson a week at school. His teacher at school allowed students to play only classical music. I took him to a music teacher's home in Pink Hill, two miles away, for one lesson a week where she taught him popular and church music. He really enjoyed practicing on the piano in the afternoons when he came home from school.

Soon after beginning piano lessons he said to me, "I have better dreams at night when I play the piano a lot."

When Melvin was twelve, I took him once a week twenty miles to Kinston where he took organ lessons at the Episcopal church so he could become our church's assistant organist. He had already begun playing the piano for Sunday school services.

When Glenn was in high school I signed with him to borrow money to purchase cows, swine, and feed for 4-H and Future Farmers of America projects. Once Lehman took some of the market-ready animals and sold them without Glenn's knowledge and kept the money. Glenn was shaken by his father's actions, but believed his father when he promised to pay off the loan. He never did. I had to pay off the loan.

Melvin and Glenn both kept good records on their 4-H club projects. Glenn was the state 4-H club winner one year on raising swine and was awarded a free trip to the National 4-H and Future Farmers of America swine and cattle shows. Melvin was the state 4-H winner in his health project. He tended our home garden and was the county winner on his 4-H Garden Record Book. Both boys were inducted into the state 4-H Honor Club.

I really enjoyed serving as a local 4-H Club leader during the years they were 4-H Club members.

Both served as local and sub-district presidents of their Methodist Youth Fellowships.

Both boys went through all the steps in Cub Scouting while I served as Cub Scout Den Mother for five years. Both completed all their merit badges to become First Class Boy Scouts before our rural troop disbanded. The Scout Master, who was a math teacher and lived in our upstairs apartment, had moved.

Melvin and Glenn earned their God and Country Scouting awards, working with their pastor.

Lehman never saw fit to work with the boys on 4-H, FFA, Methodist Youth or Scouting projects. He never went with us on Cub Scout overnight camping trips or took part in other Scout activities.

When Glenn went off to North Carolina State University after high school graduation, he stayed four months, dropped out and took a job welding. Lehman had once entered college and only stayed two weeks before dropping out.

I had grown up with the strong belief that couples should stay together until their children finished high school. I now believe this was a mistaken concept. I know now that I made a big mistake to allow my sons to have to put up with their father's misdeeds as long as I did. But I could not bring myself to make the move earlier.

A Strange Auto Liability Insurance Claim

Melvin, nine, and Glenn, seven, were at the Turner Insurance Office one day in 1951 when a policyholder came in for help in filing an auto liability insurance claim. Through the years, this claim still gives the boys a chuckle.

The man reported he had taken his family on the previous night to a movie at Pink Hill's popular drive-in theater. Like a few other moviegoers, he forgot to remove the movie speaker from his car window when he departed. However, this man's forgetfulness produced unusual consequences. As he had driven away with the speaker still on his car window, the speaker post which held the brackets for his speaker and also the speaker for the car parked next to him, was pulled out of the ground. The driver of the next car had hung his speaker on his car steering wheel. The force of the motion of the insured man's car, as he drove away, popped off the steering wheel of the next car. As the steering wheel popped off, it hit the driver in the face and knocked out his two upper front teeth!

The insured policyholder was filing a claim to recover the cost of replacement of the speaker post, two speakers and cords, one steering wheel, and the two front teeth of the man in the car next to him.

1952

The Wayward Banana Peel—
A Lesson in Littering

In August of 1952, Melvin, 10, Glenn, 8, and I were taking Milton's and Ella's children, Tom and Betty, home to Panama City, Florida after a summer visit with us.

Leaving Pink Hill at 2:30 in the morning would give us time to make progress before we stopped for a good restaurant breakfast. As usual, we took snacks and sandwich materials from home. We should arrive in Panama City by time for a late supper.

While traveling through Georgia on Highway 301, around noon, Glenn, who was in the back seat on the right side of the car, decided to make banana sandwiches for us. He was a good banana sandwich maker. We had brought along ready-made pimento cheese sandwiches.

Our car, as most other motor vehicles, did not have air conditioning back then. So, most everyone drove with car windows down in summertime. When Glenn peeled his first banana, he casually flipped the peel out the back right window, thinking it would land on the road's dirt shoulder. He didn't realize I was in the process of passing a slow moving car with the windows down.

The banana peel sailed through the window of the car we were passing and hit the driver smack in the face!

When the children saw the big, muscular driver behind us ball up his right fist and start shaking it at us and yelling madly, they shouted: "Drive fast ! Drive fast!"

The children have never stopped talking about this frightening experience. All four became anti-litter bugs for life.

Right: A 1997 picture of the little white house I built on the 140-acre farm from Lehman's mother.

Below: J. C. Carr and Garland just after marriage and before he was called to World War II, where he gave his life. She and I have been life-long friends.

Above: Glenn and Melvin dressed for Tom Thumb Wedding at Pink Hill.

Left: Melvin, Glenn and I wearing our Cub Scout uniforms seated in front of our fireplace.

Part Six
1952-1960

1952

The Duplin County Register of Deeds Office Up for Election Amid Political Turmoil

L. P. Wells, chairman of the Duplin County board of commissioners, contacted me in January 1952 to ask if I would consider filing for the May 1952 Democratic Primary for Duplin County Register of Deeds.

Mr. Wells had served as chairman of the County Agricultural Adjustment Committee during some of my eight years of service as office manager there when the Federal agricultural programs had first begun in 1933.

The office of register of deeds is a county-wide elective office carrying a four-year term. At that time, and for another fourteen years, state laws specified that it was the legal duty of the elected register of deeds to also serve as clerk to the county board of commissioners, maintaining a public record of the minutes of the board. This was in addition to the duties of recording, indexing, and issuing certified copies of official county records, such as deeds, deeds of trust, mortgages, maps, birth, death, and marriage records, military discharges, and other important permanent county records.

The incumbent register of deeds had been a bedridden invalid for the past two years, not able to visit the office. The county commissioners had been hiring the County Accountant and his staff to work part-time nights in the Register of Deeds Office to help out. The inability of many lenders and borrowers to get prompt document recording was causing great county-wide concern.

I told Mr. Wells that I would give careful consideration to this situation.

Before I decided to run for this office, there were many things I had to consider. The fact that no woman had ever filed for public office in Duplin County was the first concern. Our political situation in the county at this time was in turmoil, the worst in the County's history. The three member county committee of the former Agricultural Adjustment Administration Program, which had now been changed to the name Duplin County Production Marketing Association, had been fired for mishandling tobacco acreage allotments. The sheriff had just committed suicide and his office deputy was under indictment for embezzlement. Duplin County at that time was the only county in North Carolina which had not relieved the sheriff of the duty of serving as county treasurer. The county health officer was under indictment for embezzlement of county funds. The woman who was currently serving as office manager of the County Production Marketing Association, now called P. M. A., was suing the head of the

Duplin County Farm Bureau for fifty thousand dollars for slander. She was the head of the same office I had managed from December 1933 to February 1942.

There had been much talk about ballot box stuffing and crooked elections in the county.

Most people in the county were taking sides on the main issues involving the county officials in the current upheaval. Naturally, I wondered, with all of this political turmoil, if the voters would think this was the right time for the first woman to enter county politics and what kind of reception I would find if I was elected.

Of course, my greatest concern was Melvin and Glenn. They certainly deserved a better financial future than they could have with my present salary and Lehman's lack of interest in gainful employment. But, they needed the closeness of being able to call me on the phone every afternoon when they came home from school and during the day in summertime.

If I were elected to this office, I would be working on a long distance telephone exchange and would not be as accessible to the boys as I was in my present job. Too, the Turners were very understanding when the boys were sick and I needed to be out of work. If I ran for office, the only campaign promise I would make would be that the boys could call me long distance once during every work day.

Another negative aspect to my chances of election might be that it was not in my make-up to ever accept a campaign contribution, because I would need to be absolutely free to operate the office according to the dictates of my conscience and according to the laws of North Carolina and I would not want to have any person expecting special political favors. Bucking the reputed county political bosses would not be easy. Also, I would never want my picture on utility poles, buildings or trees during a campaign, as was the custom with political candidates in Duplin County.

It had been ten years since I had served the people of my county in the Agricultural Office and though association with them had been close when I had served them, they might not still remember my service, because ten years had passed since I left.

Not many of our people had accepted mothers working in the regular marketplace. It had not even been tried in a political office in my area. Too, I could not finance a viable campaign, so if I filed, I would just have to announce my candidacy and hope that citizens remembered my past service.

On the other side of the coin, there was the stark reality that in the future I would be entirely responsible for the care and support of our two boys and myself. Lehman had only worked at the shipyard in Wilmington long enough to evade the draft to World War II. Then he had walked off the job the day after peace had been declared. He was continuing his habit of giving worthless checks and making debts he could not pay.

I discussed my present situation with T. J. and Lynwood Turner, partners of Turner and Turner Insurance agency where I was working. We reached an understanding that I would not take any time off from my job to campaign and that if I did not win the May Democratic primary, I would stay on with the agency. However, if I did win the May primary, this would be tantamount to winning the November general election, because there was no Republican opposition. In that case, I would work on until November first and would have thoroughly trained my replacement at the insurance office before that time.

So, if I did win the primary, and thus the general election, this would give me the full month of November to study the Register of Deeds Office, analyze the conditions there and make the necessary plans for taking over the duties. I would also have time between the May primary and the time of assuming the duties to make a thorough study of the North Carolina General Statutes affecting the operation of that office.

At that time, in 1952, the register of deeds was receiving the same pay as the sheriff and the clerk of court, which was more than double the salary I was drawing at the insurance office. However, it had been so important to me that the two men who owned the insurance office had been especially kind to me and understood a working mother's responsibility to her children. This had given me great peace of mind as I worked.

The very thought of giving up the closeness I had enjoyed during the past two years with the boys and their needs as I had worked at the insurance office just two miles from home was jolting.

One of the few people with whom I discussed the prospect of running for office was Mr. Melvin Jones. He was on the Lenoir County school board and a successful businessman. His advice was, "Before you file, make sure that you can accept the results of the voting, whichever way it goes."

One honorable man in the county, who had kept records for a big merchant, had already announced his intentions to run for the office of register of deeds. The incumbent had also filed again. I knew if several persons filed I would not be able to afford the needed campaign to win. I absolutely could not take time off from my insurance job to campaign at all.

I arrived at the County Board of Elections thirty minutes before the closing of filing time and waited until five minutes before the legal closing. Only the two aforementioned persons had filed, so I paid my filing fee.

The ladies in my community helped me mail two hundred letters to people in all parts of the county, announcing my candidacy. I placed an announcement in each of the county newspapers, *The Duplin Times* and *The Wallace Enterprise*, spending a total of two hundred dollars on the campaign.

One Saturday afternoon I took my mother in my car and drove to the town of Chinquapin in the eastern part of Duplin County to talk to a few people there. Each person I approached asked me my opinion about the various unfavorable situations in our county government. I knew their concerns were traumatic, but my several contacts that Saturday afternoon showed that each person was expressing very strong feelings for or against each involved county official. And those I talked to were varying widely in their opinions on each turbulent situation.

At Chinquapin, I asked a man whom I had dealt with in the farm office if he would talk with some people for me, since I could not get off work to campaign. I had heard he had been very active in recent county politics. He told me had had already accepted and spent five hundred dollars to work for one of the announced candidates, but if I would double that amount he would change and help me instead. I explained I could not spend any money for campaign workers.

Just one Saturday afternoon helped me to thoroughly understand the county political situation. My only solution was not to make any further contacts in the county and to gracefully accept the voters' decision on 6 May.

During the time preceding the primary, I was totally unaware that the Republican party leaders in the county who had remembered me from the Agricultural Office were contacting their Democratic friends and acquaintances in the primary, urging them to "Vote for Christine. Maybe she'll manage that office like she ran the Agricultural Office." They made such remarks as, "We've got to have a change in the direction of our county government."

When the May 1952 Democratic primary arrived, voters swarmed to the polls all over the county. Many were heard to remark they were voting for Christine Williams for register of deeds to see if she would manage that office like she had managed the Agriculture Office. One elderly woman was transported on a stretcher to the polls to vote. My votes came from the rich and the poor, the black and the white. No one seemed to care that I was a woman. They were looking for someone to trust.

It was a landslide vote as people evidently caught a vision of their county government improving and gave me a majority of the votes in the first Democratic primary in May which assured my final election in November.

I stuck to my job as agreed, trained a replacement and found a good local woman, Goldie Houston, to spend each weekday at our house to care for Melvin and Glenn and to cook for them and Lehman. She did this until the boys got big enough that we didn't need full-time help. Then I went with her to our new Guilford East automotive cloth plant nearby and recommended her for a job, where she worked sixteen years until retirement.

When I stopped work at the insurance company, the Turners gave me a parting gift of two hundred fifty dollars which seemed to me a tremendous amount in 1952 for one leaving a job to take another. I had never had that much money that was not budgeted.

The full month of November was mine, as planned, to inventory the county records, study laws affecting the office and make plans and preparations to implement changes needed to modernize and upgrade office procedures to accommodate the county agricultural lending agencies and their customers who needed quick recording of loan papers to keep pace with the demands of the burgeoning poultry industry and other changing farming endeavors.

An advertisement from the Pink Hill page of the 24 April 1952, issue of The Duplin Times newspaper. It appeared each week.

Vol. 19. No. 17.

Duplin Times

KENANSVILLE, NORTH CAROLINA, THURSDAY, APRIL 24, 1952.

Straight from the Shoulder — Light from the Heart of Duplin

SUBSCRIPTION RATE: 2:00 per year in Duplin and adjoining counties; \$4.00 outside this area in N. C.; \$3.00 outside N. C.

PRICE TEN CENTS

HELPING TO BUILD A Finer Carolina

Duplin P. M. A. Office Scandal Out

County Court

County Court will convene Monday May 5th. A heavy docket faces Judge Phillips and Solicitor Maceer.

Editorial

Duplin Is In A Hell Of A Mess

By J. R. Grady

Nosey reporting is not always a cherished job of newspapers but at times there seems to be a desperate need for some. At a recent meeting in Washington City of the American Society of Newspaper Editors several of the top editors of the country sounded off on the subject.

"If newspapers had done a more thorough job," Louis B. Seltzer, of the Cleveland Press, said, "they (the federal government) wouldn't be in this incredible mess today."

Another editor, V. M. Newton of the Tampa (Fla.) Tribune, said: "You can kick the scoundrels out of Washington but unless you start the cleanup at home a new crop of scoundrels sooner or later will slip into the federal government."

The Wilmington Morning Star has this to say:

"A few days ago we mentioned that it's getting tougher and tougher for a reporter to write objectively about the news. In fact, it's tough for him to write the news at all because he's hemmed in by so many curtains and restrictions that it's practically a full-time job just to find the basis for a snot of news, let alone getting all the details and having time to present them to the readers.

"We've all read about how Washington restricts a lot of news and we're inclined to rise up on our haunches and cuss Washington out about so doing. It somehow never occurs to us that we have the same situation right at home.

1952 Cancer Crusade Begins Monday

The 1952 Cancer Crusade will begin in Duplin County on Monday, April 28.

Have your solicitor calls, people it strikes rich and poor, young and old alike.

You can strike back. You can guard your family, each member should have an annual physical examination, you can help with your contributions, you can learn the cancer's seven danger signals:

that does not heal; 2. a lump or thickening in the breast or elsewhere; 3. Unusual bleeding or discharge; 4, any change in a wart or mole; 5, persistent indigestion; 6, persistent hoarseness or cough; 7. a change in normal bowel habits.

Any of these symptoms may, if your physician, it may save your life.

The 1952 Cancer Crusade does any disease. In North Carolina, alone, 3,058 died of cancer in 1950. It is no respecter of people. Cancer is a major problem, some 22,000,000 living Americans will die of cancer. Many of them could be saved by early diagnosis and expert care.

Cancer kills more children from three to fifteen years of age than

Total 40 Candidates File For Office
L. P. Wells Withdraws; Mrs. Christine Williams Enters Register Deeds Race

The 1952 election campaigns in Duplin County began to take on shape and form last Saturday as filing time for candidates came to a close. The only new filers for county offices were L. P. Wells, candidate of the board of county commissioner, and Arthur Kennedy, county commissioner, filing for re-election and Emmett E. Kelly of Glisson filing for commissioner from the 2nd district, Mrs. Christine Wells Williams, Albertson filed for Register of Deeds Monday morning brought about the only upset in the county picture as Commissioner Chairman L. P. Wells announced he was withdrawing from the race. Mr. Wells told the Times that he had serious reasons to expect, his tenure as commissioner. He asked the people of Duplin for their fine cooperation during his tenure of office.

hard-surfaced roads under Governor Scott's road program. Some section may feel they did not get all their share of roads, the road bond, entitled Duplin County as a whole was not held in held they Chesley Williams who is all of running again, though he is retiring and losing his interest in the welfare of the county and will continue to do anything in his power to help Lady Mercer of the county court have no opposition.

The following have filed for justices of the Peace:

C. Sitterson, Bryant, Roy Sitterson, Rudolph Hanly, P. R. Stephens, and W. F. Williamson, Kenansville; L. E Brown Wallace; A. E. Williams, Chinquapin; J. L. Cates, Faison; L. J. Outlaw, Rose Hill; and F. J. He is the Board of Education held.

NOTICE

To all cancer fund chairmen: All money collected in cancer drive send to Wayne Jordan, M g r., Branch Bank and Trust Co. Wallace.

D. S. WEAVER

Duplin County HDC

North Carolinas 69,481 home demonstration club members, who will join in observing National Home Demonstration Week, April 27-May 3, are proud of their accomplishments in a statement released this week by David S. Weaver, director of the State College Extension Service.

Cpl. Bronnee A. Jones, son of Mr. and Mrs. Archie Brown of Warsaw, N. C. left Saturday, April 12, 1952 for Seattle, Washington where he will be shipped out to an overseas base. Cpl. Jones entered the U. S. Army May 7, 1951 with the Beulaville National Gu id. He received his basic training at Camp Stewart Ga. He was sent to Fort Dix, N. J. January 20, 1952

They said he was not fired. Some say it was another "McGrath Firing". At any rate Marlow Bostic of Rose Hill is no longer chairman or member of the Duplin County Production Marketing Association.

They said Mosley Phillips was not fired. Some said he had not resigned, just quit. Mosley was head of the committee in charge of measure tobacco land allotments and other detail work for the committee. Any way, they say he is out. Exum James, a member of the committee, has not resigned as of this writing but some say he is expected to resign. He failed to show up at the investigating meeting this week.

The Production Marketing Association in Duplin County seems to have taken a pattern along the lines of the Health Department and the Sheriff-Treasurer's office in Duplin County. Violations of rules and regulations, seems to have up some individuals, seems to have been the order of the day. On Tuesday of this week Raleigh officials and members of the State Committee probed the Duplin for a wholesale investigation. Farmers who had been given new allotments for growing tobacco were called in for questioning. As we go to press the department officially reports that some applications made and approved by the Duplin committee and the State committee for 1952 tobacco allotments.

As of today investigations have resulted in 36 approved allotments being recalled, 36 affirmed, and 6 still under investigation. Mr. Jim Potter, with the state department, said more applications had been approved from Duplin County this year from any other reason in the state. Among reasons given for recalling cleared lands not qualified; growing and farmer not deriving major portion of income

No Medium for Registers of Deeds in North Carolina to Share Ideas and Information and Receive Advice

After the May Democratic Primary in 1952 when I realized I would become our county register of deeds in December, I was stunned to learn there was no such thing as a guidebook or any organizational medium which could give help to new Registers of Deeds in North Carolina.

Rufus and Lillian Swain, the young married couple of high schoolteachers who occupied the upstairs apartment at our house, were attending summer school at the University of North Carolina at Chapel Hill that summer. They agreed to get an appointment with Dr. Albert Coates, Director of the Institute of Government at Chapel Hill, and talk with him about my dilemma.

The Institute is a part of the State University System and is charged with the duty of training state, county, and town officials in North Carolina.

The Swains explained to this outstanding leader that I had been in the Duplin County Register of Deeds Office only once and that was on business in 1937. Now I would be assuming the duties of this office and needed some instruction and guidance. Dr. Coates confirmed to the Swains that in 1952 there was no guidebook or any other information in print to give direction to Registers of Deeds except the North Carolina General Statutes.

He told the Swains that Eunice Ayers, Forsyth County register of deeds, had approached him about the possibility of organizing a North Carolina Association of Registers of Deeds with the purpose of assimilating and sharing information to improve the services of the North Carolina Registers of Deeds to the public.

Dr. Coates promised the Swains that he would contact me prior to the first Monday in December, when I would take office. He would notify a small group of Registers to go to the Institute of Government to form a state association.

All other elected officials in North Carolina, and many appointed officials, already had state organizations and had been receiving instruction at the Institute.

Later, Dr. Coates notified me he had decided to wait until Thursday, 9 December 1952, which would be three days after I took office, to hold this organizational meeting. He had invited the Registers of Deeds from Forsyth, Johnston, Chatham, Orange, and Duplin counties. At this meeting a State Association was formed and Dr. Coates assigned one of his assistant directors of the Institute of Government to be our advisor.

At this initial meeting, Eunice Ayers from Winston-Salem, Forsyth County, promised to send me information on every form and procedure she used in her office operations. These were invaluable.

On my summer vacation that year I had visited the six registeries of Duplin's adjoining counties and obtained information on forms and procedures they were using. I soon learned the Forsyth office was the most modern and efficient in the state and I could learn much from Eunice. She became the first president of our state association.

I served in every association office, then as president. The state group that was formed is still active and helpful.

Melvin and Glenn accompanied me every summer to annual conventions until they graduated from high school. They also drove me to Chicago to the national convention at the Palmer House in 1962 when I represented our North Carolina association as our president.

Dr. Coates authored a book, *By Her Bootstraps*, in which he paid tribute to Dr. Ellen Winston, head of our State Department of Human Resources. He also paid a tribute to Eunice Ayers and me, Registers of Deeds, and to some other North Carolina women.

Changing Procedures in the Register of Deeds Office is not Easy

As soon as I had won the 1952 May Democratic primary to become the Duplin County register of deeds, I knew I must prepare to assume the duties of that office on the first Monday in December.

The Republican leaders in the county had graciously let me know they had been as interested as the Democrats in getting that office reorganized to meet the needs of a changing agricultural economy.

Soon after I won the May Primary, I began borrowing the North Carolina general statutes from Mr. Faison W. McGowen, our county finance officer and tax supervisor. It soon became easy to see there were three current office practices in the Registry that would have to be changed to meet the requirements of the state laws:

1. All banks, other lending agencies, merchants, and some individuals had been recording charge accounts which were not authorized by state laws. There was no collection procedure. The laws required fees to be paid prior to recording of documents.

2. The system being used for office fee deposits was not in accordance with the General Statutes. Every few days, collected fees were deposited in the personal bank account of the register of deeds and at the end of the month, a check was written to the sheriff-treasurer for the amount of fees shown in the "fee book" for the month.

3. Cancellations of Deeds of Trust were not being made according to the requirements of the General Statutes.

So, just before I took office, I:

1. Notified all charge account patrons that they must either mail recording fee checks with their documents to be recorded or furnish bank drafts that we might fill in for the amounts of recording fees to deposit daily. A few complained loudly to the county commissioners, but the commissioners had given me verbal approval of the changes and were glad to see the accounting system perfected.

2. On the morning I took office, I sent the office charge account records to the home of the retiring register of deeds because I had no legal authority to collect any fees due prior to the beginning of my term. I started making bank deposits every afternoon for fees collected that day and delivered the duplicate deposit slips to the sheriff-treasurer.

3. Revising the cancellation practice to coincide with the laws was the most difficult.

The laws had long provided:

1. If an original deed of trust and accompanying note(s) are presented to the register of deeds marked by the lender or Trustee "paid and satisfied," the register of deeds may make a cancellation, or

2. If the provisions of the foregoing paragraph (1) are not met, the law requires the Trustee in the deed of trust to go into the Registry and personally sign a cancellation. The current practice being used in such cases was for the lender (not the Trustee) to go to the Registry and sign a cancellation. The law presumes that a lender might go in and sign a cancellation on a recorded deed of trust while the original document is still on deposit as security at a lending agency.

I obtained an opinion on cancellation of Deeds of Trust from the State Attorney General. He had his opinion to me on the law published in *Popular Government*, a monthly magazine sent to all county and state officials and attorneys-at-law in North Carolina by the Institute of Government at Chapel Hill.

Following is the State Attorney General's cancellation opinion as published in *Popular Government*:

FOR REGISTERS OF DEEDS
Cancellation of Deed of Trust Record by Beneficiary (Lender) Thereunder.

May the third party, or beneficiary, under a recorded deed of trust come into the office of the register of deeds and cancel the record of the instrument in person, without producing the original papers marked "paid and satisfied"?

To: Christine W. Williams
(Attorney General): It is the opinion of this office that only the trustee or his legal representative or the duly authorized agent or attorney of such trustee can make the personal cancellation authorized by the first paragraph of G.S. 45-37.

The going was tough, because the county attorney, whose duty it was to advise me on implementing the laws, had not been following the cancellation laws and he was not interested in changing. However, his clients had been perturbed at not being able to get prompt recording of Deeds of Trust and crop liens to deposit with their money lenders in order to get loan proceeds promptly. Now the new streamlined recording procedures and other improved services that I had implemented enabled them to get their recorded documents quickly. So, they were quite happy to endure the inconveniences encountered in strictly following the cancellation laws.

A few days into my new job, one of my assistants came to me with a problem I had never anticipated. The county attorney had asked her to cancel a deed of trust and back date the cancellation on the record to a week prior. He had certified a title for the Federal Land Bank indicating that this certain paid deed of trust had been canceled. He had mailed his "Certificate of Title" and had forgotten to bring the paid deed of trust to the Registry and have it canceled the same day. I had to face him and tell him I knew falsifying a public record was a felony and this could not be done. He was furious, but I never had this problem with him again.

No other attorney or office patron ever requested any help with a recording or cancellation that wasn't in strict conformity with the laws. While the county attorney was furious at first, once I made my position absolutely clear in every respect, he accepted my stand. But during my thirty-six years of service, he never mentioned one of my nine campaigns to me nor indicated whether he ever voted for me. He never gave our office any Christmas remembrance as did most of the other attorneys, Though I always felt that he appreciated the fact that he could depend on the records we created.

In just a short while, the county attorney and all office patrons were very pleased with the new recording practices and other improved services. We finally had a pleasant and cooperative situation, reminiscent of the years 1933 to 1942 in the County Agricultural Adjustment Office.

Johnson Cotton Company

In 1952 there was a general farm supply store in Wallace which also sold furniture and appliances. For each credit sale, this firm took a crop lien and chattel mortgage on which they enumerated the acreage of each of the farmer's crops and every personal possession the farmer owned, except their clothes. The store in Wallace was a branch of the home store in Dunn, North Carolina in Harnett County.

At that time, we had no photographic equipment. So, we had to type the recordings of these lien documents and proofread them, word for word.

I couldn't believe what I was reading—a customer might purchase only a plow, a ton of fertilizer, a couch, a stove, or a refrigerator. Johnson Cotton Company would not only take a lien on the item purchased, but they would include a lien on every family belonging, including the family wash pan, the children's bicycles, and the little dog the children owned. I looked for a cat or a kitten, but never saw one.

Every week the local papers advertised foreclosure sales by Johnson Cotton Company and every item enumerated in the lien and chattel mortgage would be at the sale. Usually some person with a little money would purchase the whole group of sale goods for enough to cover the indebtedness, including higher than normal interest rates.

If there were no bidders at these foreclosure sales, Johnson Cotton Company would take the bid for just enough to settle the indebtedness, and then sell separate items and usually make a good profit.

Kim Hatcher, a young insurance agent from Beulaville, has a collection of crop liens and chattel mortgages taken by Johnson Cotton Company and a few other firms. He has carefully preserved these as part of the history of his rural area of Beulaville, Chinquapin, and Wallace. Kim tells me he has seen a crop lien and chattel mortgage which took a claim on a mule and the stable manure produced by the mule, but we couldn't find one like this among his treasures.

We did find one covering forty dollars of indebtedness by a sharecropper and his wife made 28 March 1957 for the balance due to Johnson Cotton Company on two tractor tires number 400-12 purchased on that date. Not only did the crop lien and mortgage cover a lien on the tires but it also covered:

> "1 gas stove and hookup, 1 refrigerator, 1 washing machine, three beds complete with springs and mattresses, 1 three-piece living room suite, 1

kitchen table and chairs, and all other household and kitchen furniture of every kind and description that we may own. All farm tools of every kind and description that we may own. Our interest in 8 acres in corn and 6 acres in tobacco, and all other crops which may be raised on the G. B. D. Parker Estate lands and any other lands that we may tend in 1957.

This lien shows that it was insured and that it was paid in full on 30 September 1958. It is typical of the liens taken by Johnson Cotton Company and some other merchants against sharecroppers who had not learned to use more economical farm credit during the 1950s and earlier.

Attacking the Roaches

Each time the lights were turned on in the Register of Deeds Office in December 1952, hundreds of roaches quickly scampered from their positions of eating the glue on the record book covers. They went back to their breeding home under the vault rug. The office water cooler was positioned on the vault rug. The cooler, with its five gallon inverted water bottle allowed water to flow through the neck of the bottle with the neck surrounded by a bin of freshly cracked ice. When the cooler spigot was depressed, it emptied cool water into paper cups for the office staff and the public to drink. The cooler continually dripped water on the rubberized rug, making a perfect place for roaches to breed and drink. Each morning the courthouse custodian put in fresh ice and water, usually spilling some water on the rug.

The roaches had not only eaten the glue from the cloth-covered books, but they had nibbled the edges of some deed book leaves.

I immediately wrote to the State Department of Archives and History for a recommendation for a bulk roach killer. They advised visiting a farm supply store to buy a fifty pound keg of naphthalene moth flakes that farmers were currently using on their tobacco plant beds for killing insects. They suggested slinging Naphthalene flakes throughout the book shelves every Saturday at noon when we closed the office for the weekend. This finally rid the office of roaches. But, though the flakes were evaporated on Monday mornings, the lingering odor we faced each Monday was hard to endure.

Our Poor, Early Birth Certifications (1913-1961)

After the 1952 Democratic primary when I began to study the situation at the Duplin registry, the problem that concerned me most was the poor quality of the birth certificate copies on file there. These copies had been filed since October 1913 in North Carolina, but they had been seldom used.

This situation had suddenly changed for several reasons:

1. The state law requiring certified copies for school entrance had first become effective in 1952.

2. The certificates were now required for drivers licenses.

3. Farmers had just begun to pay Social Security in 1952. Some would soon begin to file Social Security claims and they would be expected to supply proof of age for all claimants born after October 1913, including proof for

underage children of deceased parents and proof of age for disabled workers of all ages.

4. All military branches had not even required proof of age during World War II, but now all applicants, when joining the military, had to furnish proof of age.

5. Employers, passport authorities, and others were now requiring official proof of age.

I tried to determine the reasons the Duplin County filed birth certificates were in such poor condition.

Birth certificates were first recorded in North Carolina in October 1913. But some midwives and doctors in rural counties, like Duplin, didn't get started until much later. Some midwives could neither read nor write, so many Duplin births either didn't get recorded or, if they were recorded, they contained errors and omissions.

Our county did not have a birth certificates prepared in a hospital until 1954. Ours had been handwritten in homes.

When the first birth registration in North Carolina started in 1913, doctors and midwives prepared and delivered birth certificates to a local registrar in the township where each baby was born. The township registrar made a handwritten copy of each certificate for the county register of deeds to file, and mailed the original certificate to the State Office of Vital Records in Raleigh.

The register of deeds listed birth certificates on family name indexes, but the handwritten Duplin County certificate copies were so poor, they were impossible to index correctly by family name. A name that should have been on the "James" page would be on the "Jones" page, et cetera. This often made it impossible to locate filed certificate copies by using the prepared index.

I finally decided that the date of birth was definitely the one most legible item on our poorly prepared birth certificate copies on file in the Register of Deeds Office. So, in order to better locate certificates I prepared a new card index by date of birth. This helped, but it didn't solve the whole problem.

Often the local township registrar couldn't read and interpret much of the data on original certificates, so they had made errors on the copies they prepared for the register of deeds. There was also the fact that local registrars received only a few cents per certificate for their work and some attached little importance to accuracy.

Before the North Carolina law became effective in 1952 requiring birth certificates for school entrance, it had been difficult for doctors, midwives, and Registers of Deeds to attach much importance to the seemingly needless task of dealing with the apparent useless birth certificates. In fact, the preparation, processing and filing of birth certificates had largely been considered hostile chores to be performed on "unnecessary records."

It had been seemingly impossible for persons charged with birth registrations to visualize that these records would ultimately become not only important, but necessary.

County Health Officers Become Registrars for Vital Records

Later on, North Carolina improved its birth registration system by abandoning its failed local township registrar plan. The new system required doctors and midwives to send original birth certificates to county health officers. These officers were required to prepare a copy for the register of deeds to file and send the original birth certificate to the State Office of Vital Records. Health officers were also charged with instructing and supervising doctors and midwives in the preparation of birth certificates.

The Duplin situation did not improve for a time, because our salaried health officer, who was forbidden by the county to privately practice medicine, including the delivery of babies, had continued to do so. He was reprimanded for this activity, but continued birth deliveries "on the side." He did not file certificates for such births.

Suddenly, beginning in 1952, the children delivered by this health officer needed birth certificates to enter school and we had to help them record their births through the complicated Delayed Birth Certificate procedure.

After this health officer resigned, he was replaced by another who had been a family doctor in the county. He, too, had delivered babies and had failed to record many birth certificates for them.

Through the years, since October 1913, when state laws first required birth certificates, there were other doctors, along with several midwives, who had failed to record their delivered births in Duplin County. So, we were beset with helping people file delayed birth certificates after they were required beginning in 1952.

Duplin County School Census Cards

In 1923, when J. O. Bowman became the superintendent of Duplin County schools, he instructed all schools to set up a school census card file. These cards documented the number of days each child attended school every year after 1923, the child's name, birthplace and date of birth, as well as parents' names and address.

As children either dropped out of school or graduated, the school census cards were sent to the county superintendent's office.

For most people needing proof of age, whose birth certificates either were not filed or contained errors, the school census cards proved to be the most reliable record available.

The Duplin County school system had changed its student records to a different system and the early school census cards had become surplus property. I was able to get the entire file of school census cards transferred to the Register of Deeds Office where they became our gold mine, because often they were the best available evidence of the facts relating to early births.

We used them in filing Delayed Birth Certificates and in preparing amendments to correct errors and omissions on filed certificates. Some organizations accepted our certified photocopies of these records in lieu of an official birth certificate.

Before 1961, when I started making photocopies of the original certificates for the Health Department to file in the Register of Deeds Office, our copy was not always exactly like the original copy sent to the state. If the state copy was correct, we could get permission to change our copy. If errors were on the original state copy, we had to prepare an amendment application, evaluate the evidence and submit the completed amendment application to the state office for approval before issuing a corrected certified copy. About half of the amendments we prepared were to enter the name of the child on incomplete certificates.

The Sad Story of My Own Birth Certificate Problems

Few people had a more distressful birth certificate situation than I encountered. My problem helped me to understand and willingly help everyone else who had a problem. This gave me desire to help not only the Duplin County people, but the ones born in Duplin but living elsewhere. This became a great mission for me.

Mother always said she named me Chrysthine after a pretty little girl in a book she read. She said she spelled it carefully, Chrysthine, for Jane Barden, midwife, and actually watched her write Chrysthine on the birth certificate she filled out at our home when I was born.

I entered school using Chrysthine and I was so proud of my beautiful name. I always thought the last part of it had a special sounding ring. My name on my school perfect attendance certificates, my scholarship certificates, my high school diploma was spelled Chrysthine.

When I went to work in the Agricultural Office, I used Chrysthine.

When my engagement was announced in the county newspapers and *The News & Observer*, in October 1937, my name was spelled Chrysthine Whaley.

I was not required to prove my age for a drivers license, so I had never had a certified copy of my birth certificate.

In December 1937, when I went into the Duplin County Register of Deeds Office to get a marriage license, I decided to look at my birth certificate for the first time. There it was, plain as could be: *Christine Whaley*.

I was in shock. I had never known Mother to be wrong when she was so positive about a matter.

In 1937, I did not know the original certificate was on file in Raleigh and that the one on file in the Registry was only a purported copy of the original, which had been copied from the original by George Edwards, Magnolia's local Registrar. He had hand copied it from the one prepared by Jane Barden, midwife. I expressed my shock to the register of deeds staff, but they just said, "Your mother must be mistaken." They never told me the original certificate was on file in Raleigh and I had no way of knowing this in 1937.

Thinking the register of deeds' record was absolutely official I made a decision that since my marriage license was my first permanent, legal record, that it should be like my recorded birth certificate, so, I had the marriage license issued Christine Whaley and changed my employment record and Social Security records.

I told Mother about seeing my birth certificate and changing the spelling of my name on my marriage license to agree with the certificate. She had the most disappointed look I had ever seen on her face. From then on I used Christine, but I always felt I gave up part of my beautiful birthright.

Until he died in 1995, brother Milton never changed spelling my name Chrysthine on every card or letter, he sent me.

The following June, after I became register of deeds in December 1952, we had the first State Registers of Deeds convention in Chapel Hill. I was seated by Charles Council, director of State Vital Records. When my two sons had been born in a hospital in Wilmington, I had been given applications to order plastic card birth certificates from his office. So, I asked Mr. Council if he would locate my certificate in the state office and prepare a plastic one for me.

The next week I received a letter from him, which read: "Dear Mrs. Williams, I am returning the fee you gave me for preparing a plastic birth certificate for you. When I located your original certificate it was spelled very plainly *Chrysthine* instead of what you are using, so I assumed you would not desire a plastic copy."

I took his letter to Mother and both of us cried because we realized we had missed the joy of using my rightful name by being misled by the certificate on file in the Duplin County Register of Deeds Office and not knowing that the one Mother had so carefully had Jane Barden to fill out correctly was on file in the State Office of Vital Records in Raleigh.

This is how Charles Council had found my original birth certificate recorded in the state office:

Now I faced these realities: In 1937, when I saw my name on my birth certificate on file in the Duplin County Register of Deeds Office, I had changed all my official records from Chrysthine to Christine. This name was now on my marriage record, my children's birth certificates, my drivers license, employment records, Social Security, financial records, and all other documents, except my school records.

Now, I had been elected to public office using Christine. This name was in our county and state election offices as well as listed with our Secretary of State. It was in the North Carolina directory of public officials, distributed to every state and county office in North Carolina.

In four more years my name would be on the ballot again and it needed to be consistent. I was fated to use this name for the rest of my life.

The only redeeming factor in my name problem was that Mother finally felt a sense of reward and release when she learned her efforts to help Jane Barden spell my name correctly on my birth certificate had not been in vain. At last she knew for a fact that the error occurred when George Edwards, Magnolia's local Registrar, had made a grievous error in copying and recording my certificate in Duplin County.

No one ever understood why I had so much patience in helping our people who said the birth certificates we had on file had errors or omissions. If anyone said our certificate had errors or omissions, I immediately called the state office to determine exactly what information was on the original certificate on file with the state.

I never discussed my own birth certificate problem with anyone except my family. So, no one else could possibly understand how anxious I was to help others avoid the heartbreak I had encountered just because I did not know I had a correct birth certificate on file in the Office of Vital Records in Raleigh.

Other Problems with Birth Certificates—Hallard's Birth Certificate

One of my first experiences with birth certificate problems came when a sixteen-year-old boy asked for a certified copy of his certificate to get a driver's license. He said his name was Hallard Miller. His certificate on file was Herod Miller so I checked the state office. The original was Herod. The boy said his school records were Hallard and he could not change them. I suggested that he ask his father to come in and bring the family Bible showing the children's names and birth dates. He did. The family Bible showed Hallard.

I asked the father, "Why did the midwife spell his name Herod?" His reply: "Well, Miss Christine, I'll tell you how it happened. The midwife, she named him Herod. But when she left, me and my wife, we got to talking about how King Herod was such a bad king that we decided to change it and name him after the Lord's Prayer, so we changed it before we put it in the family Bible."

Suddenly, I couldn't remember the word "hallard" being in the Lord's Prayer. So, I asked, "What part of the Lord's Prayer did you name him for?" The answer was, "Hallard be Thy name."

Nancy's Certificate

Soon a lady asked for a certified copy of her daughter Nancy's birth certificate so she could enter school. The child's certificate showed "Preg Nancy." She didn't want "Preg" on the certificate. I asked, "How did this happen?" Her answer: "Well, I'll tell you. When Dr. Willis was here, I went to him one time when I found out I was going to have a baby and he give me a book to read and that name was all the way through it. I liked that name, so I asked the midwife to put it on the birth certificate. But we just calls her Nancy, so that's all I want on it now for her to go to school."

Spoonbread and Cornbread

A woman from Florida wrote: "We need a certified copy of each of my five-year-old twin's birth certificates so they can enter kindergarten. My husband was a buyer on the Faison produce market when they were born there in Duplin General Hospital. Before they were born, I didn't want anything to eat except cornbread or spoonbread, so you will find in your records there that we named one of the babies Cornbread and the other Spoonbread. They are ready to go to school and we want to change their names. Please send me the papers to sign to change their names."

I had to inform her that if the twins were accurately named according to her instructions at the time of their birth, their names can be changed only by a court order obtained in a court of law in the county of current residence in Florida.

A Person's Most Important Record

During my thirty-six years as custodian of Duplin County birth records, their use changed from "seldom used records" to the "most important record a person can own for a variety of needs."

Falsified Birth Certificates

Counterfeiters all over the world have gone into the birth certificate business and in some places falsified certificates have been sold for as much as four thousand dollars each. Stringent measures have been taken to try to combat counterfeiting of birth certificates.

There was once a wave of dishonest persons going into cemeteries, taking data off tombstones, and then getting a certified copy of the dead person's certificate and using it for criminal activity.

One woman came to my house at night and offered me five thousand dollars for a birth certificate for her seventeen-year-old daughter, showing that she was eighteen. The mother said her daughter had dropped out of school and had found a job where she could go to work immediately if she could supply a birth certificate showing she was eighteen.

The mother believed that going to work would be better for her daughter than the loafing she was presently doing and the bad company she was keeping. I explained the laws to the mother and she understood my position. A few days later, the daughter was driving home in the early morning after a night out and failed to take a curve in the highway. Her car turned over several times and she was killed instantly. In the mother's heartbreak and bereavement, she came to realize that a falsified birth certificate and a job would not have solved her daughter's problem.

1953

Duplin County on the Brink of Agricultural Renaissance

Need To Modernize Recording Systems

While studying the duties of Register of Deeds before I took office, I became fully aware of the contribution that a modern and efficient system of county records could make to the overall progress of an agricultural county like Duplin.

The banks and other farm lending agencies let me know how the lack of a modern system was hampering their efforts to keep their cash flow in order and to deliver loan proceeds to the farmers promptly. Because of this awareness, I could see the record systems in the Duplin Registry must be constantly analyzed and all newly available methods studied and carefully examined as improved technology became available and our economy and needs changed. Our people must be provided with the most efficient, practical, and permanent systems available to serve the present and future needs of our county.

The burgeoning poultry industry was just beginning in Duplin County. We were said to be standing on the brink of what became labeled the "Agricultural Renaissance." This was said to have culminated in 1958 when, according to figures compiled from every county by the North Carolina Extension Service at North Carolina State University:

> "Duplin County Leads North Carolina in Total Agricultural Income in 1958 at an Estimated $44,705,647."

This headline blazed on the front pages of county and area newspapers.

Duplin County not only led in agricultural income in 1958, but it has continued to lead every year since. This position of leadership was not accomplished by accident. It was the result of hard working and dedicated county extension agents, county officials, other county leaders, agricultural entrepreneurs, and lending agencies working together for agricultural progress.

In 1959, Paul Barwick, a young journalist from an adjoining county, published a forty-eight-page magazine for distribution in Duplin County, detailing developments which contributed to what he called "New Birth" for Duplin County.

In 1958, it was very exciting to me that our county agricultural income had more than doubled since I became register of deeds in December 1952. It was gratifying that I had been a part of this progress through giving the farmers and their lenders quick recording of their

Deeds of Trust covering $4,000.00 poultry houses as our county launched into the contract poultry business.

Under the new contract plan, suppliers furnished baby chicks, feed and medications. The contract grower furnished houses, necessary heating, cooling, and labor. At that time the farmers received six and one quarter cents per broiler-size bird.

Instant Recording of Chattel Mortgages and Crop Liens

By January 1953, we had begun instant recording of chattel mortgages and crop liens for Duplin's main agricultural lender, the Kenansville Production Credit Association, a branch of the Federal Farm Credit Administration. Their organization was making 2,200 loans a year to Duplin farmers.

This was easy to accomplish and saved us much work. I simply had book pages printed identical to the chattel and crop lien forms used by the Production Credit Association. I had them punched, ready to insert into our binders. These printed pages were furnished to the Association. As their staff typed chattels and liens, they simply inserted a sheet of carbon paper in the typewriter and prepared a carbon copy on the book pages we had supplied. A carbon copy was fine, because these documents were short-lived.

All we had to do was copy the judgment that the Notary's certificate was correct, mark the filing time, and assign a book and page and hand the original chattel or crop lien back to the presenters.

We saved the laborious task of type-copying the document. The lender immediately had the original recorded document to submit to the Federal Farm Credit in Columbia, S.C. to obtain funds, thus aiding the Association's cash flow and enabling the farmers to get their loan proceeds quickly.

We saved the postage that would have been required to mail the original documents to the presenters.

Instant Recording of Land Records

After we caught up with typed recordings of the backlog of unrecorded land records on file when I took office, we started giving two-day recording service on land records. The catch-up was accomplished by bringing in extra part-time typists.

Finally, in 1960, when we moved into the new courthouse annex and had space for photographic equipment, we implemented ten-minute recording of land records following many months of planning to provide for the fast service. Only Forsyth County in North Carolina had this fast plan in effect.

The original land document was handed to an assistant or deputy register of deeds who collected probate and recording fees, certified the Notary Public acknowledgment and seal, assigned a book and page number, made a photocopy and returned the original document to the presenter, usually in less than ten minutes. This system required well-trained personnel, but the presenter had the original recorded document to use as needed. The register of deeds saved time and cost of mailing land papers to the presenters. All parties benefited.

The Cud Chewing Cow

When I became register of deeds, I employed an excellent typist who regularly chewed gum while working. Apparently at least one citizen was very much offended by the chewing.

One morning I opened a letter and found only a newspaper clipping of a cartoon, showing a contented looking cow peacefully lying under a big shade tree, with the caption: "The only difference between a gum chewing girl and a cud chewing cow is the intelligent look on the face of the cow."

I passed the cartoon among the staff and the gum chewing stopped.

Marriage Records
Prior to 1868

In 1868, Registers of Deeds in North Carolina started issuing marriage licenses. The Duplin marriage license indexes were complete since 1868, but the listing had disintegrated and needed to be retyped for use. This was one of my first projects, because all of the actual marriage licenses had not been preserved.

Prior to 1868, in North Carolina, a prospective groom purchased a marriage bond from the county clerk of court, stating his intention to marry a certain woman. Two reliable men signed his bond, making themselves responsible to see that the young man was true to his bond. The officiating officers at these weddings were not required to record official reports on the weddings performed before 1868.

In 1918, the Duplin County marriage bonds issued prior to 1868 by the Duplin County clerk of court, were in a box in the clerk's office and no indexes of them had been made.

Mr. R. V. Wells, our clerk of court, told me that when he took office in 1918, he sent the marriage bonds to the State Department of Archives and History for safekeeping.

Later, some young people from the Mormon Church prepared a listing of these early marriage bonds for the Mormon Church Library and left a copy with the State Archives and History Department.

The searching of family history was just becoming a very popular hobby when I took office. People who had once lived in Duplin, or who once had ancestors living in Duplin, began to return, searching their family's records. They often asked about the early marriage bonds.

The State Department of Archives and History was glad to supply us with a copy of the listing of marriage bonds prior to 1868 and furnish copies of the actual bonds as requested.

Genealogy, and the records searching required of this popular endeavor to determine family lineage, continues to place demands on Register of Deeds Offices to assure accurate, detailed, early data recordings, and availability of this information.

In 1988 when I retired, searching family history was said to be the number one hobby in the United States.

Paper Study

As I observed the several types and kinds of papers which had been used for recording the Duplin County records, it was easy to see that some were of much more permanent quality than others.

I contacted William K. Wilson of the National Bureau of Standards in Washington, D.C. and learned that for twenty-five dollars, his office would perform a permanence study on several different kinds of papers that were available.

The study showed that Permalife brand, acid free bond paper was the most permanent of the papers in our study. In fact, most of the paper being used for permanent recordings in North Carolina were labeled by the Bureau of Standards as "Not Suitable For Permanent Recording."

I learned that Permalife had been developed specifically for its archival characteristics with a high pH of 8.5. Most of the papers which were advertised and sold at that time for permanent recording had a pH of 7.0 which had thirty-two times more deteriorating acid than the Permalife paper with the pH of 8.5.

Tests by the U. S. Bureau of Standards showed that Permalife paper will last two and a half times the life of recording paper being promoted by some of the popular paper companies and used in county offices for recording permanent documents.

Owen G. Dunn Company of New Bern was the only North Carolina source for purchasing Permalife papers at that time. This firm acquired it in large rolls and cut it to desired sizes. We continued to use this source for recording papers.

I made copies of the results of the Duplin paper study and distributed them to all North Carolina Registers of Deeds at the next annual conference.

Later, I learned that the several State Departments of Archives and History had long been using Permalife paper.

Fourth Grade Tours
of the County Seat

The fourth grade in North Carolina elementary schools seems to be where children first begin to study county government and North Carolina history.

I noticed that some fourth grade teachers were bringing their students to Kenansville for one-day tours. So, I offered to help arrange schedules for these visits in order for the students to get the maximum benefit on their one-day visits.

At first, they visited the courtroom, jail, Office of the Register of Deeds, and the spring. When the Kenan Home restoration was completed, it was added. Later, the Cowan Museum became an interesting addition.

Later on, the county superintendent of schools designated a staff member in his office to help with the planning of fourth grade tours. When a date was set for a tour, I requested the teachers to submit data on a few students' birth certificates in order for us to be able to prepare certified copies for those students in advance of visits.

I always felt rewarded as the fourth graders showed so much interest in their own and their family's birth, death, and marriage records. Some asked to see deeds, maps, or military discharges. I invited them to return later with parents and let us help them use the records. It was surprising how many did return to learn about how their important records were kept.

It has always been a concern to me that so many children have grown up thinking the courthouse is only the place to be tried and sentenced when one gets into trouble. I enjoyed helping students learn more about the history of their county and how records are important.

A Mother Looks at Scouting

Following is the talk I made to the annual banquet of the Tuscarora Boy Scout Council held at the Goldsboro Country Club 1 December 1953:

Many years ago someone wrote a Mother's Prayer, which went like this:

> To be a Mother is an honor, Lord
> So great I stand amazed at times
> That I should have been chosen
> For such a worthy task as this.

Help me walk humbly, God
And fortify me for my task,
For well I realize
My great and grave responsibility.

What is a mother's responsibility and how can the scouting program help a mother in fulfilling her responsibility? Could it be said that a mother's greatest responsibility is to hold on to her husband with one hand and to God with the other hand in creating a home in which children can enjoy the fun of growing up and developing good character? Could it be said that her next greatest responsibility is to cooperate to the fullest extent with all agencies dedicated to the building of character?

How can scouting assist parents as they endeavor to help their children build good character happily? Cub scouting is designed to help parents plan enjoyable character building activities with their boys in the eight to eleven age group. In cubbing, boys learn to follow good leaders, to be square, happy and game; to give good will and to do their best at all times. Parents who accept the challenge offered as Cub Scout leaders not only enjoy cubbing years with their own boys but they cultivate a love for and an appreciation of all of the boys in the neighborhood gang.

For mothers who work or whose time with their boys is necessarily limited, being a Den Mother offers assurance, that time spent with the boys will be spent on activities suited to their needs and interests.

Scouting Headquarters keep Cub leaders supplied with materials needed in keeping real, live boys busy and happy during the cubbing years.

When a boy becomes eleven he can become a regular scout and take to the trails of camping and adventure. As he strives to do his best to do his duty to God and Country, to obey the Scout laws, to help other people at all times, to keep himself physically strong, mentally awake, and morally straight, he becomes a finer citizen in his home and in his community.

Surely all parents desire their boys to learn to obey the laws of our land. What better practice in obedience to laws can be cultivated than obedience to the Scout laws of being trustworthy, loyal, helpful, friendly, courteous, kind, obedient, cheerful, thrifty, brave, clean and reverent? The Scouting program gives recognition to boys for advancements made and keeps them occupied with projects suited to their age levels.

In the happy memory gardens being planted by the cubs in our neighborhood, I know there will always stand out memories of the good times we have had together in cubbing. These include: overnight family outings; a train trip; a trip to an oil terminal, an airport, a post office, a greenhouse, and a planetarium; marching in parades; visiting the underprivileged and the aged; handicraft projects; and putting on skits at our pack meetings.

In my own garden of memories there will always be among the dearest memories of the times I have worn my Den Mother's uniform and all it stands for.

Mr. B.M. Boyers commented later, "Thanks so much for your participation in our annual council meeting. Ever so many people have told me they thought your talk one of the highlights of the meeting."

Ten Years with the March of Dimes (1954-1964)

From 1954 to 1964 I served as County chairman for the March of Dimes. During that time we were still helping cases of infantile paralysis among the children in Duplin County.

Dr. Jonas Salk had made a limited trial of his vaccine in 1953. In 1954 further testing was done with a mass trial when 1,830,000 schoolchildren took part in the testing program.

Dr. Salk's vaccine was pronounced safe and effective in April 1955. The Duplin County Chapter of the March of Dimes continued to raise funds to help the patients who had been stricken prior to mass use of the vaccine, then we continued to raise funds to help with birth defects and other goals of the March of Dimes organization.

The most delightful experience I had during the ten years I served the March of Dimes was being able to deliver a March of Dimes National Foundation scholarship to Betty Anne Long, a 1961 healthy graduate of Whiteville High School. She received the scholarship in August 1961 for five hundred dollars a year for a four-year period of study in occupational therapy at the Professional Institute of William and Mary College in Richmond, Virginia. At that time there were only two schools in the United States which offered the occupational therapy course of study. The other school was in California. Five hundred dollars a year went a long way toward paying her expenses at school in 1961. She would be working some, too.

Betty Anne was the oldest daughter of Mr. and Mrs. Jesse Long, who had just moved from Whiteville to the Rockfish area of Duplin County to farm. There were two brothers and two sisters in the family. In Whiteville High School Betty Anne was active in the Future Homemakers Club and the Beta Club. She was a class marshal and ranked high in her graduating class.

Betty Anne explained, "I first read about occupational therapy in our family's World Book Encyclopedias. Then I asked our school guidance counselor for further information. I also wrote to the National Occupational Therapy Association in New York. On the basis of these three sources of information, I knew definitely that I wanted to become an occupational therapist."

A World Book Encyclopedia salesman had visited the family's sharecrop home near Whiteville where her father at first was very reluctant to purchase a set, but finally made the purchase. She had read almost every article in every one of the books in the set. There had been special interest when she read about occupational therapy, because she had never heard of this profession until she saw the information on it in her encyclopedia.

Betty Anne was one of the fifteen winners in the National Foundation's Health Scholarship program in North Carolina that year. Three scholarships were available in each of the professional fields of nursing, medicine, medical social work, occupational therapy, and physical therapy. Applications were provided through high school and National Foundation chapters by 1 April of each year. The credentials of applicants were then reviewed on a competitive basis by the Health Scholarship Division of the National Foundation. Scholarship, achievement, personal qualifications, professional promise, and financial need were the basis for selection of winners.

Meeting Betty Anne Long and being able to see her contagious enthusiasm was very inspiring. Following is a copy of the letter I received from her. She made good in her chosen field and kept in touch for several years.

Route 1, Box 195
Wallace, North Carolina

August 19, 1961

Dear Mrs. Williams:

I want to thank you and the Duplin County Chapter of the March of Dimes for making the National Foundation Scholarship possible to me.

I realize that the money comes from contributions of Duplin County citizens to the March of Dimes. I wish I had some way to say Thank You to them all. Have you any suggestions?

I received your letter, the certificate, and the forms you mailed to me. I have them ready to take with me when I leave for school on September 10.

I will send my school address to you as soon as possible after I get to school.

Thank you for your time and interest, and I shall do my best to live up to the expectations of those who have made this possible for me. I should like to keep in touch with you, and may I say it was a pleasure meeting you.

Sincerely,
Betty Long

1954
Chief Hostess—
Dedication of
Duplin General Hospital

When I became register of deeds in December 1952, the building of our Duplin General Hospital had just begun. Prior to the era of our hospital, our residents had to go thirty-five miles from Kenansville to the Goldsboro or Kinston hospitals or fifty-five miles to Wilmington.

So urgent was our need for a hospital, we had voted for a county tax to support one. There was much excitement among our population as the completion and dedication of our county hospital approached in the spring of 1954.

I had become integrated into my duties as register of deeds and clerk to the county board of commissioners. I felt so welcomed by the general public who seemed glad for me to be back in county government. This had apparently been the perfect time for a woman to enter our county political arena.

Our county commissioners asked me to serve as chief hostess for the hospital dedication. This involved selecting, training, and supervising guides to take members of the public on tours of the hospital on the Sunday afternoon of the dedication. In addition to our county people, many special out-of-town guests would be there to be guided through our new evidence of county progress.

Working in the hospital dedication project was fun and exciting. It was labeled as the greatest county event since Mrs. Roosevelt had visited Wallace in 1937. Everyone wanted to help.

The hospital dedication and the guided tours launched a new era in medical care in Duplin County and all our people felt proud to see the realization of this long awaited goal.

Joe's Big Fish

When the boys were growing up, we frequently took summer trips with Garland Carr and her son, Joe. Joe was born about halfway between Melvin and Glenn.

Most of our excursions were sightseeing. One summer when we were visiting historical sites in Virginia and eating at the seafood restaurant near the bridge in Yorktown, ten-year-old Joe ordered flounder. The others in our group ordered different fish or shrimp. The flounder was served on a platter as big as the one we use for our Christmas turkey. The fish, with its shiny eye, fins and tail, covered the whole platter and seemed to be looking up at Joe. None of us had ever seen such a mammoth fish.

Joe was small. As he stared at the fish in front of him, he seemed to get smaller and the fish seemed to grow larger. It was like an ant considering biting an elephant. All of us helped Joe stare at the big fish and watched him finally make his attack with his knife and fork before we could begin eating.

We seldom see Joe, because he lives in Danville, Virginia, but when we do, we are always reminded of his big fish.

1955

An Early Georgia Watermelon

When the boys were growing up we had a lot of fun using our imaginations to see who could tell the tallest tale.

The one they have most remembered is about a big, early Georgia watermelon I brought home. Melons from Georgia always got to our grocery stores earlier than our North Carolina melons. This one was unusually big and unusually early.

When I got home with it, the question was, "Where did you get it?"

My answer, "Do you want the truth or do you want a tall tale?"

Their answer, "A tall tale."

"Well, when I got to work this morning, a friend called and said she was flying to Florida to go fishing today. She asked If I'd like to go, so I did.

"As we were flying over Georgia, I could see the melons were big and ripe. I took out my rod and reel, put my biggest hook on and opened the plane door. My friend flew the plane down low over the watermelon field. Then I stood in the plane door, put the rod and reel out, and hooked this big watermelon. It was a tough one to lasso and bring up, but I finally did. Aren't you all glad?"

1957

First State Advisory Committee on County Records and First State-Wide Microfilm Program

In 1952, it became a great concern to me that at various times in a third of the North Carolina counties, courthouse fires had destroyed the county records, yet there was still no security program for permanent county records.

Also, in 1952, the Duplin County records vault was filled. Most vaults of county registers of deeds over North Carolina were bulging. There was no plan for retention and disposal of non-permanent and useless records. For example: A crop lien had been good for only one year, but there had been no authority to dispose of such recorded liens. We needed a statewide plan on retention and disposal of records.

Mr. H. G. Jones, state archivist, and Rear Admiral A. M. Patterson, USN (Retired), head of the Local Records Section of the State Department of Archives and History, were very interested in helping to create a security microfilm program for all permanent records.

Mr. Jones and Admiral Patterson were also very interested in helping to formulate uniform plans for the retention and disposal of county records in North Carolina and they welcomed help and support. But, they also needed support of the legislature in enacting laws to authorize such programs. We found an effective ally in Duplin's state representative, Hugh S. Johnson. He solicited the help of other effective legislators and both goals were realized.

We were able to get legislation passed to authorize the North Carolina Department of Archives and History to inventory the county records in every county.

A state advisory committee on county records was formed to work with Mr. Jones, Admiral Patterson, and the Institute of Government in deciding what records were to be microfilmed. This committee also helped prepare *The North Carolina County Records Manual*, which established the rules for retention and disposal of records.

I served on the state advisory committee on county records with registers of deeds Lemuel Johnson from Chatham County and William G. Massey from Johnston County. All other county officials were represented on the State Advisory Committee on County Records. This committee prepared a county records manual and a copy was distributed to all county officials in North Carolina.

At last the importance of North Carolina's county records began to receive the recognition which had been so long overlooked and neglected by county officials and state legislators.

Duplin County's state legislative representative, Hugh S. Johnson from Rose Hill, deserves much of the credit for the progress we were able to make during the 1950s in bringing the state laws up to date including the authorization for the use of modern methods in microfilming and other technology in our record keeping systems.

1958
Duplin County Native Moves to Washington and Becomes Jackie Kennedy's Stand-In

Ruth Wallace grew up on a farm near the B. F. Grady School in Duplin County. After a secretarial course at a Raleigh business school she quickly climbed the ladder in secretarial work. She married Douglas Shivar.

When I became register of deeds in 1952, she came to work in the Registry Office. Her husband was in the air force serving overseas. Ruth worked in the office until 1958 when they moved to Washington, D.C. She became a legal secretary for a law firm whose offices were located practically in the shadow of the White House.

As a part-time model, she was booked as the "Mrs. Kennedy" type since she bore a striking resemblance to Jackie Kennedy. Her life changed when an executive at NBC saw her picture in *The Washington Post* newspaper and needed a stand-in for the First Lady during White House rehearsals of a television program on the proposed Cultural Center.

Her work was behind the scenes at the White House but she gained instant fame with reporters and photographers. Heads were set a swivel as she walked along Pennsylvania Avenue during her lunch hour.

An article in the 12 November 1962 issue of *Newsweek* featured a picture of Ruth looking for all the world like Jackie Kennedy and stated in part: "Like her counterpart, brunette Ruth Shivar is 33, tall (5 feet, 8 inches) and willowy (35-24-34). They even use the same Washington coiffeur (Mr. Andrews at Lilly Dache), who does the Shivar hair in what she described as a 'flip with a right-direction toward the eyebrow, wing tips touching the ears, and a bouffant top.' One difference: North Carolina born Ruth Shivar speaks with a faint drawl. She said of the First Lady: 'I'm flattered that anyone thinks I resemble her. She's a perfect combination of simplicity and elegance.'"

After several years of being on the Washington merry-go-round and a divorce, Ruth returned to Duplin County. There was no vacancy at this time in the deeds office, however, Guilford Mills, a textile company, was building a plant in Duplin County just a few miles from Ruth's home. Shortly thereafter Ruth was employed as the secretary to the plant manager and worked at Guilford East in this capacity until her retirement.

She is now living a quiet and happy life with her husband of twenty-three years, Frank Wallace. They reside in the countryside where Ruth grew up.

They live only five miles from me and we get together to have lunch or go shopping as often as we can. Sometimes I go out to dinner with both of them.

1959
Duplin Gets a Copy of First Eight Duplin Deed Books for Years 1749-1784

Duplin County was cut off from New Hanover County in 1749. From 1749 until 1784 Duplin County covered the areas that are now both Duplin and Sampson counties. During these years, the Duplin Courthouse was located near the present line between the two counties, one mile from the present home office of Carroll's Foods near Warsaw.

When Sampson County was cut off from Duplin in 1784, the eight books of deed records which covered both counties from 1749 to 1784 were taken to the new Sampson County Courthouse in Clinton instead of the new Duplin Courthouse in Kenansville.

One of my first goals was to acquire a copy of these eight early deed books from Sampson, because surveyors and family history searchers had been without them since 1784.

Finally, in 1959, after the Sampson County records had been microfilmed by the State Archives, the State used the Sampson microfilm to prepare a full size paper copy of each of the eight deed books for Duplin. The State Archives staff had each book bound for our use.

The Sampson folks allowed me to take one of our staff members to Sampson and use their equipment to prepare a copy of the grantor and grantee indexes for the eight books. Our only disappointment was that the earliest deed for Duplin County found in these books was for property from Patrick Canady to Henry Byrd. It was signed in 1753 and recorded in 1754. It is not known what happened to the deeds recorded during the five years between 1749 and 1754.

At last we felt that our Duplin County records were as complete as they could ever be. We already had acquired a list of the early marriage bonds and now we had a copy of the first eight earliest deed books!

The originals of these early books had become so deteriorated that in 1849 Sampson County had employed a transcriber named, Edward Vail, to spend several months copying them by hand. As he copied the deeds into new books in 1849 and 1850 he made personal notes between some of the recordings. The most interesting one was recorded in book two at page seventy:

> "On 15 of April 1849, one of the worst and coldest snow storms came to Sampson County, North Carolina, and destroyed everything on the face of the earth."

He also noted "A big rain on 2-15-1850" and "another big snow on March 28, 1850."

He wrote about the death of John C. Calhoun, noted senator from South Carolina, at two places.

Old Courthouse Historical Marker Unveiled

In a joint effort of the Historical Societies of Duplin and Sampson Counties, a marker was unveiled on 9 April 1995 to identify the site of Duplin's first courthouse. It was completed in 1754 and served Duplin County and the middle Cape Fear region until Sampson County was established from the western half of Duplin County in 1784.

The old courthouse stood on the west side of the Old Courthouse Road (SR 1108) just off the shoulder of the road, one mile north of N.C. Highway 24, about four miles west of Warsaw. The historical marker is located adjacent to Carroll's Foods, Inc., on N.C. Highway 24, two miles west of Warsaw.

The ceremony unveiling this marker was a momentous and long-awaited event for those of us who had studied the history of our county and wished there had been a marker for the courthouse which served Duplin County until 1784 when Duplin and Sampson were one county named Duplin.

It was great to be one of the speakers at the ceremony dedicating the marker.

Duplin County Interest in Astronauts

In July 1959, Neil Collier, a painter from near my home at Pink Hill, came to the Duplin Register of Deeds Office to obtain a certified copy of his Duplin County birth certificate. He needed to attach it to his application to work as a painter for the National Aeronautics and Space Administration Launch Operation Center at Cape Canaveral, Florida. His birth certificate was a problem, as were many which were prepared in rural homes by doctors and midwives at the time babies were born.

Mr. Collier was gracious in his thanks at the time we helped him and talked excitedly about the recent naming of the first seven Mercury program astronauts on 9 April 1959. We had to share his excitement, because it was so contagious. We felt good that we would have a local man working at Cape Canaveral who would be living and breathing every astronaut adventure. What we didn't expect was that in a few days he would send us beautiful colored 8" x 10" pictures of each of those first seven pilots who had been chosen for the Mercury program.

We taped each autographed picture on to the plate glass that separated my office from the main reception office. Everyone entering the reception area had to look straight at all of them. The astronauts were air force officers: L. Gordon Cooper, Virgil I. Grissom, Donald K. Slayton; navy pilots: M. Scott Carpenter, Walter M. Schirra, Jr., Alan B. Shepard, Jr.; and marine corps pilot: John H. Glenn, Jr.

When Alan Shepard, Jr. became the first American space traveler on 5 May 1961 and spent only fifteen minutes in space, we had the feeling that he was one of our friends who had been with us in the office for several months. We couldn't have been more excited had it been a local person.

Then on 20 February 1962 when John H. Glenn, Jr. became the first American astronaut to orbit the earth three times, the excitement was hardly containable as we listened to every word broadcast on the radio, which I had brought to work that day. Every time I have heard the name Senator John Glenn or have seen his picture in a paper, it has been like hearing about a special friend. And now that he is scheduled to go back into space to study the effect of space on the elderly, he has given all elderly people reason to be proud!

We listened on 3 March 1965 as Virgil I. Grissom became one of the two astronauts on the first two-man space flight. Then we were saddened on 27 January 1967 when Grissom's *Apollo* space craft caught fire during a ground test and he and two other astronauts were killed.

Later, on 15 July 1975, our long-time friend Donald K. Slayton was on the first International Space Mission. Many people who visited our office examined the pictures of these first astronauts and shared with us their triumphs and tragedies as these seven space pioneers brought great credit to themselves, their families, to the United States, and the advancement of the space program.

In Alan Shepard's interviews, he was quick to say that while his space stay was only for fifteen minutes, this was only the beginning of things to come through space exploration. We were as thrilled for his fifteen minutes in space as if he had been our next door neighbor's son.

1960

A New Courthouse Annex

Changes to Save Space

In 1958, a decision was made to build the present Duplin County Courthouse Annex to house the overfilled offices of the clerk of court, register of deeds, county finance office, tax supervisor, and tax collector.

The county commissioners asked each official who would be housed in the new annex to draw a floor plan adequate for fifty years. I drew a plan for a reception office, a photographing room, a private office, and a 30' x 50' vault. It has been functional and adequate for thirty-nine years.

More Land Record Books Per Shelf and More Pages Per Book

As soon as we occupied the new facilities in January 1960, I set about to conserve the new vault space for future recordings. I redesigned land record book binders used for current recordings to increase the number of pages per book and to allow for storing two books per shelf instead of one book per shelf, which had been customary.

Chattel Mortgages and Crop Liens

At the time we moved into the new courthouse annex vault, the Register of Deeds Office had two hundred bound books with recordings of chattel mortgages and crop liens. There had been no authority for discarding any of these as they became obsolete until our new state advisory committee on county records, on which I served, had implemented regulations to authorize disposing of these chattels and crop lien books as their effectiveness expired, freeing up space for new land record books.

The Duplin County courthouse in 1952 when I became Register of Deeds.

Growing, Growing . . . Melvin and Glenn with their bikes. Glenn won his and Melvin worked in the tobacco fields to pay for his.

Above: The Spring and picnic grounds discovered more than two hundred years ago.

Right: Mrs. Ellen Huddler, left, had been one of my many good friends since I first explained the farm programs to her in 1934. I was reacquainted with all of my dear friends that I had known in the farm office when I went back to work in 1952.

Standing, F. W. McGowen, County Finance Officer. I was required by law to serve as Clerk to the County Board of Commissioners for my first fourteen years, then the law was changed. County Commissioners are seated.

Above: The Farm Machinery Repair Shop Lehman built in 1950 before he stopped working. It was foreclosed by the bank and has stood as an eyesore for thirty years.

Left: Jackie Boyette (left) Lucy Baker and I in the crowded vault of the office of Register of Deeds before the new courthouse annex was occupied in 1961.

Part Seven

1961-1988

1961
The Fascinating Story of the Country Squire Steak House, Established 1961—Now Seats 456

On one of the hottest days of July 1961, Amos Brinson, who owned the Kenansville Drug Store and who was a high school classmate of mine, called me and asked if I'd like to ride with him during my lunch hour two miles out toward Warsaw. He had heard Joe West was building a steak house in his father's woods and he wanted to see Joe's venture in progress.

On the way out we talked about how people were labeling Joe "dumb." He had been to college several years and changed his major several times. At this time he was teaching science at nearby James Kenan High School. But his main interest in life had been learning to be a gourmet cook, including experimenting with exotic cuisine of varying types. He spent his vacations visiting famous restaurants and studying their recipes, as well as developing new ones of his own.

When Amos and I arrived at Joe's new enterprise, he was struggling to install an air conditioner in the kitchen window. Beads of sweat were rolling down his face and his handkerchief was soaked from wiping his forehead. His shirt was drenched. He looked ready to have a heat stroke. Sitting down on a box to catch his breath, he related to us that he planned to continue his teaching at James Kenan School and serve steaks on weekends. As he continued to share his plans with us, he said he would have no lighting except candlelight or little gas flames. The Country Squire would seat sixty-one. All recipes for cheese balls, salad dressings, whipped butter, sour cream, Korean beef, and all entrees would be his very own original ones. His projected prices seemed quite reasonable.

Joe was having to do most of the labor himself, because his parents, and the local bank had refused to lend him any money. They termed his venture a foolish one. Who would go out in the woods to eat? His friends and acquaintances also thought his vision of a steak house in the woods of rural Duplin County was a foolish one. Especially the men said they would never stumble around in the dark in candlelight to eat a steak. It was just a crazy idea to think they would!

Finally, his mother's brother, a house builder, had loaned Joe four thousand dollars. Joe's Country Squire Restaurant was just a mile from the Hines farm where I had lived. I was very fond of Joe and his only sibling, Henry, Jr., who had made a good life curing fresh pork hams in his own Westwater Ham plant.

Joe's parents, Henry and Leona West, had owned and operated excellent grocery stores in Kenansville and Warsaw before the supermarket days. If they saw a customer picking over potatoes, apples, or other produce, they would immediately hurry to the back storage room and get a new supply. Nothing escaped their attention. They had been so successful in making every customer feel they were the only customer who mattered. When Joe opened his steak house, he exhibited the same trait.

The Country Squire Restaurant took off like lightning. People in the area had never tasted food like Joe served. His food was described as being flavored with romance, history, and legend from the ages. The Squire seemed to create the impression of outdoor living, as the decor changed with the seasons. The old cupboards, antiques and fireplaces seemed more like a setting for a colonial drama. The Country Squire welcomed every guest with sincerity and a genuine sense of caring for their comfort and pleasure. The names Country Squire and Joe West became household words all over eastern North Carolina.

Joe soon had to quit teaching school when he added The Pantry which was used for small parties and romantic dinners. Mead Hall was also added to the establishment at this time. These two rooms feature separate histories. The Pantry highlighted hand-hewn logs, many from the old Bowden Hotel in the port city of Wilmington. Some guests claim one of The Country Squire's ghosts inhabits The Pantry, seeking the return of the timbers to rebuild his old haunt.

Mead Hall is a commodious room seating eighty guests for dinner, reflecting the region's earliest English heritage with its brick floors, murals, tapestries, rough sawn paneling, and soft gas flame lighting. Mead Hall is one of the most popular halls, overlooking the gardens and ponds sheltered under stately Carolina pines. Here, tiny star-like holes bored in the ceiling with overhead loft lights sparkling through the ceiling holes give the feeling of dining out under the stars. Reserving a table by the windows in the Mead Hall where one can enjoy the overhead stars and look out onto the gardens has been a favorite since the Mead Hall was added.

Next, Joe purchased the old T. J. McGowen home built in the 1700s. It was joined to The Country Squire by a long hall in the English tradition of knights and their ladies. The hallway features chain-held tables, banners, and gas flame lights to reflect the history of those first Englishmen who visited North Carolina along Roanoke Island. Joe named the old T. J. McGowen house the Baronial Hall, which can seat eighty guests through use of the seating within the loft.

Finally, as the Squire's fame spread far and wide, the Jester's Court was added and seats one hundred seventy guests for dinner and dancing. This room comfortably seats two hundred visitors in a conference setting.

Joe's last addition was The Squire's Vintage Inn with sixteen guest rooms, located next door to The Squire. Each room's decor compliments the Old World charm found in the dining rooms of The Country Squire.

Joe sold The Country Squire and his recipes for a half million dollars when he was diagnosed as having an incurable malignancy of the spine with a very short life expectancy. He had surgery and treatment, and recovered.

Then he built Josef's Restaurant close by, but he was handicapped by not being able to serve large groups. He closed Josef's and soon died.

Joe West's last restaurant is presently known as The Grey Fox under new ownership and gives diners a choice in excellent foods.

Iris Lennon came to work for Joe at The Country Squire in 1974. She is a charming woman from Scotland with a Scottish brogue. She worked for the new owners after Joe sold it and purchased the whole Country Squire establishment in 1993.

Our Melvin worked as a waiter at The Squire one of the summers he was attending Duke University and saved twelve hundred dollars. Every Saturday night that summer he served a couple who drove to The Squire from their home in Chapel Hill, one hundred and ten miles away.

The Squire now owns a van which often picks up and returns dinner guests who fly to the county airport two miles away from The Squire. Residents from all over eastern North Carolina make jaunts to The Squire to enjoy the dining and surroundings. Folks from Pennsylvania and New York on their way to Florida stop by the county airport and use The Squire's van service to bring them to the restaurant to enjoy a dinner while their plane is being serviced. The county airport here is said to have the cheapest gasoline on the east coast.

The Squire's 1998 prices of regular steak dinners vary from $10.25 to $18.95. The tradition of the 72-ounce steak is still free, if the purchaser eats all of it.

During some holiday seasons the 456 seats are all reserved. A stage has been added in the Jester's Court where dinner theaters and a variety of musical programs are enjoyed in this steak house in the woods that most people considered a foolish idea in 1961.

Following are portions of the funeral service of Joseph West as delivered on 23 May 1995, by Reverend D. Gene Lakey, Jr., Minister of Kenansville Baptist Church:

> I suppose the life of Joseph Aaron West could be measured in years. Sixty-three years is a long successful life. At least that's what our mind tells us. But when it's our father, or brother, or dear friend, it's not long enough. That's what our heart tells us. And so today we would all agree that Joe was not with us long enough, was he?
>
> But the success of one's life can be measured by yet another way: one's accomplishments in life and contributions to life. Joe West accomplished far more in the sixty-three years God granted him than those who live many more years. All of us are certainly aware of how instrumental Joe was in establishing Duplin County, and particularly this part of our fine county, as a well known place to visit, to live, and especially to enjoy a good meal. Creating one of the finest restaurants in our state was the dream, born within him, and against all odds and the many who said it couldn't be done, he turned that dream into a reality. And our community is better because of it.
>
> If you knew Joe, you couldn't miss his tremendous creativity. He had the enviable gift of being able to take something very simple, something most of us would overlook and discard as useless, and transform it into something of absolute beauty. He had an eye for things, that unique taste for how things should be, whether it be cuisine or decor or flowers or landscape. His creativity was practically unmatched. Most of us here today can certainly remember Joe West for these things just mentioned. But for some of you gathered here today, the most outstanding memories you have in your heart of Joe West are of the things he did which were never written of in the newspapers, those things which went unpoliced by the crowds, those things that are probably known only to you and to God. And those memories are of his many acts of kindness and benevolence and generosity toward you and toward others. Some of you will always remember Joe for believing in you when all others had given up on you, for having confidence in you when all

others had forsaken you, for giving you a job when others wouldn't even give you the time of day. And what he did for you turned out to be just the "leg up" you needed to get going again in life.

Yes, all people now living who have ever enjoyed the food and atmosphere at both of Joe's creative restaurants will always have pleasant memories of their work, dining experiences, and association with Joe.

No doubt those who have enjoyed the fruit of Joe's labor are wishing generations to come will be able to continue patronizing these unparalleled dream places of unique cuisine and innovative surroundings.

Tar Heel of the Week

The following is an excerpt from a feature article which appeared 20 August 1961 in *The News & Observer*, daily newspaper of Raleigh, North Carolina.

Meticulous planning is the key for Mrs. Christine W. Williams, Register of Deeds in Duplin County.

It takes that kind of planning, too, for Mrs. Williams to dovetail daily her various duties as community leader, wife, mother, and housewife at Pink Hill, Route 2, with her official duties at Duplin County's courthouse in Kenansville.

In June she was elected president of the North Carolina State Association of Registers of Deeds, an organization she was instrumental in helping to form shortly after her first election to office. One of the association's goals this year, she said, is to prepare and publish a guidebook for Registers of Deeds. This will be done through the Institute of Government.

Early this month she went to Chicago as North Carolina delegate to the national convention of County Clerks and Recorders. She is an associate editor of the organization's magazine, *The County Recorder*.

Leadership For Statewide Action

From the moment she won the May 1952, primary, Christine Williams plunged deep into county affairs, her interest extending beyond Duplin's problems to embrace those of county officials throughout North Carolina.

When the central Marriage Registration Act goes into effect next January 1, Mrs. Williams will be one of several Tar Heels who will feel a sense of accomplishment, She was a member of a group of Registers who pressed the recent General Assembly into adopting the act. Until then, she pointed out, North Carolina was one of only eight states which did not have central marriage registration in their state capitols.

This lack, she explained, worked a genuine hardship at times, since proof of marriage is now necessary for a variety of purposes. In the past, if a marriage was not registered in one county, it meant that an individual might have to write or see each Register of Deeds in the State's other 99 counties in an effort to obtain the needed information.

Currently Mrs. Williams is the chairman of a committee of Registers who are working with State Department of Health officials in preparing the license form that will be used.

She is also the only woman on the nine-member State Advisory Committee on County Records authorized by the 1957 General Assembly. This committee subsequently worked hard for the passage of legislation which authorized the State Department of Archives and History to place on microfilm all county records of permanent value.

Later, the committee assisted in the preparation of the *County Records Manual* which was published by the department and distributed to all county officials in North Carolina.

A Valedictorian Learned the Business

Duplin's Register of Deeds was born in Duplin County, the daughter of Mrs. Genett Thomas Whaley and the late Mack Jefferson Whaley. She has a sister, Mrs. Norman Anderson of Mt. Olive, and a brother, Milton J. Whaley, now in Turkey with the Joint Military Aid Program.

In the depression year of 1932, Mrs. Williams was graduated from Kenansville High School as valedictorian of her class. She took a business course by correspondence and in December 1933 got the job of office manager in the Duplin County Agricultural Adjustment Administration Office.

She remained in this position until February 1942, and it provided the firm foundation of her subsequent career—during this eight-year period, she came to know Duplin County's farmers and to know them well.

She has been re-elected every four years since 1952 without opposition. Her wide personal knowledge of Duplin voters and a friendly, pleasant manner are obvious political assets.

Much of her success she attributes to her staff, a group of whom she refers in a single word—wonderful.

On December 23, 1937, Christine Whaley married Lehman G. Williams and in February 1942, they moved to Wilmington where Williams was employed in a shipyard throughout World War II.

In 1945, they returned to Duplin and the B. F. Grady section where they still make their home. The Grady section is just two miles from the Lenoir County line and the Williamses are members of the Pink Hill Methodist Church just over the county line in Lenoir.

They have two sons, Melvin G. Williams, 18, a rising sophomore at Duke University, and Glenn Williams, a rising junior at B. F. Grady High School.

Everything is a Family Affair

Mrs. Williams is a member of the Pink Hill Methodist Church's Administrative Board. She also teaches the Young Adult Class and serves as Advisor to the Methodist Youth Fellowship.

When the boys were in Scouting, Mrs. Williams worked so diligently in a variety of Scout projects. She won the Den Mother Award and The Scouting Award for Women Scout Leaders.

Duplin's Register of Deeds has set something of a record for a PTA member—she has missed only one PTA meeting since her sons started school. Currently, she is serving her second year as president of the Grady PTA.

A handsome blonde, with blue eyes, Mrs. Williams is the first woman ever elected to public office in Duplin County. In addition to her work as Duplin's Register of Deeds, she serves as clerk to the Duplin board of county commissioners.

She takes part in practically all activities in Duplin County. Among other things, she has served as Duplin chairman of the National Foundation for Infantile Paralysis and has been active in the Kenansville Garden Club. She is constantly in demand as a speaker and has made many appearances before a variety of groups.

Long-Range Planning Does It

As a mother and a homemaker, Mrs. Williams doesn't miss a beat. She now does all her own cooking, canning and freezing. Fortunately, she likes to cook.

How does she manage?

"Long-range planning," she answers promptly. "That's the secret. I'm a meticulous planner when it comes to office work, meals, household duties, and anything I'm interested in. Planning means I can do many things I otherwise wouldn't have time for.

"The boys are a tremendous help. They help with all the work around the house and yard. It's really a cooperative affair. They know if they help me, I'll have time to take part in things that interest them."

1962
North Carolina
Council of Women's Orgaizations

Continuing Education Committee

In 1962, I was invited to serve on the continuing education committee of the North Carolina Council of Women's Organizations based in Chapel Hill. Mrs. Vera B. Lawrence of Charlotte was president in 1962. Then, in 1963, Mrs. Harold J. Dudley of Raleigh became president. I served two years. Both of these ladies were dynamic and effective leaders.

My close personal friend, Senator Martha Evans of Charlotte, was on this committee.

Among the outstanding ladies who were very active in the Council of Women's Organizations at that time were Mrs. Glen Auman of Hillsborough, Mrs. J. E. Winslow of Hurdie Mills, Miss Ruth Searles of Chapel Hill, Mrs. Fred Bunch of Statesville, Mrs. J. S. Henninger of Chapel Hill, Dr. Guion Johnson of Chapel Hill, Miss Mary Shotwell of Raleigh, Mrs. Phoebe Emmons of Raleigh, Mrs. James Odom and Mrs. J. S. Barach of Charlotte, Miss Asenath Cooke of Greensboro, and Mrs. Adrian S. Lineberger of Chapel Hill.

The Council of Women's Organizations had noble goals for the improvement of women. Working with the educated, skilled, talented, and attractive ladies in this council provided opportunities to broaden my horizons and help set goals for the future of all North Carolina women. It especially gave me an opportunity to represent the women who never had opportunity for education when they were young and who, like myself, wished to continue learning as they matured into senior citizens!

I also served two years on the committee of this council which framed several laws regarding families, including the first state law to tighten requirements of parents to pay child support and provide punishment for parents who fail to support their children.

One of the council's regular activities was to sponsor an annual leadership training workshop for women, held at the University of North Carolina at Chapel Hill, extension division. I attended the 1963 session.

Moving Out—Leaving the Williams Home Place

In 1962, Lehman was loafing. His repair shop was empty. The bank was foreclosing on it for an unpaid mortgage. Melvin had been at Duke University two years and was on the Dean's List. He worked summers, had a good scholarship, but I still needed to help. Glenn was entering his senior year in high school and was planning to go to North Carolina State University with no scholarship. Lehman had insisted on Glenn spending so much time at the repair shop and not getting his lessons that Glenn had no chance of a scholarship. Also, he had heard Lehman lash out at education so much, he was apparently trying to barely skim by in spite of my having sent him to expensive summer schools for two summers and my continuing concern about his poor grades.

Lehman was still not making any contribution to our family's expenses. His disruptive behavior was getting worse. He was cursing and verbally abusing me in exactly the same manner I had heard him curse and abuse his mother for ten years when he didn't get the money he demanded.

One of Lehman's judgment holders had threatened execution. The home place would be put up and sold. I had finished paying the debt to Mr. Waller for Lehman's sister's one-half interest in the Williams' home place. I would not pay off the judgment about to be executed if the title to the Williams' eight-acre home place remained in Lehman's name alone, because his future creditors could attach more judgments. He would not agree for my name to be put on the title to prevent future judgments from attaching, even though I had paid off one-half the value. But, he did agree for us to transfer the title to the boys. So we did.

In 1962, I had to make a move. I was halfway through my third term as Duplin County register of deeds and felt fairly secure in that position. I could no longer support Lehman and help the boys get educations. I purchased a lot within a block of the courthouse in Kenansville, where I worked, obtained a low interest loan with no down payment and built a modest three-bedroom brick house with payments of fifty-six dollars a month for thirty years. Melvin, Glenn, and I moved to Kenansville and left Lehman enough furniture and fixtures to keep house.

Lehman soon moved to Raleigh. His Raleigh attorney wrote me a letter saying the property was vacated and Lehman would not be paying any taxes or insurance. I was not surprised, because he had never paid any taxes or insurance since we had been married.

Since the Williams' home place was now titled in Melvin's and Glenn's names, I decided to try to save it for them. So, I sold the house in Kenansville after five months, made a profit, and we moved back. I paid off the outstanding judgments Lehman had made while the title was in his name.

Glenn was in Raleigh in mid-August 1964, and Lehman contacted him saying he needed a divorce, because he was having to marry a woman eleven years younger then he. I obtained a divorce on grounds of two years separation and sent it to him.

Lehman married the woman and when the baby boy she soon had was one year old, Lehman took the baby and went to a nephew's house some distance away. While the nephew and the nephew's wife were at work, Lehman took their credit cards and went through South Carolina, Georgia, and Florida, visiting relatives and acquaintances and running up credit card debts on his nephew's cards.

The last communication I had regarding his finances was when he was in Florida with the baby boy, supposedly in hiding from the boy's mother. An elderly sounding woman called me by phone. She said Lehman was in a Florida hospital and owed her eighty-two dollars of child care. She was planning to turn the little boy over to Social Services if she didn't get paid. Lehman had asked her to call me and ask me to pay her eighty-two dollars. I wired her the money, but questioned whether the boy wouldn't have fared better to go to the care of Social Services. I never had any further repercussions from Lehman since that time.

The woman Lehman married in Raleigh has never tried to locate him or her son, which Lehman took. Lehman finally came to Kinston, twenty miles from my home, where he married a woman with a house, but after some unhappy years, she asked him to leave.

The boy Lehman took from his second wife has had a hard life, quitting school at sixteen and being put out of Lehman's third wife's home. Once when I saw him, he followed me to my car and asked me how he could locate his mother who had never tried to locate him. He said Lehman had never even told him his mother's first name and didn't want him to know it. I assumed he had been told that I had worked with birth, death, and marriage records. I suggested an attorney, but he said he couldn't afford one.

Lehman spent his last days in rest homes and then in a nursing home. When Lehman died, I saw the boy he took from his second wife. He seemed like a sad, never married, thirty-two-year-old, whose life has been beset by alcohol, drugs, and bankruptcy. He doesn't even own an automobile. On the day of Lehman's funeral, I gave the young man a photocopy of his mother's marriage license to Lehman. It showed her full name before she married Lehman and her parents' names. He just said, "Thank you," and smiled.

Mother's First Television

When Milton came to visit Mother Christmas of 1962, he delighted her with her first television. He set it up on a table in her living room, turned it to Channel 7, Washington, North Carolina, and adjusted the rabbit ears. Mother was keen on many subjects but television was a totally new experience for her.

She felt that she had become in touch with the whole world. During the coming year, she watched major civil rights events. President Kennedy's assassination, and a parade of other national and global events.

Her daily evening routine had focused around watching channel 7 news at 6 P.M., *Dragnet* at a quarter after six, then Huntley Brinkley news at a quarter until seven.

When Milton visited Mother the next Christmas, he asked how her television was doing. She really made him feel rewarded by saying what a good friend it had been all year.

He asked, "How many channels can you get?"

She replied, "What do you mean?"

He answered, "You know, when you change from one channel to another, how many different stations can you get?"

Her reply was, "Milton, you didn't tell me there was more than one station on that thing."

She had watched only channel 7 for an entire year but she wasn't complaining because it had opened up the whole world during a year of great events.

1963
Need for More
County Development

In 1963, there was a lot of talk in Duplin County that though the county had enjoyed the greatest agricultural income of any county in the state every year since 1958, our county desperately needed more available jobs. Our young people were leaving the county in large numbers to find jobs elsewhere.

C. W. Surratt, Jr. from Rose Hill was a leading citizen interested in more job development for Duplin County. In 1963, he and some others led the effort to organize the Duplin County Industrial and Agricultural Council. This was a non-profit county-wide volunteer council organized to promote agricultural and industrial development in Duplin County and to promote enabling legislation and referendum to establish a full-time Duplin Development Office with a paid staff.

Serving as secretary and treasurer of this volunteer organization seemed a worthwhile cause. The referendum was successful, a tax was approved, and a fully staffed development office was established.

The county commissioners asked me to serve on the first board of directors of the new Duplin County Development Commission from 1970 to 1974.

The Day President John F. Kennedy was Assassinated

On Friday, 22 November 1963 I was delayed in going to the Jones Cafe in Kenansville for lunch. The Jones Cafe was within a block of the courthouse. It was owned by Roscoe Jones and his wife, Ruby. At 6 A.M. every weekday, Roscoe started making his famous apple, cherry, and peach pies and put a ham and beef roast in an oven to cook. At that time, this was the only place in town to eat, so most of the county workers ate their noontime meal with Roscoe and Ruby. There were many traveling salesmen who arranged their schedules to allow for eating at Jones Cafe.

On this day, when I arrived, most of the people had already eaten and left the cafe. Stephen Worth, a little hunchback man, about sixty years old, who was a whiz as a court reporter and who had his own school in Fayetteville, North Carolina for training court reporters to use Stenotype machines, was in the restaurant. He was eating alone at the table in the rear next to the television. Roscoe provided the television for his local guests to watch the noon news, followed by the soap opera, *As the World Turns*, at 12:30 each day.

Every time I ran into Mr. Worth he always had some sort of current joke to get my attention. On this day as I sat at the table to eat with him, he asked, "Have you heard about the proclamation President Kennedy issued this morning?" He wanted my answer to be, "No, what was it?" So, I obliged. He said, "President Kennedy declared that the people in the United States cannot drink any more orange juice." He wanted my question to be "Why?" So, I obliged again. His answer was, "Because it reminds him of Goldwater." Senator Goldwater had already announced he would be running against President Kennedy in 1964.

As Mr. Worth finished saying the name "Goldwater" a flash interrupted the television program in progress, blaring: "President Kennedy has been shot in Dallas, Texas. Jackie held his head when he collapsed. Governor Connally also shot."

Unlimited tears started streaming down my cheeks as the television continued to give available details on the tragic event in Dallas. My tears were flowing not only for the implications of what this tragedy would mean for our country, but I also felt a keen sense of personal loss.

When John F. Kennedy had come to Greenville, North Carolina, seventy miles away, during his presidential campaign, and had spoken from an outside platform to thousands of people, I had gone early and stood within a foot of the platform. His shoes were level with my eyes. I became intrigued with how the soles of his shoes had been built up to about two inches thick and the heels to about three inches, enabling him to be seen above the crowd.

Such a dynamo of power, strength, and charisma I had never beheld as he outlined his vision for the future of our country. I got the feeling that he stood for all that would be right and against all that would be wrong for the people of the United States. And now he had been murdered!

I had followed everything that had been printed about First Lady Jacqueline Kennedy, beginning with the *Life* magazine issue which portrayed her fairy-tale marriage to this handsome Senator from Massachusetts, to the births of her three babies, the loss of little Patrick, and the stories about Caroline and John John.

I somehow felt closer to Jackie, because Ruth Wallace, from my community, who was living in Washington, D.C. at the time, had won the Jackie look-alike contest and the right to stand in for her during the trial shots made by NBC of Jackie's tour of the new cultural center at Washington, D.C.

As I watched this film on television, I had felt a special kin to Jackie as I envisioned that I was watching Ruth in Jackie's place. Ruth and I had been friends since her high school days and she had been my secretary before she had gone to Washington to live a few years. She soon returned to our community to live and we are still friends.

1964
Governor Sanford
Forms Commission
on the Status of Women

On 5 March 1964, I received the following letter from Governor Terry Sanford:

STATE OF NORTH CAROLINA
Governor's Office
Raleigh

Terry Sanford
Governor

March 4, 1964

Mrs. Christine W. Williams
Register of Deeds, Duplin County
Kenansville, North Carolina

Dear Mrs. Williams:

I am enclosing copy of my Executive Order establishing the Governor's Commission on the Status of Women and the announcement which was given to the press. I consider the Commission's work most important and hope that you will be willing to serve as a member of the Committee on Education Beyond the High School and Expanded Opportunities for Mature Women, chaired by Dr. Bonnie Cone.

I will look forward to hearing from you as soon as possible.

With best wishes always,
Sincerely,

Terry Sanford

This was a statewide committee made up of twelve persons. Six of the committee members had Doctorate degrees.

Our first meeting was on 19 June 1964 at 10 A.M. at the Methodist Building in Raleigh with Dr. William Archie, Director of the North Carolina Board of Higher Education.

The leaders of the several education groups in the state which were then interested in education beyond the high school and expanded opportunities for mature women met with our committee that day and gave us their prospective on what could and should be accomplished through an expanded program of education and opportunities beyond the high school for women, mostly through the state community college system.

Serving with North Carolina educators on this committee was interesting and rewarding and gave me great satisfaction. These subjects have always been concerns of mine.

I was still interested in continuing education when I retired in 1988 at age seventy-three. I enrolled at Mount Olive College in a creative writing course and found it just as challenging and interesting as I found learning when I was much younger.

1965

The Kenan Family Donates Liberty Hall to Duplin County for a Museum

The town of Kenansville, the county seat of Duplin County, was named for the Kenan family which came to America in 1736. The men in this family were active leaders in the military, civic, religious, educational, medical, and legal fields.

In 1922, when we moved to the Hines farm and attended the one-room Kenansville school, we walked by the vacant Liberty Hall, the Kenan family home. We also passed it on the way to school at the new brick Kenansville consolidated school, beginning in 1927. We were always curious as to what this empty house looked like inside.

During the more than forty years when the Kenan home was vacant, it was owned by Dr. Owen Kenan, who lived in Wilmington. He made frequent visits until he died in 1964. For most of the vacant years, Perry Dobson, a local mail carrier, who lived two doors from Liberty Hall, served as the Kenan property caretaker.

Ghost Stories

During these years there were so many fascinating tales, including ghost stories, told about this empty Kenan house. These stories caught the imagination of teenagers who many times crawled over the high fence which surrounded the property and walked around the grounds looking for ghosts.

On a moonlit night in 1958, my next door neighbor's son, who has led an exemplary life of accomplishments, called his parents from the Duplin County Jail to tell them he and a group of our B. F. Grady High School students had climbed the fence at the Kenan property and had been walking around the grounds, peeping into the windows. They were spied by Perry Dobson, the caretaker. They had not planned to do any harm; they just wanted to look for ghosts and satisfy their curiosity.

The parents of each student were required to go to the jail, identify the students, and take them home. None were indicted.

The ghost story that fascinated me most was the one which maintained there was a lady's big pocketbook in the home, stuffed round with bills of money. Each time anyone stooped down to pick up this pocketbook, it would jump, so no one was ever able to lay hand on it.

A Prime Target for Thieves

Not only did this closed home catch the imagination of teenagers, but several times vandals entered and stole objects.

In 1960, two young men from Wilmington, fifty-five miles away, who had recently worked for a Wilmington contractor repainting the Kenan home, broke in and stole several objects. They were being tried in Duplin Superior Court in Kenansville for breaking, entering, and theft.

Dr. Owen Kenan's attorney, Vance Gavin, the presiding judge, and the solicitor suggested to Dr. Kenan that they would like to go to the home and see how the thieves had entered and then go inside and observe the condition of the home after the break-in. Vance invited me to go with them on this tour. Seeing inside this fascinating place had been on my wish list since 1922. So, I was delighted.

It was interesting how the beds in the house had been left with linens on them when the Kenans had moved out. Expensive and decorative objects were tastefully in place on some of the antique furniture and some pictures were still hanging on the walls.

I was not surprised at the many years of cobwebs hanging from the ceiling and under pieces of furniture. Everything was covered with layer upon layer of dust. What had been elegant silk wallpaper created in New York by special designers was in pieces, and at some places in shreds, hanging from the ceiling and walls. This had apparently been caused by long years of the house being closed with no heat and air conditioning.

I saw the stolen objects which had been returned. It appeared that the young men doing the stealing had selected the least valuable among an array of expensive treasures. For example, one of the stolen pieces was an aged, black leather chair with oxen horns on the arms. Dr. Kenan had brought this chair from the house he occupied in Paris for many years before moving to Wilmington. The chair was probably close to being worthless.

I was using a rather big pocketbook on the day I toured the Kenan home, and as we came out, I had the feeling Dr. Kenan was giving my pocketbook a real hard look, wondering if I had taken something. He was quite aged at the time and had been troubled by vandalism for so many years, so it was easy for me to understand any suspicions he might have.

Miss Mary Lily Kenan

From our childhood as we had walked by the abandoned property, we had been intrigued by the story of Miss Mary Lily Kenan's marriage in the home. It was in August 1901 when she was thirty-three that she married Henry Flagler, a multimillionaire, age seventy-one.

Mr. Flagler, with John D. Rockefeller, one of the wealthiest men in the United States, had founded the Standard Oil Company. Later, he had set out to develop the east coast of Florida and had become the biggest property owner in that state.

The wedding party, which included guests from New York to Palm Beach, Florida, had come by train to the town of Magnolia where Mr. Flagler had arranged for the guests to be driven to Kenansville in horse drawn carriages. The guests included members of a fifteen piece orchestra.

I was charmed by the news story which stated that following the wedding Mr. Flagler presented Mary Lily a five thousand dollar oriental pearl necklace and three million dollars in cash and bonds. As a further wedding present, he had built the famous White Hall Mansion in

Palm Beach, which, according to newspaper reports, cost one-half million dollars to build and one and one-half million dollars to furnish.

I have twice visited this elegant home at Palm Beach, which is open to the public as a museum. Mr. Flagler's private railroad car sits on the lawn of this palatial exhibit of wealth where every item and every explanation by the guides interested me.

Mr. Flagler died in May 1913, leaving an estate of one hundred million dollars to his widow, Mary Lily.

Mary Lily later married Robert Bingham from Louisville, Kentucky, whom she had known in Asheville during her college days.

Mary Lily Kenan Flagler Bingham died in Louisville, Kentucky. Her body was brought to Wilmington for burial. Her many paged will is recorded in the Duplin County clerk of court's office, because she owned property in Duplin. I found her will extremely interesting. In the early 1960s, after the Duplin Register of Deeds Office acquired copying equipment, visiting Superior Court Judge Robert Gavin, who was holding court in Duplin, asked me to prepare a copy of Mary Lily's will for him. So, I made a copy for myself to enjoy at the same time.

When the book, *Henry Flagler*, was published I purchased a copy. The same author later published *The Binghams of Louisville* and I checked it out from our local library to read.

Kenans Give to Duplin County

When the 1949 performance of *The Duplin Story*, sponsored by Duplin County government, was over, a twenty-five thousand dollar profit had been realized. This money was used as a nest egg to start a building fund for the Kenan Memorial Auditorium in the town of Kenansville. Through generous donations from the Kenan family this facility was completed and later refurbished to include comfortable seats, a large stage, and efficient heating and cooling. This auditorium is one of the finest in North Carolina and has been host to all kinds of meetings, catered luncheons and dinners, as well as basketball tournaments.

The Kenans also built an outdoor amphitheater behind the Kenan Auditorium. It is first class in every way, with comfortable individual seats, and effective outdoor lighting and sound. It has served the area well for the production of outdoor dramas and musical shows.

The consolidated high school, serving the Kenansville-Warsaw-Magnolia communities, is named James Kenan High School, for a member of this family.

The University of North Carolina at Chapel Hill

Through the years the Kenan family has been generous with support of the University of North Carolina at Chapel Hill and other educational endeavors. The football stadium at Chapel Hill is named Kenan Stadium.

The School of Business at the University at Chapel Hill has been a special project of the Kenan family with teaching fellowships endowed.

Liberty Hall as a Museum Today

In 1965, philanthropist, Frank H. Kenan, of Chapel Hill, deeded the Liberty Hall property to Duplin County and endowed it for use as a museum. Young Tom Kenan, III, of Chapel Hill, supervised the restoration, renovation, and refurbishing of Liberty Hall to restore it to its original elegance. It now contains the restored wedding dress Mary Lily Kenan wore in August 1901, for her marriage to Henry Flagler.

After the first renovations in the late 1960s, the Kenan family later added several interesting outbuildings, replicas of the original eighteenth century structures. Then a handsome and functional visitors center was added. Among other niceties, this center has a visitors assembly and viewing room which enables visitors to enjoy a professional video presentation of the Kenan family legacy. The Kenan compound now seems complete, but the digging of a pond on the property is now in the works.

Liberty Hall has become the main tourist attraction in Duplin County. Colorful brochures on the home are now available at North Carolina visitor centers for tourists as they enter our state.

The Tar Heel Fine Arts Society

After the Kenan Auditorium in Kenansville was refurbished, a number of our citizens continued to discuss how the auditorium would be a perfect center for performances similar to the ones many of our citizens were driving to Raleigh to enjoy. We continued to discuss the possibility of an organization to sponsor such concerts and other art endeavors.

On 15 February 1965, I joined eight other citizens, including the president of James Sprunt Institute, at the home of Dr. and Mrs. Glenn Rasmussen to consider the formation of the Tar Heel Fine Arts Society to plan, coordinate, promote, and sponsor cultural activities of all types of fine arts, including drama, painting, music, and literature.

The nine of us contributed five dollars each to be used mostly as postage during our first year. We made plans to secure unpaid artists to give performances that first year and charge ten dollars for season tickets. We had no trouble in finding obliging performers and made enough profit to engage paid performers for the next year.

At our first meeting we made the decision that following the first year, the Society would always have in hand the funds to contract for performances for the next annual concert series. This plan worked well.

The incorporation of the Tar Heel Fine Arts Society as a non-profit organization was perfected in October of 1965. A board of directors was formed with at least one representative from each area served. It was vested with the authority to govern the organization by directing its policies and operations in all matters relating to the objectives for which it was formed. Either the president of James Sprunt Institute, or someone designated by the president, served on the board. Since most board members were working, all board meetings were held at lunch time at the Country Squire Restaurant.

Memberships were ten dollars each annually, with a season ticket provided to each member. Annual contributions were solicited from sponsors and patrons. A season concert ticket was given to patrons for each ten dollars contributed. For several years, more than two thousand season tickets were distributed.

Our Tar Heel Fine Arts Society was the only county-oriented art organization in North Carolina. I served as the first secretary and later served as president, during the 1974-75 concert series.

One of our first goals was to purchase a Yamaha grand piano and donate it to the Kenan Auditorium. This goal was soon accomplished and the piano still serves the needs of various programs and performances in the auditorium.

So successful were our efforts that we were able to sponsor some of the same performances being enjoyed at the "Friends of the College" series at North Carolina State University in Raleigh.

Among the concerts we sponsored were the Preservation Hall Jazz Band, located at St. Peter Street in the heart of New Orleans' French Quarter, and Jose Greco and his Spanish Dancers with Nana Lo, Flamenco Dance Theater.

During the 1974-75 concert series when I was serving as president, we sponsored Fred Waring and his Pennsylvanians. How exciting it was to introduce Fred Waring to our audience of over two thousand Duplinites and members from adjoining counties! At that time Fred Waring was still giving performances and conducting summer music camps for young people and Elder Hostel in an effort to perpetuate his unusual style of music, which appealed to young and old alike.

After twenty years of sponsoring annual concert series in Kenan Memorial Auditorium, the Tar Heel Fine Arts Society disbanded when the cost of an annual concert series that would appeal to the people of our area became prohibitive. We donated the funds on hand to James Sprunt Community College (no longer an institute).

During the year 1975, when I was president, we were able to organize the Duplin County Arts Council. How happy I was to sign the application to obtain a state grant to start a county arts council! Our council now owns a building with a paid staff. It sponsors all types of art endeavors in the county schools and in many other areas of Duplin County life.

Uniform Commercial Code Saves Space

In 1965, our state representative, Hugh S. Johnson, appointed me as one of three Registers of Deeds to serve on a two-year commission to analyze the proposal to implement the Uniform Commercial Code in North Carolina in 1967. The Uniform Commercial Code which was implemented in North Carolina in 1967 provided that all documents representing encumbrances on crops, farm implements, household appliances, and other personal property could be filed in loose folders and discarded as their life expired. The use of bound books for personal property documents was eliminated. This saved future cost of books and saved valuable space in record vaults.

This commission on which I served designed functional, easy to read forms for the loose filings provided by the new code. County vault space required for storing the new Uniform Code filings was reduced to less than ten percent of the space used prior to 1967 for personal property encumbrance documents.

After the Uniform Commercial Code was enacted as state law in 1967, I arranged a training course on its use for Duplin County banks, lending agencies, and businesses. The course was held at James Sprunt Community College, where Attorney Richard Burrows and I served as instructors. Bank and business leaders from as far away as Kinston attended because our course was the only one held in our section of the state.

1967

The Warsaw Garden Club

If I could belong to only one organization in addition to the church, it would be a garden club.

In 1967, when the Kenansville Garden Club disbanded, I joined the Warsaw Garden Club and served as vice-president and program chairman more than once. When I retired in 1988, the Warsaw ladies claimed I had implied that when I retired, I would serve as president of the club. After all, I had received all benefits of lunching with these lovely ladies and enjoying excellent and timely programs for many years. So, I was happy to serve from 1992 to 1994 as president and I plan to continue to be active in this club as long as I can.

My happiest moments are when I'm growing flowers and sharing them with shut-ins. Just to feel free "piddling around" in a terminally ill patient's home, arranging, rearranging, discarding, and watering flowers creates a gateway to speaking a caring and comforting word to patients and their families. These are times when they most need the outreach of a non-family member who is not being paid and who is not under obligation to help and comfort.

There is so much to be learned at garden club meetings, not only about flowers, but birds, shrubs, trees, conservation, garden therapy, civic beautification, horticulture, anti-litter, and recycling. And there's still so much I don't know! But one truth I do know—the power of God's creativity is most visible when involved in making wise use of anything God has entrusted to us.

The Warsaw Garden Club was organized 27 October 1949 by Mrs. Henry L. Stevens, Jr., my high school history teacher and my special friend.

Duplin has Its First Astronaut

Dr. William Thornton, from Faison, was one of eleven scientist/astronauts named in 1967. He had attended Faison schools and the University of North Carolina at Chapel Hill, where he graduated in 1952. He married an exchange student from London, England, and they have two sons.

One day in 1975 I had a telephone caller at the Register of Deeds Office who asked: "Is this Mrs. Christine Williams?" My answer was, "Yes." Then the caller said, "This is Dr. William Thornton, Jr., from the Houston Space Center. I need a copy of the legal description of my mother's property in the town of Faison. A question has arisen about a property line."

What a surprise and delight it was to speak with our own, real live Duplin County Astronaut!

After Dr. Thornton soared into space on 30 August 1983, he visited his hometown of Faison, where a big homecoming celebration was held. It was a special treat to me to shake his hand and talk with him at the celebration, to relive the sheer excitement I had known when he had called.

Dr. Thornton was kind and friendly and thanked me for sending him a copy of the legal description of his mother's property.

It was great to see him again on 19 April 1998, when he returned to Faison to experience the joy of introducing Betty Ray McCain at her special day set aside by the Town of Faison to honor its favorite daughter. He and Betty played together growing up and had many incidents to relate to the crowd gathered to honor Betty.

1968
Mother Succumbs

The Re-Election was Too Much

It had been twenty years since Daddy died. Mother had enjoyed living in her little house in the center of Beulaville where she had been a shut-in much of the time with frequent trips to the hospital.

Brother Milton was in Turkey ten of those years and in Norfolk, Virginia, the other ten. Alma was living in Mt. Olive and seldom visited Mother or me. I had assumed the total responsibility for Mother's day-to-day care during those twenty years.

There were times when she needed a companion in her home for several weeks. Sometimes I could not find a person available in Beulaville and I would bring her to my home near Pink Hill where there would be a local person available to care for her while I worked.

Five months before Mother died, she seemed unable to prepare any of her meals and needed to make permanent plans. The ladies in the Beulaville area who had lived in homes as companions for the elderly had taken jobs at the growing number of local assisted living homes where they only worked eight hours a day for five days a week and went home. When they lived in as a companion for Mother, they worked around the clock, except weekends when I had to take over.

A big textile plant had come to my area where the ladies, who had stayed with Mother several times at my home, had found permanent employment with good wages. All other ladies in my area who desired work had found jobs in the plant.

After much exploration and deliberation, Mother decided to enter an assisted living home in Kenansville about two blocks from the courthouse where I worked. She had a private room and seemed happy there. It was easy for me to see her every weekday and often bring her to my home for weekends.

I had been in office sixteen years with no opposition since I was elected the first time. I was fifty-three years old and hoped I would never change jobs again.

When I ran for office the first time, in 1952, there was a lady my age who had been talking of running for the office. So, I had waited to file until the last five minutes before the close of filing time, because I didn't plan to file if she did.

In 1952, this lady was keeping books for a fertilizer dealer and decided to continue with him. Now, he had died and his office was closed. She was working in 1968 for a small newspaper. She took a long leave of absence from her job and filed against me. She contacted voters all over the 819 square miles of Duplin County, day and night. A young man with no office experience had also filed.

Normally, Mother had a beautiful spirit and attitude. She was a positive thinker regardless of how she felt. She could always see that things would get better, but this was a very stressful time for her. She was now seventy-four with advanced bronchitis, pulmonary fibrosis, emphysema, and chronic heart failure. She found it hard to accept the thought of anyone trying to get the job that had worked so well for me and enabled to do so much for her for sixteen years.

I assured Mother that I felt confident I would be reelected. I told her that during the current campaign I would continue looking after my work and her, and just take a vacation the week before the Democratic primary on 4 May to get out and see the voters.

I stuck with my plan until about a week before the 4 May voting. On Saturday, 27 April, I called sister Alma and asked her to spend the day with Mother in the assisted living home while I contacted voters. Alma visited her until 7 P.M. They had a nice time together, except Mother told Alma she was extremely concerned about the election and that she didn't believe she could survive if I lost.

At eight o'clock that same evening an aide checked Mother and she had died in her bed. I felt so badly that she never knew the election which took place in just another week was a landslide and I would serve a total of nine four-year terms, until age seventy-three.

Now I had lost the compass I depended on for fifty-three years and I could hardly endure the realization that she died so concerned about my reelection.

But in retrospect, I should really not have been so surprised, because she had so depended on me for so long. I remember when brother Milton had been in Ankara, Turkey for ten years, how much I wanted to go for a visit, but each time I discussed going, Mother would physically get worse until I gave up the idea. She was not "putting on." Her health and general condition was so poor she couldn't bear the thought of my being so far away. Now, she couldn't bear the thought that I might lose my job that I loved so much.

I missed my daily contact with Mother. She had always been my Rock of Gibraltar, always there, and we shared so much. I never forgot how fortunate I had been to have her and my Daddy for my parents.

Due To The Unexpected Death Of
My Beloved Mother
Mrs. Jeanette Thomas Whaley on Saturday April 27.

Mrs. Christine Whaley Williams

I Will Not Be Able To Get Out
And Contact VOTERS Every Night
The Last Week of Campaigning As
I Had Expected To

I Will Thank All Those Who Are Interested In Keeping
Experience, Efficiency and Integrity In The Duplin Register
Of Deeds Office To Work Harder This Final Week During
this Period Of My Sorrow and Bereavement When I Cannot
Contact The People of Duplin County Personally.

YOUR VOTE AND SUPPORT
ON MAY 4
WILL BE APPRECIATED

Mrs. Christine Whaley Williams
Canidate for Reelection
As Duplin County Register of Deeds

A copy of a paid political ad I placed in the local newspapers the week after Mother's death.

1972

One of Forty-Two
Biographical Sketches

I was one of thirty-six men and six women of Duplin County, living or deceased, included in the 569-page *Flashes of Duplin's History and Government* by Faison and Pearl McGowen.

Christine W. Williams

Christine Williams is the daughter of Mack Jefferson Whaley and Genett Thomas Whaley. She attended Duplin County Public Schools and graduated from Kenansville High School in 1932. She was valedictorian of her class. Christine completed a business course by correspondence from Southeastern University, Rock Hill, S.C.

She is a graduate of the County Administration Course, Institute of Government, University of North Carolina, Chapel Hill, North Carolina.

In 1937 she married Lehman Guy Williams. They have two sons, Melvin Guy Williams and Joseph Glenn Williams. Christine is a member of the Pink Hill United Methodist Church, and has served as president of Women's Society of Christian Service, Sunday school teacher for thirty-four years, Counselor for Methodist Youth Fellowship for six years, and a member of Board of Stewards of Pink Hill Methodist Church for the past ten years.

She was Manager of Duplin County ASCS office 1933-1941.

In 1952 she was elected Register of Deeds of Duplin County, being the first woman elected to public office in the County. She has been re-elected every four years since.

Christine is a past president of the North Carolina Association of Register of Deeds; serves as chairman of the State Board of Health Advisory Committee on birth, deaths and marriage records; a member of the State Department of Archives and History Advisory Committee on County Records, and member of Legislative Committee of North Carolina Association of Registers of Deeds for the past ten years.

Her civic services include: Secretary-Treasurer Duplin County Agricultural and Industrial Council; member Board of Directors of Duplin

County Development Commission; incorporator and treasurer and president of the Tar Heel Fine Arts Society; Charter Member and past secretary Duplin County Historical Society; active member and past president B. F. Grady Home Extension Club; past president of Kenansville Garden Club and Kenansville Junior Woman's Club; Member of the Continuing Education Committee of Governor Sanford's Commission on the Status of Women; past co-chairman Continuing Education Committee of North Carolina Council of Women's Organizations; now active member Beulaville Garden Club; Den Mother for Cub Scouts; Adult Leader for 4-H Clubs; and vice-chairman of Duplin County Democratic Executive Committee.

Christine was "The Tar Heel of the Week" in August 1962; "Farm Lady of the Week" for the *Goldsboro News Argus* newspaper, in 1954; received Scouting award from Tuscarora Council of Boy Scouts of America in 1955, and was listed in "N.C. LIVES," 1962.

1973

Snow Brought Me to My Knees

Though I lived fourteen miles from my work at the county courthouse, I believed I owed it to our people to be there during office hours, regardless of the weather. I learned this lesson from my parents when I was walking two miles to school every day.

When we had bad weather, I always remembered that so many of our people in the 819 square miles of Duplin County lived long distances from the courthouse.

Many of the Duplin County people chose to come in to search records when they couldn't very well work outside. I especially considered the three land surveyors in the Wallace area who usually came in the twenty miles from Wallace to the Register of Deeds Office in bad weather to search records. So, I tried to have the office open during all regular office hours.

We seldom have really dangerous roads from snow and ice in eastern North Carolina, but on Saturday, 10 February 1973, there began four days of snow and ice. The highway officials in our area did not own enough equipment to keep the highways safe and passable. During this storm many farmers used their tractors to pull ambulances and automobiles from outlying areas into the county seat to the doctors and hospital.

I was content to stay at home during the storm on Saturday and Sunday, but when Monday morning came and I saw some passenger cars on the highway going by my house, I knew there would be some people going to the Register of Deeds Office for service. I decided I should be there.

By driving slowly, I arrived safely at the office and parked directly across the street at the jail. As I was crossing the street, I could see that the cement gutter, sidewalk, steps, and porch at the office door were covered over in slick ice and had not been traveled since the storm began. No one was in sight. If I should fall, there might be no one to rescue me. My safest bet appeared to be to start crawling! I knelt at the gutter next to the office, preparing to crawl over the gutter, sidewalk, steps, and porch, because it seemed to me certain that no one could survive walking without falling.

Just at the moment when I had knelt to crawl, a county ambulance came around the corner of the courthouse. Two emergency service workers in the ambulance spotted me. The ambulance stopped. The two workers immediately jumped out of the vehicle, quickly removed a stretcher from the back of it and headed for me. I realized they thought I had fallen!

Making their way over to me, they called, "Are you hurt, Miss Christine? Can we help you?" I told them I had decided it was safer for me to crawl on into the office than try to walk.

Eight citizens came in that day for services. A couple in their thirties came for a marriage license. The woman had been stranded in her car on the highway because of the snow and ice and had taken refuge in a house nearby, which was the home of the man's mother, where he also lived. They met there for the first time, had immediately decided for sure they had always been meant for each other, and after three days they were ready for a marriage license. Their wedded bliss lasted longer than their courtship, but dissolved in about two years.

The county commissioners declared that day a non-work day at 11 A.M., but I stayed on until 3 P.M., when the sky suddenly turned dark gray and I slowly made my way safely home.

1975
State-Wide Uniform
Land Record Forms

In 1960 when Duplin County began photographic recording, it was evident that valuable vault space could be saved by redesigning the North Carolina standard four-page form deeds and deeds of trust that were being used all over the state.

A little experimenting with rearranging some of the printing on the standard forms, showed that both the standard deed and deed of trust form could be printed on fourteen inch, two-page forms instead of the current four-page form being used.

I gave a rough draft of these revised forms to the Wallace Enterprise Printers. They prepared them for sale.

While some attorneys preferred to have their deeds and deeds of trust personally typed, other attorneys and many lending agencies liked the new two-page standard form which used only one-half the space of the old four-page ones. (While working on the Uniform Commercial Code Study, 1965-67, we had already designed a simple short form for use in personal property encumbrance filings in North Carolina.)

By 1974, most counties were using photographic recording and there was a need to begin a massive effort to conserve vault space in every county by revising Land Record forms.

Our State Association appointed Jean Ramsey, Register from Rowan County, and me, as co-chairs of a committee on uniform forms in North Carolina. The goal of this committee was to work with the real estate instruments committee of the North Carolina Bar Association to develop uniform deeds and deeds of trust forms to be used in North Carolina to save valuable recording space in county record vaults and to more adequately meet the needs of attorneys, Registers of Deeds, and the general public than the variety of forms then being used.

As co-chair of this committee, I made a collection of ideas for uniform deeds and deeds of trust forms from the one hundred Registers of North Carolina. These ideas were summarized into sample forms for consideration of a larger committee of ten Registers of Deeds who met in Raleigh on 10 January 1975, for adoption of recommendations for the co-chairs to present to the North Carolina Bar Association committee on 23 January 1975.

Sample deed and deed of trust forms finalized at the 10 January meeting were presented by the Registers' co-chairs to a meeting of Real Estate Instruments Subcommittee of the North Carolina Bar Association at the North Carolina Bar Center in Raleigh on 23 January 1975.

Attorney M. Marshall Happer, III, of Raleigh was chairman of this subcommittee. Also attending the 23 January meeting were Attorney J. Troy Smith, chairman of the Real Property

Committee of the North Carolina Bar Association, William M. Storey of Raleigh, who was executive vice-president of the State Bar Association, and Allan B. Head, Executive Secretary of the State Bar Association. Attorney J. Troy Smith's family was from Magnolia.

This meeting and some others which followed taught me how much the State Bar Association appreciated our interest in working together with the State Bar to better serve the people of North Carolina.

While some attorneys still preferred to have their land record documents personally typed, the new space-saving forms were widely used in many areas of the state to conserve county vault space.

New Notary Public Laws for North Carolina

When the county clerks of superior courts in North Carolina were transferred to the state courts system, the task of judging the notary public acknowledgments on deeds and other land records was transferred from the offices of the county clerks of superior courts to the registers of deeds.

Also transferred by state law to the registers of deeds was the duty of maintaining records of notaries public commissions, corporation records as well as records of partnerships and assumed business names. County clerks of court went under state courts system at various times. The Duplin County clerk was transferred to the state system in 1969. All aspects of the transferred duties went well, except that in 1969 Duplin County had 416 commissioned notaries, who had no training or access to a handbook or guidebook for notaries. Most of these notaries were employed where they needed a notary commission for only certifying acknowledgments on documents executed in the establishment of their employer. But, many of them certified signatures on land documents presented to the registers of deeds for recording.

North Carolina laws had considered certain instruments would be of such importance that they were required to be signed by the maker in the presence of a public officer to prevent fraud and forgery. But, it was clear that notaries public had not been informed on the significance of their function. Working with our county notaries clearly indicated that North Carolina needed a system that would help our notaries public be aware of their responsibilities and how to effectively fulfill them.

I discussed this problem with Secretary of State Thad Eure, to whom the duty of issuing notary commissions had been transferred from the governor's office. We formed a committee to work with the secretary of state on improving the notary public situation.

Finally, in 1975, we were able to get state legislation to require new notaries to attend a three-hour workshop, studying the laws covering their duties and responsibilities. The required three-hour workshop training course was established through the state community college system.

Teachers for the course were required to be trained by the secretary of state. The Institute of Government at Chapel Hill prepared a *Notary Public Guidebook* for use in the workshops taught at the community colleges. I took the training and taught the first workshop for Duplin County notaries at our James Sprunt Community College.

1976

Installation of Geodetic Markers on all State Highways in Duplin County to Aid Land Surveys

Prior to 1976, only a small portion of Duplin County's state highways had geodetic markers for use by surveyors and engineers in preparing accurate land surveys. Markers were desperately needed in the remainder of the county.

Since the county's establishment, land deed descriptions had been tied to such temporary markers as "a small pine tree", "a small red oak," et cetera. Such descriptions were no longer adequate to locate "the goodly lands of Duplin County."

State personnel for the statewide project of installing geodetic markers was limited to twenty-two people for the entire state. Requests for installation of these markers were being given preference where the interest in these markers was sufficient for the county to make arrangements for two local people to assist state personnel in this project.

Duplin County had not been interested in budgeting funds for such a project.

In 1976, I was able to arrange for the state geodetic marker installers to be assisted by two residents of the Kenansville Youth Center which is a part of the state correction system.

It was exciting, at last, to get the project launched to complete the installation of geodetic markers on state highways to eliminate concern and controversy among land owners.

A legal land description which shows the land's location in relation to a geodetic-marker, actually shows the position of the land on the face of the earth, because each marker is reported to and made a part of the record of the National Geodetic Survey Control.

As work progressed on the 1976 project, many citizens wanted to know: "What's going on with stakes, flags and yellow arrows pointed along State highways; little triangular tags nailed to poles, posts, and trees; holes dug and then filled with concrete and a bronze disk; and State employees working at night by the use of flashlights?" We tried to give publicity to the fact that we had requested geodetic markers to aid surveyors and engineers in preparing accurate surveys for property boundaries, maps, and engineering projects.

Geodetic markers were placed along state highways at the most permanent locations which would maintain a line of sight between each marker. The installation was not made along secondary roads, however surveyors preparing land descriptions along these roads can tie such descriptions to the geodetic markers along state highways if they use electronic equipment, which all surveyors are now doing.

Most of the work of installing these markers had to be done after sundown because atmospheric conditions are more favorable for accurate instrument readings at night. Some folks claimed that the installers were stargazing and, quite frankly, they were! They were observing the North Star. The exact location of certain stars in relation to the Earth is known at any given time. Measuring angles to these stars gives the most accurate bearings on which to locate geodetic markers.

So satisfactory was the performance of one of the youth center residents in the geodetic marker project that upon his release, he was given permanent paid employment by the State Department of Natural Resources in other county projects where he gave good performance.

State-Wide Study Commission on Volunteers Within the Criminal Justice System

In 1976, Governor Jim Hunt asked me to serve on a state commission to study the subject of volunteers for the North Carolina criminal justice system. This commission, made up of volunteers, met periodically for two years and made several recommendations regarding plans to expand volunteers in all areas of the criminal justice system.

At the end of our study, Governor Hunt awarded all commission members "The Order of the Longleaf Pine," in appreciation of our efforts.

Yokefellow Prison Ministry

Prior to the time of the study on volunteers in the criminal justice system, I had helped to organize a Yokefellow Prison Ministry at Kenansville Youth Center, a unit of the State Department of Corrections.

While serving two and one-half years as executive secretary for the Yokefellow group, soliciting volunteers and refreshments for meetings, I became concerned about the lack of a chaplain at the Kenansville Youth Center. I wrote to then Governor Jim Holshouser expressing my concern.

Soon I received a letter from David L. Jones, state secretary of the Department of Corrections, which read in part:

> A request from Governor Holshouser's Office has been received regarding your concern about the availability of Chaplains within the Division of Prisons and the Division of Youth Development.
>
> A four-year plan has been developed by an Advisory Group with initial emphasis on the placement of full-time Chaplains at the Adult Institutions within the Division of Prisons. The second year of the plan calls for the placement of six area Chaplain Coordinators, one of which would be designated to cover the Kenansville Youth Center.
>
> Let me take this opportunity to express my personal appreciation to you and to the other members of the Yokefellow Prison Ministries for their efforts in behalf of the development of religious services for offenders in the North Carolina Department of Corrections. It is through such individual effort of people who care enough to involve themselves personally in these matters that the real goal of rehabilitation will be accomplished.

A Woman Who Never had Any Problems

One day in 1976, I received call at the office from a woman who said, "If you are free for lunch today, I'd like to take you to The Country Squire. There's something I want to talk to you about."

I was delighted to accept her invitation but I could hardly concentrate on my work for wondering what this woman wanted to discuss with me. I had known her husband through professional dealings but I had never seen her.

I was aware that her fine educated son had married the daughter of one of my friends and lived some distance away. But I would not recognize this woman. She knew me only through what she had heard and read in her local paper.

When we were seated in the candlelight at The Squire, she began: "You have always appeared to me to be a woman who has never had any problems. So, I want to tell you mine!"

She had enjoyed the same efficient full-time cook/maid for thirty years who even did her hand washing for her. There was nothing left for her to do.

She had discontinued serving as musician for her Church. She had served long enough. It was time for someone else to do it.

Her son and his family lived away and did not come home often.

Her husband was attentive but still worked and was away all day.

She was absolutely bored to tears. Her life was void of any sense of achievement or belonging. She was not only bored all day, she couldn't sleep well at night, so she suffered from night-time boredom too. She was relying on sleeping pills but thought they made her feel sluggish during the day.

She was absolutely correct in thinking I had never had any problems like hers. Every night I was going to bed completely exhausted but had to take a few minutes to reflect on all the lives which had touched mine during the day, and how much those lives had enriched mine.

In no day did I ever accomplish all that I had set out to do. There just wasn't time. But I was always thankful there would be another new day with more opportunities. I felt very helpless but I began to make suggestions.

The residents in the nursing home and boarding home near her home would love to have her go play the piano in their dining rooms, or write letters or run little errands for them. Many had few or no guests to call. But she said that wasn't her cup of tea.

At that time I was working in the Yokefellow Ministry at our youth center and I mentioned how much they loved to hear the piano played during their meals. Most of them were long distances from home and had few visitors. To go in a correctional center was not her cup of tea either.

When I enumerated all the interesting courses being taught at her community college, none appealed to her. They would be an absolute waste of time.

First and second grade schoolteachers were crying out for adults to volunteer to listen to little children read. Just once a week would be a big help to some child who had no one at home to listen. She had taught her own child to read. This was the parent's responsibility, not hers.

When I mentioned some other situations which seemed to afford great opportunities for service and enrichment, none appealed to her.

The lunch was delicious and the lady was charming but I was left with a feeling of emptiness. This lovely and talented lady had not experienced the joy of reaching out and helping others and thereby enriching her own life.

Not long after that day, she went to visit a relative in a distant town and died in her sleep. I never saw her death certificate but I suspected the actual cause of death was boredom in the midst of opportunities for service.

1978

Creating Modern 16mm Computerized Microfilm for Public Use of all County Records

The 35mm microfilm of all county records produced by the state under the 1959 law provided some feeling of security, because one-third of all North Carolina counties had lost records by fire.

But soon after the Duplin records were microfilmed, we obtained a few rolls from the state and found that it not only could not be adapted for use in the modern instant reader-printers being made but there was no method available to get good prints from it. This was because in haste to complete microfilming of the records of all counties, the State had made only one image of each two pages in the bound deed books. The center part of each two-page image could not be read in copies made from the microfilm. To get good copies from microfilm, there must be a separate image for each page.

When these determinations were made, I began a serious study of a plan to re-microfilm Duplin County's 228 years of records, using 16mm film that could be stored in cassettes and used in instant reader-printers by the public with copies of the microfilm stored for security.

Contracting with a commercial firm to prepare suitable instant image location microfilm was not an option for two reasons. The cost was prohibitive and our records from the early founding of the county until 1940 were handwritten with varying inks and papers and many would not produce good microfilm images. Most of the poor book pages could be deciphered with the naked eye but needed to be typed before microfilming.

One of my goals was to personally supervise and complete this task while I was serving as register of deeds. We received a grant for purchasing a planetary microfilmer suitable for preparing excellent microfilm from bound books.

In 1978, with two years of help by two CETA workers paid by the Federal government and one year's help of a worker under a Federal training program, we launched the re-microfilming of all records.

The resulting film could be used by the public in making excellent copies, thus relieving our staff of copy-making.

The job training worker used four dozen black numbering machine pads in replacing unreadable page numbers on the old deed book pages on which light red or blue numbers had almost faded. She used twelve dozen art gum erasers in getting rid of long years of finger smudges on pages to be microfilmed. The job training worker also checked all loose-leaf deed books to make sure no pages were missing. Two pages of one deed were missing, but I was able to locate the name of the missing deed on our index. I contacted the land owner, got the original deed and re-recorded it. These pages had been missing when the state microfilmed, but their men had not checked the books for missing pages.

One of our regular staff carefully examined each developed microfilm image and flagged the page in each deed book which had not produced a good readable high quality microfilm image. Then the legal description of each flagged page was carefully interpreted with the naked eye and typed into eight new books, marked "supplemental." A cross-reference was then made to the "supplemental" book on the original poor recording in the deed book.

After the re-microfilming of all records was completed, the microfilming was kept current as new documents were recorded.

One copy of all microfilm was placed in a cassette for public use in instant viewing and copying. One copy was stored in the county library which can either be available if increased public use requires an additional copy, or if the courthouse microfilm should get damaged by fire, storm, et cetera, the library copy can be available immediately.

The original copy was stored in a climate-controlled, fireproofed, bomb-proofed vault under a mountain in Pennsylvania. Only Duplin and Forsyth counties in North Carolina have such a records security storage program. However, Duplin is the only county in North Carolina where a register of deeds has tackled such a program of personally planning and supervising the highly technical task of creating such a microfilm program for all records dating as far back as 1749.

There are commercial concerns which, for enormous prices, perform microfilm services, but when they take a contract, speed in completion is important in order to make a profit. It is not possible to get as good, finished microfilm as when a concerned local person watches every detail. This is especially true on old records such as Duplin is fortunate to own.

So, for two whole years, 1978 and 1979, visitors to the office of the Duplin County register of deeds in taking care of routine business, overheard staff conversations regarding such strange subjects as blips, density readings, voltage settings, exposure, meter settings, static, positive and negative page problems, contrast, light reflection, film magazines and press tapes, as our staff members went in and out of a dark room, busying ourselves with new equipment, cleaning and numbering old books, and deciding which pages of deed and map books would have to be recopied in order to create good microfilm images.

But when our two-year microfilm project was completed, we had a treasure that set us apart from any other county with as many old records. It was hard for visitors from other counties to believe how easy it had become to search records and punch in page numbers to get record copies.

The more than eight hundred rolls of new microfilm not only saved our staff time in making record copies for the public, but they saved wear and tear on our record books.

Recommendation for Medical Disability

About 1970, the pain in my neck area became almost unbearable especially when I found it necessary to sit at my office desk continuously for long periods at a time.

Dr. Corbett Quinn, at Magnolia, was my family doctor. He had been Mother's doctor for the last twelve years of her life. His wife, Ruth, a splendid nurse, was his office manager. They were not only a skilled and efficient medical team, they were and still are, wonderful people and good friends.

Osteoarthritis was spreading to all of my bone joints. I tried all of the available arthritis drugs, but because of my long-time sensitive stomach, I could not tolerate any of them. Mother had been plagued by osteoarthritis, but had been able to take drugs to help her some. Her shoulders were badly humped from osteoarthritis and osteoporosis.

I could only tolerate Tylenol. So, since the early '70s, I have been taking two Extra Strength Tylenol every four hours around the clock. I only sleep for short periods of time. The Tylenol helps the pain, but is not anti-inflammatory; therefore, it does not deter the spread of the arthritis.

I discussed my ever-present neck pain with Dr. Quinn and he set up an appointment with an orthopedic surgeon in Wilmington. The Wilmington surgeon found that vertebrae numbers six and seven in my neck area were deteriorated causing constant pain to radiate down my left arm.

This surgeon scheduled an appointment to fuse pelvic bone into my neck area. This would result in a stiff neck, but should help alleviate some of the constant pain.

Dr. Quinn and I decided we needed a second opinion. An appointment was made with Dr. Donald S. Bright at the division of orthopedic surgery at Duke University Medical Center.

Dr. Bright doubted that surgery on the deteriorated degenerative C6-7 of my neck area could possibly be successful. He believed any improvement in the pain that could result from the fusing of pelvic bone to C6-7 would be short-lived, because it would not hold.

During several visits to Dr. Bright, he made recommendations for strengthening the muscles in my arms, shoulders, head, and neck areas.

My good friend, Dr. Donn Wells, was engaged in family practice in Fort Lauderdale, Florida. His father had been our school principal. His mother taught both of our boys in fifth grade. Donn had been our Cub Scout Den Chief. He had been my personal physician before he went to Fort Lauderdale. He is still my health advisor. Dr. Wells is an exercise enthusiast.

He prepared an order for a skilled therapist at our Duplin General Hospital to work out a twenty minute routine of exercises for me to perform while lying on my bed every morning upon awakening. These exercises are designed to strengthen all other parts of my body without causing strain on my neck area.

Dr. Bright, Dr. Wells, and Dr. Quinn recommended that I not get overtired and take rest periods.

Finally, in July of 1978, my pain was still increasing and Dr. Bright recommended that I take medical retirement from my job:

DUKE UNIVERSITY MEDICAL CENTER
Durham, North Carolina 27710
Department of Surgery
Division of Orthopedic Surgery

July 28, 1978

TO WHOM IT MAY CONCERN

RE: Christine Williams
Duke No. A 5 6 131

Dear Sir:

Mrs. Williams was seen by me on July 21, 1978 regarding the continued pain she was having in her neck radiating down the arms and also in the median nerve distribution.

After clinical evaluation and confirmation by x-ray that she has osteoarthritis with degenerative changes at C6-7 and interspinous ligament calcification, I recommend at this time that she be given medical retirement from her job. If additional information is needed, please let me know.

Sincerely,
Donald S. Bright, M.D.
Assistant Professor
Division of Orthopedic surgery

DSB:gmn

I was finding it more and more difficult to live with the constant pain in my neck, which radiated down my arms. But, I weighed every aspect of my total situation and made the decision to try to work on until I had completed all of the county record projects that I had planned.

In late fall of 1987, when again it seemed impossible to continue enduring the pain, I went to see Dr. Bright. I wanted to know what additional changes had taken place. He ordered an MRI, which showed there were more degenerative changes in the neck area of my spine. Now a total of five joints were degenerated with interspinous ligament calcification. After studying my MRI results, it was then Dr. Bright's opinion that while surgery with bone fusion was not desirable and might not be successful, there was now no other possible effort available if I could not continue to tolerate the ever-increasing pain.

He advised me that when I decided I could no longer tolerate the growing pain, for me to call his secretary for an appointment with the psychologist who worked with him in spinal surgery and get an appointment for a pre-surgery consultation.

My pain was growing, but I could not bring myself to setting a date for surgery without another opinion. So, I took the MRI to Dr. Ira Hardy at East Carolina Medical Center at Greenville, North Carolina. He studied my MRI results and made a myelogram. His conclusion was that I was not a candidate for surgery, and such a procedure, at my age, with the great amount of deterioration would be futile, and most likely dangerous with little chance of helping the pain.

Without mentioning my escalating pain, I immediately announced that I would not run for office in 1988 and would retire in December 1988, when my current four-year term was ended. I would be seventy-three years by that time.

Two times since 1988 I have been to Dr. Hardy for more tests and evaluations and once for another myelogram and learned that the deterioration and calcification increases as time goes on, but the wisdom of corrective surgery lessens.

My Searches for Learning to Live with Constant Pain

I was in my early fifties when I was forced to begin the search for solutions to learn to live with pain. I finally realized that it was up to me to plan and organize my life so as to cope with constant pain in the best possible way.

First, I had to accept the fact that there is no magic formula to learning to live with excruciating pain. It is a never-ending struggle.

There were a few simple, practical adjustments that I could make to pursue comfort, such as the use of a special pillow with a roll under my neck, the use of a firm mattress, and a metal heating pad for use when I wake up at night with a stiff, arthritic back. I could wear sensible shoes and stand and sit correctly.

My twenty minute exercise routine on my bed upon awakening in the morning must never be skipped. It helps the stress on my neck area and exercises every other part of my body.

Most days and during most nights, I exercise my shoulders in a rotating motion at several different times. I also rotate my arms at intervals during every day and every night. Some days at intervals and nights, I lie down on my bed or the floor and rotate my feet and legs just as I do in the early mornings. Then I use massage or heat treatment or cold compresses whichever seems to help.

It seems that pain, in itself, makes us tired. So, I learned I needed to avoid utter exhaustion by using alternative periods of rest and activity. And I learned to cultivate the habit of saving my energy for things that matter most.

My diet has always been centered around fruits and vegetables to try to stay strong physically and prevent diseases. Since I never had any childhood diseases, this must work for me. So, I must continue my quest for fresh fruits and vegetables. My friend, Louise Wells, calls me Tutti-Frutti because of my love for and seeming addiction to fresh fruits.

We read that pain causes stress as well as stress causes pain. So neither of these are good for the other. Together, they can cause depression. So far, I've never been depressed. I must continue to avoid it.

Then there are means of distracting the pain by such efforts as keeping busy, being with others, engaging mental stimulus, using meditation, and relaxation. It is so easy to say we can't do this or that. But I find that tackling every job I reasonably can, gives some use to the parts of my body which aren't in pain and helps them to stay useful.

I've found that learning to live with pain can motivate me to achieve, in a variety of areas, where I may develop hidden, creative talents, or invest my energies in some worthwhile causes for the good of other people.

It seems agreed by all authorities on pain that everyone's pain threshold is different. I find it helps to believe that there is a pattern in everything that befalls us. That belief helps me to handle my pain. I now believe it is possible to discover something positive in everything that happens to us, including pain. At first, I found it difficult to find the positive. But, after searching long enough, I've found it.

I've found good therapy in doing things I enjoy and I've found it is possible to broaden my horizons and find new things to enrich myself. Just a few years ago, I had never taken the time to learn to play cards. I didn't even know how many cards or suits were in a deck. I've been learning to play bridge for a few years by playing two Monday nights a month with some Pink Hill ladies. We have formed a bridge club. I reflect on how George Burns played bridge until he was one hundred and praised the benefits of bridge. I find it is an excuse to get with friends and an excuse to entertain friends in your home.

Above all, we are told more and more that we must absolutely cultivate seeing the funny side of life in little things. We must learn to laugh at ourselves.

The American Association for Therapeutic Humor, an organization of six hundred doctors and healthcare professionals, would like to see laughter become a part of every patient's prescription. They say laughter is a sort of internal jogging, that it increases the immune system activity and decreases stress-producing hormones. This association claims that laughter boosts activity of body cells that attack tumor cells and viruses.

When people come to us for help and advice, living with pain has made us more sensitive and understanding. And the older we get, the more people seek our help because as we get older, we become symbols of endurance.

Enduring pain can help us speak from the heart to others who are suffering pain, terminal illness or other tragedies.

Some Spiritual and Mental Truths I've Learned

The first truth I learned about pain is that I must face life with genuine optimism in spite of my pain, because positive people cope best with life.

I made these decisions:

1. I must learn endurance.

2. I must accept my pain without bitterness or grumbling.

3. I must learn to how to live a life full of meaning and purpose in the midst of pain.

4. I must find positive ways through my situation to give me strength to bear my pain.

Sometimes we wonder: Is there a meaning in this pain? When life is going smoothly, we often don't listen. Pain makes us stop and ask questions. It keeps us humble.

Pain is never good, but with study and searching for the best advice we can take the worst things that happen to us and use them for our greatest benefit.

When I was searching for direction, I read that Benjamin Franklin once said: "Those things that hurt, instruct." Pain can play an important part in helping us to grow up and mature as human beings.

Pain turns our attention to the important questions of life. It also brings us to the end of our own resources and enables us to rely on the best advice available and rely on a power greater than we are.

I discovered other truths:

I have no right to try to make others suffer just because I'm in pain.

I must avoid self-pity, because it is one of the worst pitfalls. And I don't need a pitfall, because living with pain is pitfall enough.

I must major in the good activities I can still enjoy.

I find it helps to think of other people's problems until thinking of others becomes an ever-present habit. This helps me to avoid self-absorption. It seems that persons who think only of themselves and their families exist in a very small space. When I practice thinking of others and offer any help I'm able to give, I can always find some act of love to perform in words or action.

I have found that to get maximum benefit from any act of love I perform, it must be totally unselfish and I must not expect or accept anything in return. It is so hard to remember to count our blessings. I am now in my tenth year serving as a volunteer with terminally ill patients for Hospice. I find it is easier to count my blessings, to name them one by one, when I am giving of my time, effort, and attention to the dying than at any other time. As I watch them I can't help counting the parts of my body which are not in pain. And for these parts, I am grateful and I count them as blessings.

In the very act of saying we can't do something next month, next year, two years from now, we are cutting ourselves down and projecting our prediction of failure. Being positive in looking to the future takes practice and a special mindset when one is in constant pain. But fear about what might happen in the future makes us tense and anxious and can adversely affect our pain, for without planning for the future, we're cutting ourselves off where we are.

Keeping My Body as Fit as Possible

When I retired at age seventy-three in 1988, Dr. Corbett Quinn, who had been my personal physician at Magnolia, would be twenty-one miles from my home, and he was preparing to retire. My long-time gynecologist, Dr. Sam Parker, at Kinston, was retiring, too.

Young Dr. Edwin P. Little had begun family practice in Pink Hill, just two miles from my home. He had gained a reputation for being friendly, caring, concerned, and effective with no reluctance to refer his patients to specialists in Kinston or Greenville when a situation warranted referral.

During the last days of terminally ill patients, he makes home visits and he is cooperative with Hospice nurses. Since I reside in one of the four counties in North Carolina which have the most incidents of cancer, diabetes, strokes, and heart problems, these are important considerations. So, when I retired I felt so fortunate and grateful to have Dr. Little as my personal family physician.

For many long years I have been allergic to dust, pollen, and mold. I get my vaccine from my allergist in Kinston and go to Dr. Little's office once a week for injections. He allows his friendly and efficient staff to take blood pressures of his patients who are on blood pressure medication. This helps me to decide when it is time for me to take some "slow down time."

I read that one elderly person said: "Nearly every part of my body hurts and what don't hurt, won't work." So, of all people, I feel most fortunate to have Dr. Little and his fine staff helping me to keep the parts of my body "working that don't hurt."

Ministry to the Elderly, Beginning 1980

From 1980 until retirement in 1988, I visited the five county nutrition sites for the elderly once a quarter and tried to deliver inspirational talks on timely subjects in which I sought to emphasize good diet, exercise, a positive attitude, humor, spiritual values, and doing simple deeds for others.

Since retirement in 1988, I have talked to senior groups in Duplin, Lenoir, and Wayne counties.

My two favorite stories I love to tell the elderly are:

Many sincere elderly people make the mistake of stumbling through life overlooking what is rightfully theirs. It is easy for us to be like the old man who saved his earnings for many years to take an ocean trip to Sweden. After paying for his ticket on the ocean liner, the man was almost penniless. So, he stocked up on crackers and cheese and ate the meager fare alone in his cabin. That's all he had to eat on the entire trip. Finally, on the last day of the voyage he asked the steward, "How much would it cost me to eat in the dining room today? I'm sick to death of crackers and cheese!"

"How did you get on this ship if you didn't buy a ticket?" the steward asked him.

"Oh, I have a ticket," the man said, as he dug in his coat pocket and handed it over.

"Look here," the steward showed him, "It says, 'Meals Included'!"

So, we don't have to be satisfied with a lonely, cheese and crackers existence when there are people just waiting to enjoy the feast of some little contact with us. It might even be just a phone call.

And:

Then, there is the story of an elderly woman who shared an experience that helps us realize no matter how old we are, we can still be useful.

She was resting in a lawn chair at the end of the day, thinking to herself: "I'm old and useless to others. At my age, what good am I on this earth? As she sat gazing at the sunset's vibrant colors, another thought came to her mind: If the sun can be beautiful and bring warmth and light in its final hours each day, surely man's final years of life can be beautiful and useful, too. Even old trees still produce fruit and are vital and green if they get the right fertilizer, plenty of sun and rain.

There is no retirement role for doing little things for other people. Even in old age, we can be vital and growing in our ability to cheer others. There are some tasks we can do, no matter what our age.

Above all, in our sunset years, we can bring to others a compassion born of suffering and trials, and a richness of experiences that we did not have to offer when we were young.

Laughter

I love to talk to the elderly about laughter. Seniors seem to have to take a lot of medicine. But, more and more we are being told that laughter may be the best medicine of all.

More medical experts are saying that humor is not a substitute for competent medical care, but it can be a powerful and delightful aid to patient therapy and rapport. It's a sort of internal jogging, a kind of sitting still aerobic exercise.

There is now evidence that laughter enhances blood flow, speeds healing, strengthens the immune system, affects heart rate, blood pressure, and muscular tension.

We are admonished to keep a file on funny and entertaining experiences and stories. You should see mine! I miss my brother, Milton, since he died in 1995, mostly because he, my sister, and I spent so much time reminiscing and laughing about the funny and ridiculous things that happened to us as children.

Exercise

We used to read advice such as: "Ask your doctor before you start exercising." Well, chances are if you ask your doctor today, you'll be told: "Regularly exercise every part of your body that will move."

The results of a study were announced in 1997 that showed four hours of exercise a week even reduces chances of breast cancer. It was found to reduce hormones that cause cancer.

At this writing, I am a Hospice volunteer for a seventy-eight-year-old pulmonary fibrosis patient whose twin sister is her caregiver. Five months ago, her lung problems had caused her heart to be in very poor condition, even though she was using oxygen around the clock. She asked the local rescue squad to take her to East Carolina Medical Center at Greenville, where she hoped to get a heart pacemaker. The Heart Center advised her that it does not install pacemakers unless a doctor judges the patient will be able to live at least three months. The doctors judged that she would not live three months. That was now six months ago. On her last doctor's visit two weeks ago, she was told to return in three months.

This patient told me her doctors advised her to take regular exercise but gave her no demonstrations. I laid on the carpet in her bedroom and demonstrated the ones I do for twenty minutes on my bed upon awakening each morning. She has now been walking with help around the outside of her house every day for some time. Of course, her companion keeps oxygen handy. When she reenters her house, she reconnects to her regular oxygen system.

The news that she was judged to live less than three months never seemed to change her positive attitude or her love of laughter. She and her twin sister have become an important part of my life. I tell them that, at first, I went to take flowers and goodies to cheer them up. Now I go not only to take flowers and goodies, but to get cheered up, to laugh with them, or enjoy a video or musical tape. Most of all, I enjoy the laughter and banter. It seems to give me new strength for the day.

1981

Duplin's Most Unusual Murder

Duplin County being the county in North Carolina known mostly for having the biggest agricultural income has never been known for violence or murder. But it has endured one unusual murder that sets it apart from other murders in North Carolina.

Mary Jernigan Williamson froze in the front hall of her mother's house on the morning of Tuesday, 22 April 1981.

Two men employed in her mother's business, Jernigan Tractor Company of Kenansville, had called Mary. Her mother, Inez Jernigan, had assigned these men to report to her home that morning to perform yard work on her well-kept landscaped premises. They hadn't been able to get Inez to answer her door. This was not like their smart and dependable employer, and they were concerned.

As Mary entered the front hall, she panicked when she saw blood spattered on the floor and on the walls in her mother's strangely silent house. She ran next door for help.

Moments later, a neighbor discovered the savagely beaten and stabbed body of fifty-three-year-old Inez Jernigan.

A wood dining room chair was tagged with Inez's hair and blood indicating that it had been the death weapon used to beat her. Blood had gushed out of two deep stab wounds made in her throat, apparently by a large butcher knife. Her two diamond rings for which her now deceased husband, Clifford, had paid twenty-four thousand dollars were missing from her fingers. There were no signs of forced entry to the house.

A neighbor called Sheriff Elwood Revelle, who responded with his investigators, Glenn Jernigan, Rodney Thigpen, and Alfred Basden. The State Bureau of Investigation was called in to help.

Word of the brutal murder spread quickly. Area residents were jarred and disturbed. Every person entering the Register of Deeds Office that day was stunned and expressed shock.

Mrs. Jernigan had helped her husband operate their successful tractor company for twenty-six years. At Clifford's death five years previously, she became the owner. The business had still thrived under her masterful management.

In addition to their daughter, Mary, the Jernigans had one son, Clifford, Jr. who resided at our state's Caswell Center for the severely afflicted at Kinston, thirty miles away.

Mrs. Jernigan had become deeply involved in developing mental health facilities in Duplin County and was a member of the First Duplin County Mental Health Advisory Board.

The county's first appropriation for a local mental health effort had been seven thousand dollars which Inez Jernigan somehow quickly turned into forty-five thousand dollars through state and federal grants and private donations. She remained on the County Mental Health Board during a merger with adjoining Sampson County and was still serving on the joint mental health board for both counties. The 1981 budget for the Duplin-Sampson Mental Health Board was over two million dollars.

It was Inez Jernigan's ingenuity that led to the creation of group homes for the mentally retarded in Warsaw and Magnolia where the residents could live close to their home communities. She helped overcome resistance and hostility so these homes could be created.

The question on everybody's mind was, "Who would so brutally slay this smart business woman who had used so much of her time, talents, and resources for the good of the unfortunate and often neglected mentally retarded?"

Mrs. Jernigan had been a frequent visitor at the Register of Deeds Office in the process of recording and canceling the conditional sales contracts on tractors and equipment sold by her firm located less than a mile from the court house. Always pleasant and businesslike, she was a favorite patron.

On the night after Inez's beaten and stabbed body was found, I joined a multitude of friends and acquaintances paying respects at the home of her daughter. Mary's husband grew up a mile from my home and his family still lived near me.

I was at Mary's home when Inez's minister, the Reverend Sheldon Howard, came in with his Bible in his left hand to make the funeral arrangements. When he entered the living room, he was told Mary and her husband were in a back bedroom with friends.

Reverend Howard went to the bedroom but quickly came out through the living room, Bible still in his left hand. There had not been time to plan a funeral which would be held at Inez's beloved Church, Pearsall's Chapel Free Will Baptist. Mary's husband, James, later told me that he informed the Reverend Howard that Mary had engaged the services of another minister to preside at the funeral. I thought this was very strange because Reverend Howard had preached Inez's husband's funeral five years ago and the families had remained good friends. But then I realized sometimes shocked and grieving families often make strange decisions.

The $20,000 Unpaid Loan

What I and the general public didn't know until some time after Inez Jernigan's funeral was that she had been dating a man from Kinston. The Kinston man had been with her the Sunday before her murder. This had been Easter Sunday. They had brought her son Clifford, Jr. from Caswell Center home for a visit.

Inez had confided in her Kinston friend that two years earlier she had loaned Reverend Sheldon Howard twenty thousand dollars and had been unable to collect it. She had written Reverend Howard that if he didn't repay her by Tuesday, 22 April, she would take legal action. She had been murdered the night before her ultimatum would become effective.

When the Kinston friend heard about the murder, he immediately hurried to Mrs. Jernigan's home while Sheriff Revelle was still there and told him what Inez Jernigan had shared with him about the unpaid twenty thousand dollar loan. Sheriff Revelle informed Mary Jernigan Williamson who had not known about the transaction.

The Investigation and Arrest

Several acquaintances of the murdered woman were questioned by the sheriff, his investigators, and the SBI. Some took lie detector tests. All passed with flying colors.

Word gradually leaked that her minister was being investigated. His parishioners at the North East Free Will Baptist Church at Mt. Olive where he was then serving were hostile at the thought of their pastor being investigated. Area Free Will Baptist ministers were disturbed at law enforcement for even thinking a minister was the guilty one. After all, Reverend Sheldon Howard held a Master of Divinity Degree from Wake Forrest University. He had served as a Bible professor at Mt. Olive College, owned by the Free Will Baptist Denomination.

Reverend Stephen Smith, a Free Will Baptist Minister from Beulaville was the most outspoken: "They're after the wrong man. It's like blaming Jesus Christ."

Young Dewey Hudson, the Assistant District Attorney helping investigate the murder, attended one of Reverend Howard's Sunday morning church services. As Hudson exited the church while Reverend Howard was shaking hands with his church members who had attended the service, Dewey Hudson could see the blood rush to Reverend Howard's face and see him tremble as Hudson introduced himself and shook his hands.

Discrepancies and conflicts developed in Reverend Howard's evidence. His brother-in-law in Wilson, North Carolina, corroborated the minister's claim that on the night of the murder, Reverend Howard spent the evening with the brother-in-law's family in Wilson. He later retracted the claim saying Reverend Howard had asked him to lie about the visit. Other holes in all of the minister's claims caught up with him.

The arrest finally came on the first Friday night in October after the murder in April. The Howards and another couple were about midway through watching a movie at a Goldsboro theater. He offered no resistance.

On the following Sunday morning, Reverend Howard's attorney read a statement from the pulpit of his church saying: "Reverend Sheldon Howard is innocent of the charge of murder. He will be completely exonerated and he will be back in your pulpit next Sunday."

After the arrest, my sister, Alma, shared with me an experience she and her husband recently had when they spent a day at the Howards installing wallpaper. She described him as bouncing around the house like a little bantam rooster finding fault and criticizing his gentle and attractive wife, Hilda, and all things in general. He had been especially critical of the pattern of wallpaper Hilda had allowed their Cub Scout son, Don to choose for his room. It depicted airplanes in flight and, at that time, it was the favorite selection for boys Don's age.

Prior to a probable cause hearing at the courthouse for Reverend Howard the Wednesday following his arrest, I watched several Free Will Baptist ministers stand on the courthouse lawn in a circle and hold a prayer service. Bond was denied by the judge and Reverend Howard was returned to jail to await trial.

The Confession

By the last of November, Reverend Sheldon Howard had reconstructed the crime for Phil Hardy, state probation officer, and directed authorities to Inez Jernigan's two diamond rings missing since the night of the murder. He had hidden them in a small plastic bag under a pile of brick left over from a recent construction job at the church he was serving at Mt. Olive.

He also provided information on how he disposed of the bloody clothes the night of the slaying and how he disposed of the butcher knife he used to stab her twice in the throat. He had wrapped the knife in one of her paper towels and thrown it in Goshen Creek on his trip back to his Mt. Olive home after the murder.

The Mt. Olive and Duplin County communities were still reeling in late November when Reverend Sheldon Howard, age forty-four, entered a guilty plea to second degree murder in the death of Inez Jernigan. He is still serving a life sentence.

The Howards' son, Don, came down with bone cancer. One leg was amputated. He died at age fifteen. Hilda Howard obtained a divorce, re-married, and is trying to make a new life in a new community. Both of his parents have died since he entered prison. Some say they died of broken hearts.

1982

Current Land Record Indexes on Line with County Computer

In 1982, thirty-six county registers of deeds in North Carolina were using computerized land record indexes. The registers' offices were key-punching index data and sending the data to the Cott Index Company in Columbus, Ohio, or some other commercial index company, to complete the index printing. I had made trips at no expense to the county to the Cott Index Company and to Hall & McChesney Index Company in Syracuse, New York, to study their highly skilled computerized index operations, but decided the costs were prohibitive for Duplin County.

Creating our own computerized index program was complicated, because our county programmer was not familiar with creating records for public use. But, it was worth the effort in order to get quicker service for record users and save a great amount of taxpayers' money.

So, we became the first county register of deeds in North Carolina to use a central county-owned computer to print daily sensitized index strips for applying to temporary public indexes and store the index entries in the county computer for an annual merged printout of all computerized indexes at the end of each calendar year.

Our computer terminal which we used to feed entries into the county computer, was located in our 30' x 50' records vault.

By working on until I was seventy-three, in 1988, I could monitor the system for six years and feel that it was working well.

1983

Co-Chair of State Study Commission on Computerized Information Systems of Public Records in North Carolina

An Act of the 1983 North Carolina General Assembly created a state commission to make a two-year study of the statewide computerization of information systems of public records in North Carolina. It was anticipated that the study would aid not only the state criminal justice system, but all other areas of municipal, county, and state governments, as well as members of the general public. It was to cover a study of present and anticipated computerization of county, municipal, and state records, including but not limited to recorded deeds, deeds of trust, birth, marriage, adoptions, wills, and estate records.

The act required the commission to particularly examine the storage and retrievability of such records, corrections, and updating. The commission was directed to examine questions relating to access of public records and issues concerning the rights to privacy.

Longtime state representative George Miller from Durham and I were appointed co-chairs of the commission. Working with Representative Miller was one of the most enjoyable experiences of my career. He had authored, introduced, and shepherded through the legislature many public bills for our state and had always appeared to have the interests and concerns of the public at heart.

The act authorizing the commission had mandated eighteen voting members, appointed by the governor, the president of the senate, and the speaker of the house. It was mandated that the voting members be made up of two state representatives, two state senators, and one from each of the following organizations: clerks of court, registers of deeds, sheriffs, city police chiefs, district attorneys, members of the news media, the state administrative office of the courts, the state bar, the governor's crime commission, the state department of justice, the administrative office of crime control and public safety, and two members-at-large.

My service on this commission did not cost my county because the act provided that the state pay for mileage and meals for making the trips to Raleigh to attend meetings of the commission, which were mostly held on weekends.

Working for two years with this outstanding group of public servants gave me insight into how the views of the involved professions may differ, but all representatives on the commission seemed to be dedicated to the group of people they serve, as well as to the general public.

I felt a keen responsibility to represent all Registers of Deeds and the people of my county as well as all the people in North Carolina.

After hearing testimony and proposals for two years, our commission reached a decision that except for the statewide computerization of data regarding drivers licenses and criminal offenses, the cost at that time, of creating and maintaining an effective, efficient, and continually updated system of all other public records was prohibitive.

The commission's decision was a disappointment to a wide range of people who had envisioned keying a name into a statewide computerized system and obtaining data from all public records of the state, municipalities, and counties for a named individual. But, because of high cost, the time just wasn't ripe to launch such a system in North Carolina.

At the conclusion of our study, all commission members were presented the North Carolina Distinguished Service Award for our two years of work.

1984
Trying My "Hands" at Bridge

For more than fifty years, Mrs. N. B. Boney wrote the social news at Kenansville for the local newspaper. She never failed to write about the meetings of the two bridge clubs.

Every word about the bridge clubs fascinated me. It was especially interesting that Mrs. Boney could always seem to serve cantaloupe a la mode when she entertained her bridge club.

Then, during 1951 and 1952 when I worked in Pink Hill at Turner's Insurance Agency, Wednesday afternoons were the most exciting time at the office. I could look through the two big plate glass windows of the office and see the Pink Hill ladies, wearing their prettiest dresses, go walking by the windows on their way to play Wednesday afternoon bridge.

Seven of the bridge club members lived within a block or two of the insurance office and walked if the weather was nice. There was Mrs. Etta Turner, Mrs. Helen Turner, Mrs. Ruby Tyndall, Mrs. Carrie Jane Smith, Mrs. Helen Ruffin, Mrs. Belle Jones, and Sarah Worley to watch go walking by.

The looks of anticipation on their faces clearly showed their fondness for getting together to play bridge. All of these bridge-playing ladies passed on, and for several years, there was no bridge club in Pink Hill.

I never thought I had time to play cards. I didn't even know how many cards were in a deck or how many suits there were or how many cards were in each suit. Then, a few years ago when I was heading for retirement, some Pink Hill ladies decided to form a bridge club of nine players so two tables of four each could play and one member could be hostess. They needed one more person and invited me to join. I kept hearing the famous George Burns tell how he played bridge at his club three hours most days and he seemed to believe that it was good for him to keep up with four suits of thirteen cards each.

I joined the bridge club and one of the ladies and I went to Kinston two times to lessons taught by the community college, but when the teacher moved, the classes were discontinued as there was no replacement. I bought a book on bridge.

Then Belle Stroud, Mildred Turner and Sarah Worley patiently played with me on the two Monday nights each month when the club was not meeting. I seemed like a slow learner, but they put up with me and tried to help.

Bridge has been a most wonderful way to empty my mind of whatever is on it and it is such a lovely way to keep up with family activities of the players. Too, it encourages cleaning the house every so often and preparing refreshments to entertain the bridge club.

Duplin Register Office Wins Award

In 1984, the Neuse River Council of Governments, an organization of nine eastern North Carolina counties, presented its first award to a county Register of Deeds Office. All staff members participated in the presentation.

The award was for productivity improvement in the Duplin records management programs of:

1. Instant recording of documents

2. Computerized microfilm back to 1749

3. Daily computerized indexing using county computer

4. A continuous repair and restoration program of county records.

1985
Eunice Ayers
Distinguished Service Award

In 1984, the North Carolina Association of Registers of Deeds originated an annual award to be presented at future state conventions to honor Registers who made unusual contributions in implementing the goals of the association to improve services to the public.

This award was named in honor of Eunice Ayers, register of deeds for Forsyth County, who had served as first president of the association in 1952-53. Until her retirement from office, she had been instrumental in helping other Registers in statewide promotion of our goals. Though she had retired, she was invited to attend our 1984 state convention, to be presented the first of these awards.

In 1985, she was invited to attend our state convention to present the second Eunice Ayers Distinguished Service Award to me. It was such a treat to have this award presented by Eunice, because more than anyone else, she had helped me to set goals and make decisions on how to plan and create record systems and service for our Duplin County folks and to work for improvements needed on a statewide basis.

I never forgot how late she stayed up with me one night during my first week in office when Dr. Albert Coates had invited a few of us to the Institute of Government in Chapel Hill to form a State Association for Registers of Deeds to share information and improve services.

More than all else, Eunice's help to me when I was new at my job and inexperienced, gave me the inspiration and motivation to help other new Registers of Deeds through the years.

When is He Going to Stop Practicing and Really Do It?

Bonnie Robinson, a longtime paralegal for Wallace attorneys, had her young son visiting with her at the Registry one day. The son was enjoying pushing the buttons on a microfilm reader-printer to locate page images and make copies.

Robert West, a Warsaw attorney, came by the reader-printer and stopped to chat. Bonnie said to her son: "This is Mr. Robert West. He has been practicing law for fifty years."

Whereupon the son innocently looked up into his mother's face and asked: "When is he going to stop practicing and really do it?'

1987
To China

The Fulfillment of a Childhood Dream

During the days of my childhood, I was charmed by our next door neighbor's sister, Miss Katie Murray, as she told stories about the Chinese children. She was a Baptist missionary to China until the expulsion of 1949, when the communists took over and the missionaries had to leave. Every two years she came home on furlough and kept us spellbound with the stories of how receptive she found the children of China.

It was easy for me to envision Miss Katie seated with a group of Chinese children, telling them about Jesus loving little children. She made her work in China sound so exciting, she inspired me to set my goal in life to become a Presbyterian missionary to China for at least one two-year term.

When this goal moved out of my reach because I couldn't go to college to get the required preparation, I never gave up on my desire to visit China to see what I had missed.

Finally, in October 1987, my longtime friend, medical and health advisor, Dr. Don Wells, invited his mother, Louise Wells, and me to accompany him and thirteen other doctors and their wives on a seventeen-day medical study tour of China.

We visited Beijing, Xian, and Shanghai on the mainland of China, then Hong Kong.

Our government-trained guide, who was with us on the mainland visits, was a twenty-three-year-old Chinese college graduate who majored in English.

The Chinese government emphasizes taking visiting tourists past emperors' palaces and tombs, and the Chinese temples. Tourists are taken to the grounds of "The Forbidden City," allowed to walk around and see all the paintings of dragons, but they are not allowed in the buildings.

At Tienamien Square there was always a long line waiting to see Mao's tomb, averaging ten thousand visitors a day. Tombs and temples surround the Square area as far as one can see.

The Chinese also like all tourists to see the Empresses' Summer Palaces some four thousand years old. The artwork on the ceilings and on the mammoth vases around the palaces were reminiscent of emphasis on art in past centuries.

We studied the best hospital in Beijing where there are six patients in every room. Patients bring their own peasant clothes to wear in the hospital.

Each patient keeps his own "eating dish" in his room and washes it at the room lavatory after meals.

Physicians prescribe patients' diets which are dipped from one of the four pots on the worn and aged food carts passed at mealtime.

Commodes are holes in the floors. But the American hotels where we stayed had American bathroom fixtures.

After a simple hernia operation, the patients stay in the hospital a full week, because upon being discharged they must ride on a bus then they usually have to walk a distance to their homes.

Louise Wells and I talked at length with two bright young hospital surgeons in their late thirties. Both said they wanted to marry, but couldn't afford marriage. They lived in the hospital dormitory while both were on the waiting list for a small government-owned apartment. They said many young couples get tired of waiting until an apartment is available, so they often marry and move in with their parents in their tiny apartments. At the time of our visit, these two surgeons were drawing government wages equal to sixty American dollars a month. All four of their parents were schoolteachers and still giving them some financial help.

We asked about the current law allowing only two children per family. They said if a couple has a third baby they must vacate government housing and lose all government benefits.

In 1987, fifty percent of the people in mainland China lived in government high-rises. These buildings contain many small family apartments built since the communists took over the mainland in 1949. Construction of new high-rises dotted the landscape. Our guide told us they hoped to have all the Chinese people in government housing by the year 2010. Those who are not living in government high-rises mostly live in deplorable old houses, many with crimped tin roofs held down by loose bricks or cement blocks.

Very few citizens own automobiles. Salaries only allow for purchases of bicycles which are used, rain or shine. All bikers carry umbrellas and plastic capes.

Buses are everywhere. The cities have taxis, many with dented bodies. Traffic in cities is very crowded. I decided I would never apply to be a taxi driver in Shanghai—dashing in and out of the crushing street traffic.

The government owns all the land and allots vegetable plots according to family size. In 1987, government overseers were taking forty percent of harvested vegetables for taxes. Farmers could use their sixty percent of the vegetables they grew for the family, or sell the surplus on the street. Usually they used their own push carts for displays and sold some of their share.

"Good Neighbor" stores, where the best merchandise is sold, are government operated, but street merchants were still allowed to sell linens, trinkets, et cetera. Often the street merchants spread a cloth on a sidewalk and laid their wares on the cloth, enduring wind and dust. When rain came, they closed shop by simply folding their wares in the cloth and quickly taking cover.

The greatest tourist attraction on mainland China was the Emperor Quin's six thousand life-size, terra cotta figures of warriors at the foot of Lishan Hill near Xian. Xian was the former capitol of China.

In 1980, two sets of large bronze chariots with horses and drivers were unearthed. Excavation, which has cost millions, began in earnest in 1984 and still continues. Several unearthed areas are as large as football fields. Some are covered to protect the excavators from the uncertain weather. Our guide explained that when the terra cotta figures were made, they were all visible, but centuries of dust and dirt blown by winds had covered them with soil. Tradition has it that Quin believed the terra cotta warriors, chariots, horses, and drivers would protect him after he died. The discovery of these ancient relics has provided valuable objects for the study of Quin Dynasty history.

Quin ruled from 221 to 206 B.C. He established China's first central government and started the four thousand mile Great Wall of China, which took many years to construct over rugged mountains. Thousands of Chinese lost their lives during construction. Quin is said to believe China would be forever free of northern invaders when the wall was completed.

The Chinese museums we saw were truly windows to the past. They contained mostly terra cotta statues of animals, exquisitely carved jade objects, and artful antique vases.

It was amazing how big and fat the live pandas were in the Beijing Zoo. They were about the size of our two hundred pound hogs.

We saw the world famous Shanghai acrobats perform. When children are selected to join these acrobats, they live as a group in one of the mansions in Shanghai which were taken from foreigners in 1949. The children get private schooling at the mansion and visit their families on vacation.

We stayed at hotels owned by Americans who have ninety-nine year leases on the land. The same situation applies to most Chinese factories owned by foreigners. They, too, have ninety-nine year land leases.

In 1987, the average monthly factory pay was twenty American dollars a month. I understand it is around forty American dollars in 1997.

I was concerned that on streets and in tourist parking lots, all street sweepers we saw used a broom and big dust pan and were poorly dressed, elderly women. We were told their government pensions, in 1987, were around twenty American dollars a month and were not enough to support them without this work. Our Chinese guide tells me that now, in 1997, his parents receive government pensions equal to around forty American dollars per month.

We thoroughly enjoyed the food. All meats and vegetables were cooked separately, except the last course was always thin vegetable soup with cabbage in it.

We saw no egg rolls, chow mein, or fortune cookies. All restaurant tables seated ten. We never had a dessert or cheese in China. There was always a tray on each table with either ten big persimmons, apples, or tangerines. Fresh, raw fruit or dried fruit in paper twists was everywhere, even on the coffee tables on riverboats.

Our guide told us his goal in life was to come to America to live. We kept in touch. Three years later he married a lovely American girl who works in Washington, D.C. for the Federal Housing program. They live in Wheaton, Maryland, just over the line from Washington, D.C. They now have three children and have visited my family twice, bringing his parents once who were here on a visit. My family has visited them once for several days. They are Catholic and their oldest child is in Catholic pre-school.

After visiting China I fully understand why this vast country, which reached a billion residents in 1996, has always been so attractive to missionaries of every religion.

We spent three days in Hong Kong where twenty-six-year-old Faith Dietrich from our county was serving as a missionary for "Youth With a Mission." Her mother had sent her my schedule. She spent two days showing me the best places in Hong Kong to shop and giving me details on how all religious faiths have used modern and progressive Hong Kong as a springboard to reach mainland China ever since the communist occupation of China in 1949.

Faith loves the Orient because she was born in South Korea while her parents were medical missionaries there.

When we were in Hong Kong, the British rule seemed very open and progressive. It has had an elected governor since it came under the British in 1841. There were cars on the streets, fast electric trains under ground, and beautiful, clean harbors with sparkling waters.

The Victoria Hotel where we stayed had ice sculptures in the dining room along with a tasty dessert tray, cheese, and bread trays.

We ate fabulous food once at the jumbo floating restaurant, reputed to be the biggest floating restaurant in the world.

We saw people with their children flocking to the McDonald's fast food restaurants.

For the trip back to San Francisco, we boarded a Singapore Airliner which gave me my first glimpse of their young airline attendants, who were more handsomely dressed than I could imagine, serving the best airline food I had ever tasted.

Hong Kong has only 410 square miles, just half of the 819 square miles in Duplin County, North Carolina. But in 1996, Hong Kong's population was six million, nearly the same as the whole state of North Carolina.

In 1841 when Great Britain gained Hong Kong, it was made up of only a few fishing villages with a total population of 3,500 inhabitants.

In 1987, every man, woman, and child we saw in Hong Kong was well dressed. Jobs were so plentiful, people were daily coming in on boats to seek work. Hong Kong's population is said to be ninety-eight percent Chinese.

Our United Methodist Women's 1997 study book, *The Enduring Church in China and Hong Kong* by Gail Coulson, portrays how there were only 700,000 Christians on mainland China in 1949 in spite of all the missionary efforts in China since the beginning of time. It has been so exciting to learn from this book that in just forty-seven years, since 1949 when all missionaries were forced to leave, there were, in 1996, 11,300,000 additional Christians in China, making a total of 12,000,000 out of the one billion mainland Chinese population of 1996.

Hong Kong has been a British Crown Colony since 1841. It went back to the government of China, now under communist rule, as of 1 July 1997.

I am helping the whole world watch to see how missionary efforts and other causes will be affected. Studying China and Hong Kong for myself in 1987 was the fulfillment of one of my greatest childhood dreams, even though I didn't experience it as a missionary.

1988

"I'm Sixty-Five, Don't Expect Me to Know What I'm Doing!"

Many seniors give themselves the same credit as a woman who came into the County Registry the week before I retired at seventy-three.

The woman said, "I want to get a copy of my will!" I explained that the wills were in the clerk of court's office, down the hall.

"Oh, no. I was here about a year ago and you made me one," she said.

I enumerated the different kinds of records we kept, and when I came to powers of attorney, she yelled, "That's it! That's it!" Then she added, "I just turned sixty-five last week, so don't expect me to know what I'm doing."

Left: The courthouse annex occupied January 1961, contains Register of Deeds office and vault complex 80 x 30 feet for which I drew the plans.

Right: The Country Squire Steak House, 1997, can seat 456 guests.

Left: The Gray Fox Restaurant. The original part of the building dates back to 1805 and has been beautifully restored and redecorated. It is adjacent to The Squire.

Right: The three-bedroom brick house I built on the block next to the Courthouse in Kenansville in 1962 when the boys and I moved out of the homeplace and left Lehman.

The closing banquet of the state convention of Registers of Deeds the year that I was president. Governor Terry Sanford, back row, second from left, was the featured speaker. Dr. Albert Coates, back row, fourth from left, the founder of the N.C. Institute of Government, also spoke.

Picture made in the winter of 1967 to be used in my newspaper announcement that I would file to run for a fifth four-year term in 1968.

Josephine Waters at her marriage to Austin Anderson.

Austin Anderson

My sister, Alma Anderson, and her husband, Norman Anderson.

Duplin County Officials attend the National Convention of County Officials in Washington, D.C. and visit with Congressman David Henderson.

A flower for North Carolina Governor Dan Moore when he attends the district Democratic convention in Duplin County.

TAR HEEL OF THE WEEK
CHRISTINE WILLIAMS
A Duplin Mother Leads in a County Role

Tar Heel of the Week

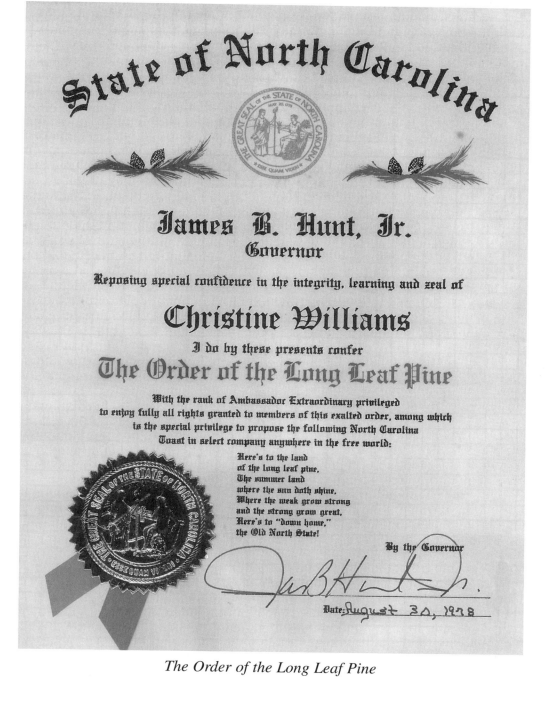

The Order of the Long Leaf Pine

A Young N.C. Governor Hunt attends Duplin Democratic Convention during his first of four terms as Governor.

A kiss from Secretary of State Thad Eure

Left: Eunice Ayers, retired Forsyth County Register of Deeds, presents the 2nd Eunice Ayers Distinguished Service Award to me as the Beaufort County Register observes.

Right: Attorney Richard Burrows and I teach a class at James Sprunt Community College to bankers, merchants and others on The Uniform Commercial Code.

Left: Teenager Randy Sandlin and I chat back stage with the famous Fred Waring at his Duplin County performance with his Pennsylvanians.

The Guilford East Plant, established in Duplin County in 1972. It employs 689 people in the distribution of automotive fabric world-wide.

Left: Friend Louise Miles and I enjoy a little sight-seeing ride in Hawaii.

Right: Louise Wells, Dr. Don Wells and I in the city square of Beijing, the capitol of China in October 1987.

October 1987, the hostess at a Japanese wedding reception at The Victoria Hotel in Hong Kong takes my picture with the bride and groom.

Fall mums and a pink mandevilla brighten the scene at my front porch.

Part Eight
1989-1998

1989
Meeting My First
Retirement Goal of Becoming
a Hospice Volunteer

In 1967, I read about Dr. Cicely Saunders founding the first Hospice in London. Dr. Saunders began the family-centered concept of home healthcare for people dying of an incurable illness. The Hospice concept emphasizes a team approach. The team includes the patient, the family, physicians, nurses, social workers, members of the clergy, and volunteers.

Since 1967, I carefully watched the spread of the Hospice idea to our country and finally to Duplin County in 1986.

I had continued to relive the deaths of my little fifteen-year-old brother in 1937, and my sister's twenty-seven-year-old son, who came down with cancer in December 1962 and died in April 1963. Also, in December 1962 my thirty-two-year-old efficient top office assistant was diagnosed with cancer and died in April 1963.

As I headed toward retirement, I kept thinking how really great it would have been to have had the help and comfort of home care and Hospice when we were painfully watching the lives of these three young people slowly come to a close. How wonderful it would have been to have known the joy of how much trained Hospice volunteers could have lightened our loads!

Then came March 1988, when brother Milton's forty-eight-year-old son, Tom, employed by the U. S. Army in South Korea moved to Satellite Beach, Florida, to wait out terminal leukemia until that October. He and his Korean wife, who spoke little English, had a six-year-old daughter.

His Satellite Beach doctor engaged the services of the Merritt Island Home Care and Hospice. I was there for four several-day visits where I saw Hospice at its best. My nephew's mother had died prematurely with a malignant brain tumor and he had since depended a lot on me.

Tom had a male volunteer who sat with him to relieve his wife and took him to his doctor's visits.

Tom's wife had a woman volunteer who drove her to the grocery store, ran errands for her and kept their six-year-old daughter most weekends to play with her own daughter. The family had the services of a Hospice visiting nurse, a caseworker and a nurse's aide. His wife never could qualify for a Florida driver's license until a month after he died.

After Tom died in October, his widow called to say she wanted to cook a big Korean luncheon meal for the five Hospice workers who served them and she wanted me to be there. Saturday after Thanksgiving was the first day I could fly to Satellite Beach.

One of the most delightful, heart-warming and touching experiences I have ever enjoyed was sitting on big Korean floor pillows to eat at low Korean tables with five, dedicated Home Care and Hospice workers, my nephew's widow, her little daughter, and the Korean friend who had been at the home all night helping to prepare the delectable Korean food.

An observer would have believed that all of us had been born and lived in Korea if we were judged by the way we adapted to crossing our legs in typical Korean fashion and using our chopsticks like Korean pros.

Observing Hospice so effectively at work in Florida in 1988, reaffirmed and enhanced my goal to volunteer with Hospice when I retired.

Another great factor in my zeal to become a Hospice volunteer was the realization that Duplin County is one of four North Carolina counties having the highest incidence of cancer, diabetes, strokes, and heart problems. The other three counties are in eastern North Carolina and have large agricultural areas within their counties.

What I saw was a very real opportunity to use my experiences for the benefit of others.

My first patient was an elderly Indian man. A story about him follows this story. I have served a black man and two white men. All others have been women.

My last patient, at this writing, has been seventy-seven-year-old Estella Edbanks, on continuous oxygen, with pulmonary fibrosis. She was breathing out of only twenty-five percent of her lungs. Her doctor had told her she had less than two months to live at the time she requested a volunteer.

Four of her six children live in Utah, one in Dallas, Texas, and one is Maryland. Her twin sister, Rosella Barnette, who lives about five miles from her, moved in to care for her. Rosella did not drive, so they needed an errand-runner. The uplifting and positive spirit and attitude of these twins was contagious and kept Estella living six months.

I would say to the patient's sister, "How fortunate she is to have you." She would reply, "How fortunate I am that I can care for her."

Her six children and twenty-eight grandchildren arrived from seven to three days before she gave up, and what a great reunion this lively Mormon family had before their mother took her leave.

The volunteer tasks I have enjoyed have ranged from taking flowers from my yard, to food, to running errands, to just visiting, to making two casket blankets using my own yard flowers and greenery. Most of all, it's just letting folks know that someone outside the family cares for them when they most need caring, and it helps to minimize the volunteer's health problems, for it is impossible to dwell on your own feelings when you are trying to make life easier for dying persons and their families.

In 1997, our Duplin County Home Care and Hospice had one hundred twenty paid employees and forty volunteers.

The volunteers are true rainbows that shine in all their vibrant and refreshing colors at intervals during the rain and dark clouds of terminal illnesses.

My First Hospice Patient

He Considered the Lilies—How They Grew

By Christine W. Williams, Hospice Volunteer
Published in *The Wallace Enterprise*

Lindburg Chavis, a Robeson County Lumbee Indian, was living alone in Detroit, Michigan, when he developed a terminal illness. He came to the home of his sister, Julette Fields, in Smith Township in Duplin County, near my home. He knew she would care for him in his last days and take his body back to Robeson County for burial.

When I became his Hospice volunteer the first of this year, I had potted two amaryllis lilies which were almost ready to bloom—one white and one red. Both were the giant variety from the Terra Ceia Dutch Bulb Farm near Pantego, N.C. For several weeks, they filled a need in Lindburg's life.

As he lay on his sick bed of pain and suffering and watched the stalks grow and the blossoms unfold, he reminisced about happier days on a tenant farm in Robeson County. There he had bought wildflower and phlox seeds to sow along the road area near his home and people would stop their cars on the side of the road to marvel at their beauty.

First, one lily bore two stalks with four snow-white, trumpet-like blooms on each. The stately white flowers represented to him the Hospice angels who came to care for him. As he watched the lilies grow and their beauty unfold, there was a calmness in which he tuned his sensitive Indian ears to the sounds of approaching vehicles on the road which runs just a few feet from his sister's house. It was unbelievable how he could identify the sounds of the car of each of the dedicated Hospice workers long before they applied their brakes to stop. The car of each case worker, nurse, and aid had its own special sound to him as it came down the road, and each brought him a special joy as they came to minister to his needs and change the bandages around the tubes which kept his body functioning.

The red lily bore three stalks with four blossoms each. From his lying position, he could see only three of the trumpet-like blooms on each stalk. He often said that each stalk with the three blood-red flowers that he could see reminded him of Jesus hanging on the cross and the agony of the blood that He shed. Frequently talking about the likeness of the red flowers to

Jesus on the cross seemed to help him bear his own pain and discomfort and prepare for his approaching departure about which he talked freely.

As the blossoms on each stalk withered and closed, we cut off the stalks. This gave him opportunities to observe how much like the flowers we are as people on this earth. We grow up and blossom forth, then wither and die like the lilies.

We had cut off the two bloomed-out stalks on the white lily. The third stalk on this lily had grown up healthy and strong, but the little pre-bloom buds had been very slow to open. Finally, two days before he died, only one single large white bloom unfolded and pointed its trumpet-like image directly toward him. This represented to him a single angel standing by to welcome him home. His departure was at hand and he was ready. In just 48 hours with the single white lily pointing toward him, Lindburg withered and peacefully died.

He was buried in his beloved Robeson County with a homemade blanket of colorful shrub and tree twigs covering his grave. Then his bereaved sister became the recipient of the beauty of the mysterious, large, single white lily blossom which lasted much longer than any of the others. The faithful Hospice professionals went on to comfort and care for other terminally ill persons.

Creative Writing Course at Mount Olive College

Retirement in December 1988, at age seventy-three, brought opportunities to make many ventures that had been laid aside for retirement.

First, there was Hospice volunteering, which definitely came first.

Next, there was writing the book that so many "scraps" had been saved for. But, before starting to write, I thought it would be helpful to go to nearby Mount Olive College and enroll in a writing course of some kind. So, I enrolled for one semester in Professor Janice D. Morgan's English class.

This was a great experience, to be in a class with bright, young college students. I was especially delighted at the depth of the thinking of the youngsters, particularly when we were assigned team role-playing and I could work with them one-on-one.

When Professor Morgan gave the assignment "A Person Who Meant a Lot To Me" I wrote about my daddy, Mack Whaley.

When she gave the assignment to write about "A Place That Means a Lot to Me" I wrote about my front porch.

My current event writing was on the San Francisco Earthquake of 17 October 1989: "Earthquakes, Garbage and Lives."

My "opinion" assignment was "A Great-Grandmother Looks at Schools Then and Now."

In 1989 when I was taking the English course, a nephew, Jimmy Williams, who grew up across the highway from me, was working in the administrative office of the college. He had handled my class enrollment for me. I left my writing assignments with him to read. Following is the letter he wrote when he returned my assignments to me:

MOUNT OLIVE COLLEGE
209 North Breazeale Avenue
Mount Olive, N.C. 28365

February 20, 1989

Aunt Christine:

I read with great interest the writing that you left with me today. Thank you for sharing.

I was especially impressed by the one about your father and also the one about "Earthquakes, Garbage and Lives." The qualities that made your father a great person are the same ones that made you a great person. I recognize so many of the traits that you described as being so much a part of you. I like to think that observing these in you and other members of the family have helped me also. It constantly amazes me as I grow older how much my "roots" mean to me and you are such an important part of those "roots."

I hope that you have a very happy Holiday Season. Please give my regards to all the family.

Jimmy

Following are the assignments I wrote on "My Front Porch" and "Earthquakes, Garbage, And Lives."

A Place that Means a lot to Me— My Front Porch

My front porch is the most pleasant place in the world to me. The first thing I do each morning is walk onto the porch and evaluate the new day. It serves as my gateway to the rising sun because it faces the east. At night, it is my gateway to the rising moon, and the stars. My last activity at night is to open the front door and soak up the view from the porch.

During all four seasons, the panorama of nature is delightful when viewed from this special porch. It is cool and shady on hot summer afternoons. At one end there are two white metal chairs with a table between them. The other end holds a matching white steel chair with a small table by it, and a multi-colored lounger made of plastic strips. In the center a glass table with four chairs provide a restful atmosphere for dining. A 4-speed, rotating electric fan above the table assures refreshing breezes.

A hanging basket and green plants complete the pleasing and restful surroundings. A big, white cement pot next to the front steps holds five red geraniums in summertime and pansies in winter. These seem to enhance the American and North Carolina flags which hang from the flagpole that my son, Glenn, constructed and erected next to the post lantern which sheds its rays from dusk to dawn.

A large bed of pink geraniums and pink begonias welcome guests at the driveway in summer and seem to invite them to the cement pathway leading to the front steps. From October to May this bed holds yellow pansies with faces that glow all winter, surviving snow and ice storms. These flowers give their beauty not only to the adjacent front porch, but to passersby on the highway. The porch is protected on the north by the garage, so on cool mornings it provides a sunny respite from the north winds.

I often told my brother, Milton, after he retired I thought he loved to visit me mostly to sit on my front porch, even when the weather is cold.

This porch has endless purposes. It is often my family's haven. All meals at my house are served here when weather permits. It is the center for our family to watch the grandchildren and great-grandchildren scamper on the wide, front, cushiony centipede grass lawn, or play volleyball, badminton, soccer, or lawn golf.

When the azaleas and camellias are blooming among the pines on either side of the house, we view them from the porch, and sometimes get a view which invites us to stroll among them for a closer look. Games are played on the glass table.

Even the birds cannot resist my front porch. In summer, hummingbirds entertain us with their frolickings and flights as they frequent the feeder hanging from the porch eves. The larger bird feeder near the porch attracts all sorts of birds during winter months. There are times when quail and dove walk on the front lawn when I am alone and there's no activity around.

The porch lounger provides a perfect place for me to have solitude, to read or write or watch the birds, with no interruption, or enjoy seeing the local farmers go by in their pickups, and watch cars and trucks on the highway.

Where else would I be for perfect peace? Burning all night, the coach lantern at the front steps and the two at the corners of the house make the lawn, shrubs, flowers and trees look like a Fairyland, even if the rain is falling.

The moon seems to shine brighter from my front porch than any place I know except when I call up the indelible picture etched in my mind and heart of how bright it shined on the waves the sand, and the offshore boats as I gazed at it with Ivey Cooke when we strolled along the beach at Oceanview, Virginia. I thought back then: "This is paradise."

Now, when the moon adds its light to the scene from my porch, I feel closest to heaven and to my unfulfilled romance with Ivey. And I am happiest.

Earthquakes, Garbage and Lives

At 5:04 P.M. on 17 October 1989 a 7.1 earthquake, the most severe in our country since the San Francisco quake of 1906, shook the San Francisco and Oakland, California areas, crumbling roads, buildings, and neighborhoods. Cars and houses became death traps. Sixty-five lives were lost, over 2,300 injured, and 1,400 people left homeless. The price tag on earthquake repairs has evaded the experts. Destroyed, for the present time, are all such popular dreams as the proposed ninety-six million dollar, 45,000 seat sports stadium to replace the windy Candlestick Park on San Francisco's China Basin Waterfront, and the proposal to spend fifty-five million dollars in improvements to the Oakland Coliseum. With freeways closed and so many people homeless, all attention has now focused on repairing earthquake damage.

In October 1987, on my way to China, I spent three days in San Francisco. I strolled casually down to the beautiful Marina District to watch the Air Force Blue Angels perform in the skies above, to the delight of hundreds of attentive viewers. We had no thought that this particular section of San Francisco was the most vulnerable to earthquakes.

The heaviest damage in the recent October quake was to areas like San Francisco's Marina District, that was constructed on landfills—garbage. At the same time, entire suburbs built on what was once swampland survived. Scientists and engineers studying what happened to structures built on the many garbage landfills around San Francisco Bay have concluded that areas built on non-compacted, undried garbage failed to withstand the quake. The portion of the freeway that collapsed, crushing cars and passengers, was the portion built over untreated garbage. Geologists and engineers advised twenty years ago that the collapsed freeways needed heavy reinforcements. "Non-compacted, undried garbage had turned into a heavy fluid, like Jello before it sets," said Robert Darragh, geologist for the engineering firm of Dames and Moore in San Francisco. "The process is called liquefaction. Loose, wet, and sandy soil combine with garbage to form a quicksand-like material," according to scientists. On the other hand, nearby Foster City withstood the quake. It was built on eighteen million cubic yards of garbage fill beginning in the 1950s. The garbage under Foster City was compacted and dried before it was brought to the site.

Most San Franciscans forgot long ago which areas suffered most in the 1906 earthquake. They were the same areas that were most devastated in 1989. Earthquake construction techniques that have been recommended as necessary since the 1906 quake were not followed in the areas devastated in 1989. Most houses in these areas sit atop garages and have large windows which do not provide the support and reinforcements needed to survive earthquakes, engineers say. Buildings that had been built to earthquake specifications are still in good shape.

On 17 October 1989 every single person in the quake area was terrified at exactly the same instant for exactly the same reason. Not just terrified, but the most frightened that most can remember being. While those in the San Francisco and Oakland areas buried their dead, took care of the injured and homeless, and evaluated their damages, the invisible social walls that divided the people by sex, race, and class shook to their foundations and came tumbling down. The poorest of the poor were the first to risk their lives bringing victims down from the freeway. People who had nothing displayed uncommon compassion toward those whose circumstances had been much better before 5:04 P.M. The people were a community coming to grips with reality.

The people in the earthquake areas learned lessons about building communities on untreated garbage. Never again will building permits be issued there for structures that do not conform to earthquake specifications. Other areas of our country located in quake fault lines are reexamining their situations and preparing for the inevitable. All areas of government—local, state, and national, are taking new looks at the mounting problem of garbage disposal.

Just as the recent earthquake showed that the buildings and freeways not built on solid foundations with good reinforcements cannot withstand nature's earthquakes, the earthquake was a grim reminder that lives not built on good foundations—with untreated garbage still undergirding them, cannot withstand the quakes that come to individual lives. We were reminded that tremors and quakes can come at some time in the lives of all people. The recent California quake has given all people everywhere cause to reflect on their lives and ask: Is my life built on a solid foundation, or, is there some underlying untreated garbage? Does my life have the reinforcements to withstand the shocks of illness, sorrow, disappointments, and tragedy without crumbling? Is my life a structure that is separated from others by sex, race, or class? Have I been willing to get my life on a level where I am engaged in helping others, or am I waiting for a quake to show me how to level?

If my life is built on solid foundations, if I have survived the quakes of my life, what are my obligations to others who are enduring illnesses, sorrows, disappointments, and tragedies?

Anti-Litter—"Keep America Beautiful"

For many years there has been hardly a day that I have not picked up litter from my front yard as I go or come from my rural mailbox. Litter seems to have become a national plague.

Our Warsaw Garden Club has long sponsored an anti-litter poster contest in the third grades of the Warsaw and Kenansville Elementary schools. The third grades were selected because this is where students begin the study of protecting the environment. Our garden club members believe the third grade is the best time to make the most impression on our students against littering.

Cash prizes are awarded for the best posters. I have helped judge them and the originality of the ideas portrayed in the posters has been surprising and rewarding.

After I retired, I began the search for suitable videos and other materials to use in anti-litter programs for the third grade at our B. F. Grady Elementary School near me. This is where my children, grandchildren, and now two of my great-grandchildren have attended.

I learned that the Wake County, North Carolina "Keep America Beautiful" committee in Raleigh was very active and outstanding. My phone call to this committee resulted in receipt of a copy of the words to the new and easy to learn song, "Keep America Beautiful." They also gave me the address of the "Keep America Beautiful" national headquarters in Stamford, Connecticut, where I could order the sheet music for this new song, for around ten dollars. For $19.95 I could order a 3.2 minute professional video of a dynamic group of children singing this song.

For another $19.95 I could order a 9.22 minute professionally made video produced by RJR Nabisco, entitled "How Did This Get Here?" It was made in Raleigh and its opening narration is by the Raleigh mayor. This video depicts the carelessness of citizens in littering and the cost to city, county, and state governments in cleaning up litter.

It seemed like a good investment to purchase all of these supplies and start an anti-litter program and poster contest in the two third grades of our local B. F. Grady Elementary School. This idea was welcomed by our principal and the third grade teachers. Each year our Duplin County "Keep America Beautiful" committee has supplied official "Keep America Beautiful" car litter bags and imprinted lead pencils for all third graders.

A local committee of retired teachers has judged the anti-litter posters and it has been an enjoyable experience each spring to use a third grade class period for giving a short pep talk on anti-litter, showing the video "How Did This Get Here?" and teaching the song by use of the video.

Supplying the total of thirty dollars for cash prizes and rosette ribbons for the winning third grade posters has been a good investment.

Words to the song are left with each third grader.

Keep America Beautiful Theme Song

Verse:

The time has come to take a stand,
We're the keepers of the land,
Side by side and hand in hand,
Take care of America.

Save the rivers, trees and shores
Clear across the great outdoors,
Let's protect what's mine and yours,
Take care of America.

Chorus:

Keep American beautiful,
Show her we deserve her trust,
Take pride in her yesterdays,
Tomorrow depends on us.

Keep America beautiful,
If one by one we try,
We can make the diff'rence,
Together, you and I.

Verse:

Grow a garden, save a tree,
Be a part of history,
This great land needs you and me,
Take care of America.

Save the air we live and breathe,
Save the land we use and leave,
What we give we'll all receive,
Take care of America.

Chorus:

Keep America beautiful,
Show her we deserve her trust,
Take pride in her yesterdays,
Tomorrow depends on us.

Keep America beautiful,
Together if we strive,
We can make the diff'rence,
Keep the land we love alive.

The sheet music for the song was given to our public school music teacher for use with her students.

During the 1996-97 school year, the Duplin County "Keep America Beautiful" committee furnished enough official car litter bags and pencils for each B. F. Grady student in kindergarten through eighth grade.

Five years ago the third grade teachers at Pink Hill Elementary School, in Lenoir County, two miles from me, were interested in the anti-litter program. While they do not have a poster contest, the students really enjoy and benefit from an anti-litter pep talk, the video, "How Did This Get Here?", learning the "Keep America Beautiful" song, and using the official car litter bags and the pencils.

It seemed that it might be good for our Duplin County superintendent of schools to have the two videos, the sheet music, and the words to the "Keep America Beautiful" song for distribution to the several county schools. So, it was a pleasure to donate them.

The most striking, and the only sad aspect of dealing with the third grade students on anti-litter, has been that after all of the programs which I have presented except one, as the children were receiving their car litter bags and pencils following the programs, one or more of the boys or girls have whispered in my ear "My daddy (or, my mama) throws litter out of the car." Two students have asked: "How can I make them stop?"

The haunting question comes: Have we missed educating the generation of the parents of our present day students on anti-litter?

Mt. Olive Just Older Youth Group

What could be a better effort to make upon retirement than to join a JOY group? My sister had commented so often about how much she had been enjoying the monthly luncheon JOY group at her Baptist Church in Mt. Olive, twenty-two miles away.

This group is made up of "Just Older Youth" from all Mt. Olive churches with some Older Youth from Calypso and surrounding rural areas.

The Older Youth come at 11 A.M., bring one covered dish and a lot of Joy to the spacious church fellowship hall. The hall is seasonally decorated and tables arranged by a church-appointed committee, which also arranges the food attractively on the buffet tables.

Bersha Lewis, an Older Church Youth, is director of the JOY group as well as other Older Youth church activities, including area trips in the church van to attend plays and musical performances.

You can't look at Bersha without catching some of her Joy germs, and when she opens the meeting with the group singing "It's Joy That Makes the World Go Round," you get infected with a full blown case of Joy.

Meetings are from 11 A.M. to noon, and then the luncheon meal. Guest performers or speakers, arranged by Bersha, present around thirty minute programs. These are geared to entertaining the Older Youth and helping us to remember to live joyfully always, in spite of what life brings us.

We are reminded that Joy is not a product of circumstances, because circumstances can change so quickly and so severely that our source of Joy needs to run deeper than the surface of our lives.

We are admonished to avoid dissatisfaction, self-pride, and self-focus and to live with an attitude of gratitude. Even in the unpleasant things we're reminded to search for a vein of gratitude and Joy.

These JOY meetings are a good place to make new friendships and JOYfully renew old ones.

1990

Kinston Arts Study Group

A keen appreciation for all types of art seemed to be mine from the time I was a little child. But because I had been so concerned about making a living and caring for family, I never felt I had time to devote to arts study or participation in the application of the arts. There always seemed to be so many other concerns that needed my time. So, I had mostly participated in art by being an appreciative onlooker of finished art.

I can't make a glance at any part of my home without sighting skillfully finished paintings or ceramics done by my sister. And each glance makes me grateful for the way each object represents the development of her talents when she needed consolation in her bereavement from the loss of her only son.

After retiring, I was invited to join the Kinston Arts Study Club, which is limited to sixteen members. Two ladies from Pink Hill, who have been members of this club for many years, submitted my name for membership when there was a vacancy.

Monthly meetings are held in the homes of members, October through May. As stated in its constitution, the purpose of this club is "to promote the appreciation of art in any form, the development of the mind, and the understanding of the human spirit."

The Kinston Arts Study Club looks at art in the broad sense, as skill in making or doing. Its members believe there are many arts—as many as there are kinds of deliberate, specialized activities for human beings to engage in.

In this club we study not only painting, writing, music, dance, poetry, sculpture, theater, and costuming, but many other forms. Some of the art themes studied during my membership have been drama, arts in the land of the Cross and the Crescent, North Carolina arts and crafts, the arts of the Golden West, art collections, selected artists, and classical studies. Each year, in March, an art theme is selected for study throughout the coming year.

This is a most cultured, concerned, dedicated, and interested group of ladies. They made it very easy for me to serve as their president during 1995-96 and 1996-97.

Participating in this group has been one of my most enjoyable experiences since retirement.

1992
Need for a Hospice Foundation

While Medicare and most hospital insurance policies pay for Home Care and Hospice benefits, we found some people came down with terminal illnesses but had no resources of any kind.

In 1993, we formed the Duplin Home Care and Hospice Foundation a non-profit corporation to raise funds to pay the Home Care and Hospice expenses of patients without the ability to pay.

The foundation is governed by a volunteer board of directors. Serving on its board for the first three years and then rotating off, was a rewarding experience which I would label "Love in Action by a Lot of People."

Fundraising activities have been many and varied and quite successful, because it is easy for the general public to see the funds of this foundation in action in their communities, ministering to the terminally ill.

Qualifying expenses covered are those incurred by Home Care and Hospice employees and, upon request and approval, can include travel expenses incurred by the families or neighbors transporting the terminally ill patients to appointments and/or treatments.

A group of dear elderly ladies, living near Kenansville, formed "Aunt Dinah's Quilting Club." They make quilts for themselves and also make quilts to donate for Hospice benefits. These ladies are classified as Hospice volunteers and are invited to the annual volunteer recognition dinners.

1993

Betty Ray McCain

My long-time friend, Betty Ray McCain, a former Duplin County girl, has been the Secretary of the North Carolina Department of Cultural Resources since 1993. Under the umbrella of this department is the North Carolina Symphony, the arts museum, arts council, the preservation office, the Department of Archives and History, the State Capitol, Tryon Palace, and twenty-two state historical sites.

In 1996, Betty had the honor of being named one of the most powerful women in the North Carolina Triangle area of Raleigh, Durham, and Chapel Hill. She received an Honorary Degree of Doctor of Laws at the University of North Carolina at Chapel Hill, on 17 May 1998.

Betty's home was Faison in Duplin County until 1955, when she married Dr. John McCain and moved to Wilson. They have two children.

When one looks at the long, dazzling list of accomplishments of this former Duplinite, including becoming the first woman to head the North Carolina Democratic party, the question comes, "How has she accomplished so much?" The answer has to be entwined in her ever-flowing laughter which accompanies her spirit of accomplishment. Betty always makes you glad you are in her presence. Her laughter is contagious.

During each speech she makes in Duplin County, she tells that she wrote to me once for a copy of her birth certificate to apply for a passport. She tells I informed her we had on file a birth certificate for an unnamed male child born to her parents on her birth date. If she would send me two dollars, I could get her name put on it and get a sex change.

The people of the Faison area are so proud and grateful for the services and accomplishments of this gallant favorite daughter, they scheduled Sunday, 19 April 1998, as Betty Ray McCain Day to pay honor for the good she has brought to her home town and to North Carolina.

Duplin's Selfless Hospice Volunteers Saluted

Christine Williams Is Honored As Hospice Volunteer Of The Year, 1994

By Jo Cameron Jones, Staff Writer
(Copied from *The Wallace Enterprise*, by permission)

"This wonderful woman makes every day special for everybody she touches!" declared Evelyn DeVane, RN and Duplin Hospice Coordinator, as she saluted the 1994 Hospice Volunteer of the Year, Christine Williams.

Williams, a retired Duplin County Register of Deeds with an innovative and distinguished record in her former profession, was recognized for outstanding Hospice volunteer service by her co-workers at the seventh annual Volunteer Recognition Luncheon held Thursday in the Fellowship Hall of the First Baptist Church on Church Street in Kenansville.

A Salute To Volunteers

Lynn Hardy, executive director of Hospice services in Duplin County, welcomed volunteers and guests on behalf of the organization

Hardy saluted the fifty some local Hospice volunteers who give so selflessly of their time and their compassionate hearts as special care givers to patients and their families as they undergo the final great challenge every human being must face.

Duplin Hospice volunteers are pledged to make that final challenge a rich and meaningful experience that no one must face alone.

Diane Leaming, RN, shared "Because He Lives" a gift in song dedicated to the memory of a fellow worker.

Jack Blair, NSW, read the group a poem that emphasized the work Hospice volunteers do.

"Hospice work is emotionally complicated and very demanding, and often we blame ourselves when we cannot do more," Blair said.

"But it is important to remember that we are simply human beings trying the best way we know how to help our fellow human beings leave this world with some measure of tranquillity," he stressed.

Reverend Leo Bracken, a Hospice Chaplain, spoke of the "ministry" of volunteers.

"You volunteers are valuable because you are following the Biblical example of Christ, the world's most famous 'volunteer,' who comforted the sick and brought to them the peace of God," Bracken said.

"You are doing the very same thing," he added.

Darlene C. Leysath, CCSW Volunteer and Bereavement Coordinator who presided at the luncheon, praised in detail the volunteers in the Duplin Hospice program.

"If it were not for volunteers, there would be no Duplin Home Health Care and Hospice program," said Leysath.

She and Evelyn DeVane stressed that volunteers suggested that a Hospice program be set up, and that volunteers wrote up the first grant application.

Volunteers serve on the executive and the advisory boards.

"They are our eyes and ears to the community," Leysath said.

Above all, volunteers raise funds so that Hospice activities can go forward and expand to serve the needs of an ever larger group than is served at present.

"And finally," said DeVane, "Hospice volunteers, undergo intensive training for four weeks, then go on to devote as much as forty hours a week or more to those they serve. Our volunteers are truly a blessing in all our lives.

"Christine Williams is just such a volunteer," she said.

"Hospice volunteers provide companionship, emotional support, run errands if needed and give family caregivers a respite from their duties," DeVane said.

"Christine does all that and more," she said.

Christine Williams As A Volunteer

"She brings flowers she has grown and arranged herself to her clients. She is an absolutely fabulous cook who spoils both her Hospice patients and we, her co-workers, with all kinds of goodies," DeVane smiled.

"Christine provides books and tapes to those she serves and reads anything from the Bible to the newspaper to them, just as all our Hospice volunteers are trained to do," DeVane went on.

"But one thing that makes this most living and elegant lady so special as a volunteer is the fact that she gives her services to patients and their families in two counties, not just here in Duplin," DeVane added.

"That's why it's both an honor and a pleasure to recognize Christine Williams, as Hospice Volunteer of the Year," said DeVane.

1995
The New B. F. Grady School

My children, some of my grandchildren, and now two great-grandchildren have attended the B. F. Grady School, named for an early local educator. It is two miles from my home.

The original B. F. Grady brick school was built in 1928, one year following the new school I attended at Kenansville in 1927.

Melvin graduated from B. F. Grady when it was first through twelfth grade. Glenn graduated the year grades nine through twelve merged into East Duplin High School at Beulaville during the Christmas holidays.

A few years ago all middle school grades in Duplin County had been removed from the K-8 schools, except B. F. Grady, Beulaville, and Chinquapin. Plans had been made to build a new middle school at Beulaville for a merger of the middle grades of these schools.

Dr. Alice Smith Scott, a B. F. Grady parent, was on the County Board of Education. She believed a new middle school at Beulaville would not be the right decision for these three schools because of the long distances to be traveled by some students, up to twenty-five miles.

The parents of the three schools did not believe merger was the best answer. They signed petitions to keep these three rural schools K-8.

A consultant was paid forty thousand dollars and his study showed that B. F. Grady, Beulaville, and Chinquapin middle school grades should not be merged.

The B. F. Grady school district has always been famous for parental support and participation. Support is evident throughout the year. But, each fall there is a festival to raise funds to purchase equipment and supplies which are not otherwise available. Most area residents attend and join in the fundraising.

The spirit and attitude of the B. F. Grady community is so clearly exemplified by an opinion Lloyd Stevens, a former principal expressed a couple of years ago when he and his son were dining in a Goldsboro restaurant and invited me to join them to chat.

Lloyd asked, "Who is the principal at B. F. Grady now?"

I told him.

He then remarked: "That is the only school I know where it really doesn't matter who the principal is. The teachers in that school are so dedicated they could run the school without a principal."

B. F. Grady K-8 occupied a modern new building in 1995. The 1928 building has been demolished and the grounds it sat upon are now school playgrounds.

During the 1997-1998 school year, the Hispanic enrollment increased to 175 students out of a total enrollment of 650. This is twenty-seven percent of the total student body. Most parents of the Hispanic children work at the turkey plant or in the swine and poultry growing houses. Both the B. F. Grady and the North Duplin Elementary Schools are literally bulging at the seams because the children of the 1,100 Hispanics who work at the turkey plant send their children to one of these two schools.

Tutoring Great-Grandchildren and Supplying Educational Materials

My first opportunity to tutor my great-grandchildren came three and four years ago when I tutored a great-grandchild in the first and second grades in school.

His younger brother was only four, but decided he wanted to come to Grandma's to do homework. He looked very motivated coming in with his book pack on his back, containing his preschool books.

These are my only great-grandchildren living nearby, only six miles away. Two live forty miles away in Goldsboro, where I see them frequently and talk to them often on the telephone. The others live much further away.

Watching a little child learn must be one of life's greatest pleasures. The older great-grandchild was interested in getting his homework assignments and in doing special projects. He made good progress. He especially did well in reading, learning to tackle new words.

I also worked with him in the summer before he entered the third grade and he was on the honor roll the first grading period. Then his parents made arrangements for someone to sit with the boys at their home. He did not make the honor roll again in the third, fourth, or fifth grades.

The younger one had so much fun in his pre-school lessons, especially did he enjoy applying stickers to each completed page. He loved to be at my house and cried every time he had to go back to the home where he was staying while his parents worked.

Both boys were a real joy and I am grateful for the good times we had learning and the good memories we created.

I purchased for each of my granddaughters and their families all of the World Book products: the pre-school *Early World of Learning*, Child Craft books, with encyclopedias and dictionaries to take them through high school.

When I was tutoring the second grade student he had such a special interest in and aptitude for computers, I bought him and his brother a twenty-five hundred dollar computer and printer, which included a five-year maintenance contract. I could see both of them becoming computer whizzes. I took the older one to summer computer camp for two weeks and paid tuition of one hundred dollars.

It seems that in order for children to do well in school, parents or some other person must be interested in the children's homework, encourage them and give help when needed. It's easy for children to pick up on what parents and family consider to be important.

Both Melvin and his wife Scarlette, graduated from college. Their daughter, Stephanie was an outstanding student at East Duplin High School where she served as president of the student body. She is a registered nurse working with Wayne County Home Care and Hospice at Goldsboro where she and her husband, Brian Childers and their two little boys, Cody and Collin live. The boys are enrolled in three and four year old Church pre-school.

Brian is the manager of the complex of the tire store, the convenience store, and the ABC store on Seymour Johnson Air Force Base at Goldsboro. They live the good life, enjoying their boys. They take them on jaunts to the North Carolina Zoo and other meaningful children's outings, and to Myrtle Beach to see such shows as "Snoopy on Ice." The boys delight in talking on the phone, relating what they have seen and heard, not only on family outings, but during their days in Goldsboro.

On 20 April 1998, the family went to Orlando, Florida, for a week's vacation to visit Disney World and be there for the grand opening of Disney's Animal World and to see Sea World.

Duplin County Partners for Health

In 1995, the Duke Endowment Fund awarded a grant to East Carolina Medical School at Greenville to make a long term health study of the four counties in North Carolina experiencing the greatest number of cases of cancer, diabetes, strokes, and heart disease.

Duplin County was one of the four counties selected for the long term study. The other three counties are also eastern counties with large rural areas: Hertford, Martin, and Pitt.

A county organization called Partners For Health was formed to participate in and promote the study. It was made up mostly of health professionals with a few community representatives. Representatives of East Carolina University Medical School served as advisors.

I was asked to serve with Partners For Health as a community representative because I live in the large rural area of Duplin County where there are no medical services and where the four diseases to be studied are rampant.

The first meeting of our Partners For Health in 1995 was devoted to selecting five health objectives for study. Those selected were:

1. Healthcare Delivery Systems

2. Nutrition

3. Physical Fitness

4. Abuse of Tobacco, Alcohol, and Other Drugs

5. Mental Health

Many meetings followed in which we heard lectures by authorities on various aspects of the five selected health objectives. Duplin County problems relating to these objectives were defined.

Eleven hundred Duplin County households were enumerated with five hundred of these scientifically selected for in-depth studies of how these families relate to the five selected study objectives.

When the study was completed in 1998 and the results analyzed as to the strengths and weaknesses of our Duplin County families as they relate to the five priority areas we had chosen, we divided into three action groups as follows:

1. High Risk Behavior in Adolescents

2. Depression And Anxiety Disorders

3. Prevention of Chronic Diseases

Each group chose a chair person and a recorder, defined assets, goals, and objectives, and identified the county resources available to develop strategies to accomplish selected goals.

I joined the action group on Prevention of Chronic Diseases.

During the discussion on Depression and Anxiety Disorders, it was reported that the study of all county middle school students revealed that 27% had considered suicide. Eleven percent had planned or made failed attempts.

It was also noted that a recent Health Department study showed that Duplin County's adolescent pregnancy rate is the highest in the state. Also, the Partners study found that the percentage of adolescents who have tried a drug substance is higher than the state average.

It is estimated there are at least two thousand undiagnosed cases of diabetes in the county. My chronic disease group chose getting these people diagnosed and into treatment as our first project. The other two groups selected projects. It is believed we will be working on the problems of these groups for a long time.

The health history of my own family and working as a Hospice Volunteer for my tenth year, mostly with cancer patients, causes my greatest health concern to continue to be our high number of cancer cases.

One 4.4 mile rural secondary road known as the Seth Turner Road, which runs within a mile of my home, has one of the worst cancer patient records in Duplin County. There have been ten cancer deaths on this road in the past two years. I have helped usher most of them into eternity after visiting with them and keeping them supplied with fresh flowers from my yard. At this writing, there are three arrested cancer cases on this road and one terminally ill person with a brain tumor.

Seth Turner Road extends over into Lenoir County where four men have died of cancer during the past two years within a short distance of Duplin County.

Seven-Day Alaskan Inside Passage Cruise

A trip to Alaska in July 1995 provided my only experience in viewing a place more breathtakingly beautiful to the natural eye than shown by all of the book pictures and videos I had ever seen on this our most northern state where I had always wished to visit.

My longtime friend, Sarah Bolin, of Beulaville, and her son, Dr. Paul Bolin, and his wife, Linda, of Greenville, invited me to go with them on an Alaskan cruise from Vancouver, Canada, to Juneau, Skagway, Haines, and Ketchikan.

We flew to Seattle, Washington, and spent the weekend. My brother's grandson, his wife and two little girls, who live near Seattle, came to our hotel and we had a five-hour visit at the hotel's pool-side area.

A rental car gave us a scenic drive from Seattle to Vancouver, where we boarded the *Nordic Prince* cruise ship for the Inland Passage voyage to Juneau.

When we were sailing, Dr. Charles Stanley from Atlanta, Georgia, and two other ministers led Bible studies in the ship's three lounges. These lectures seemed more meaningful sailing amid icebergs and sparkling waters than in churches at home.

I was surprised at seeing so many seals sunning on small icebergs in the waters of the Alaskan Inside Passage.

Each time we docked there were planned tours.

At Juneau we toured the city and salmon fisheries and attended a public salmon bake where, for a fee, tourists can see and smell fresh salmon steaks being grilled over hardwood coals. We could eat grilled salmon with accompanying delectable foods prepared by Alaskans, until we could eat no more.

At Skagway, we took a four-hour ride on the White Pass Scenic Railway over more beautiful mountains than I had ever imagined.

A city and cultural tour at Haines highlighted the early history and handicrafts of the Haines area.

The Indians at the Saxman native village at Ketchikan, with their native costumes, drama, and dances made us feel we were visiting Ketchikan before the white men arrived.

It was difficult for us to imagine what Alaska might be like in the rain, because we never saw a drop from the time we left home until we returned to Charlotte, North Carolina, on our way home. We only saw Alaska with the July sun blazing on it, allowing us to view it in its most dazzling light.

28 October 1995—80th Birthday Celebration

Until brother Milton lived to be eighty in 1994, folks in the Whaley family just hadn't survived that long. He had his eightieth celebration at my house with his family and his best high school chum.

Twenty-eight October 1995 would mark eighty years for me. Sons Melvin and Glenn Williams thought it was time for a great celebration. So my eightieth celebration was held at 1:30 on Sunday, 29 October, with a catered luncheon at the B. F. Grady Elementary School cafetorium. Guests were seated to dine facing the cafetorium's massive stage.

Individual birthday cakes with a single candle on each marked the places for guests. Miniature match books reading "October 28, 1915" were placed on the tables. Small vases of pink begonias and blue ageratum lined the tables. A fall arrangement of pumpkins, gourds, and yellow chrysanthemums graced the front center of the stage.

The whole affair was like "old home week" with guests lingering to enjoy visiting with old friends and family.

Following is Iris Raynor's report in the 9 November 1995 edition of *The Wallace Enterprise* newspaper, describing my birthday party. Used by permission, excerpts from the report include:

> Christine Williams' family and friends really pulled out all the stops and added all the great elements to celebrate her 80th birthday with flair and in an impressive style. Two hundred-plus people came from all over Duplin County, from throughout North Carolina, and from several other states to help make this a most memorable birthday celebration. The event, featuring food, fun, fellowship and a musical performance, was held at the new B. F. Grady Elementary School cafetorium on Sunday, October 29.
>
> Anyone would have thought (if they had not known better) that they were at Myrtle Beach attending one of those musical productions staged at any one of several theaters. The atmosphere of the celebration was electric and exciting. Everyone was having a great time. Everyone could see family and friends talking and laughing, enjoying themselves.
>
> Wanda Stroud played the piano as the guests arrived at this special occasion. Glenn Williams, Christine's younger son, welcomed everyone to the delicious barbecue luncheon and gave the invocation. Afterwards, at

every place setting there was a square slice of birthday cake with each piece having a single candle placed in the center. Then, the lights of the building were turned off. All were invited to light their candles.

It was a sight to behold, to look over the entire room at all the candles lit in celebration of the 80th birthday of this outstanding, respected and admired Duplin County woman. It sent chills down one's spine as the event took place.

Everyone chimed in to sing "Happy Birthday" to Christine.

Several people came up to the microphone and made remarks about having known Christine over the years, including her sons, Melvin and Glenn. Some of the remarks were from family members recalling childhood days. Others spoke of having known her in her professional years as Register of Deeds of Duplin County.

Christine Williams—always gracious, charming and poised—came up to the microphone and recognized family and friends. She reminisced about people, places and events that have taken place throughout her life living and working in Duplin County.

Melvin G. Williams, Christine's elder son, spoke to the guests about his mother and mentioned several events in her life. He surprised her by reading and presenting a letter from President Bill Clinton and First Lady Hillary Rodham Clinton, as well as a letter of congratulation from Governor Jim Hunt of North Carolina. Melvin ended his remarks by saying, "Mother is the youngest eighty-year-old lady you will ever see!" (Everyone heartily agreed.)

Guests were entertained by an impressive stage production by the Mount Olive College Singers, under the direction of Irene Patten. The young ladies singing and performing wore red sequin tops with black skirts and the young men wore white shirts with black sequin vests and black trousers. The entertainment lasted over thirty minutes and was absolutely great. Most songs were from the 50s, 60s and 70s. Included were, *This is a Lovely Way to Spend an Evening*, *Going to Take a Sentimental Journey*, and many other selections.

As a climax to the Mount Olive College Singers' program, one of the young men came down off stage as the chorus was singing *Earth Angel*, and taking Christine by the hand, ushered her onto the stage as the chorus sang this special song just for her. The honoree was given a standing ovation.

The gathering of Christine's family, friends and co-workers will be long remembered.

The Emmaus Walk— A Spiritual Retreat

In January 1995, two of our church members and I accompanied our pastor to Jarvis Memorial United Methodist Church in Greenville, North Carolina to hear lectures on opportunities for the year in the Methodist churches of the Greenville district. Descriptive materials were available.

The lecture on *The Emmaus Walk* by Dr. Rick Herbert described a most interesting sounding spiritual retreat weekend, beginning Thursday, 2 November with supper, and ending on Sunday, 5 November at eight o'clock in the evening. The retreat would be held at a comfortable, brick, motel-like camp, with a large dining and assembly building, overlooking a small, picturesque lake near St. Paul's, North Carolina. Rustic wooden benches near the lake would offer a restful view of the foliage, sunsets, fishing piers, and ducks.

The speaker mentioned the requirement that persons going on Emmaus Walks must be sponsored by former attendees. A sponsor is required to transport a new participant to and from the Emmaus Walk.

Dr. Herbert and his wife, Barbara, were listed among the members of Jarvis Memorial United Methodist Church who had attended previous Walks and who would sponsor persons. I called the Herberts and they graciously agreed to be my sponsor.

Barbara was serving as a volunteer on the staff of the 2-5 November Walk, so it was easy for her to pick me up on her way to St. Paul's and drop me off on her return trip.

It was so good to get to know the Herberts. He is a professor at East Carolina State University and she is a Ph.D. qualified family counselor.

The Emnaus Walk is presented with great integrity and authenticity. It is informative and practical. You leave with information and insights that can help you all your life. It is also spiritual, offering the opportunity to participate in daily worship and celebration of Holy Communion.

There are fifteen lectures by clergy and lay persons on such subjects as "What are your priorities?", "Growth through study takes commitment," "Christian action," "Discipleship," "Perseverance," et cetera.

Surprising to some, Emmaus Walks are fun! You laugh and eat until your sides ache. You share fellowship and foolishness in a wonderfully meaningful way. But, most of all, you receive more love than you ever expected—from the volunteers who serve at your Walk and from dozens of people whom you will never meet. The people are former Walk participants who work behind the scenes, serving food, refreshments, and furnishing favors.

Most importantly, Emmaus Walks help remind us that we are never alone, that we just need to learn to open our eyes and become inspired, challenged, and equipped for Christian action, wherever we are.

Emmaus Walks are non-denominational. But in eastern North Carolina the main participants seem to be Methodist.

The seventy-two hours on an Emmaus Walk can be the impetus we need, no matter what our age, for the renewal of a lifelong Walk filled with the strength, joy, and peace for which we all yearn.

A gathering of area pilgrims who have participated in Emmaus Walks is held every third Friday night of each month at the Mt. Olive Untied Methodist Church. This Church is twenty-two miles from my home and is on the same street where my sister lives. The music, singing, talks by former pilgrims, communion, refreshments, and fellowship are inspirational and are reminiscent of our attendance at our own Walk.

1996
Governor's Outstanding Volunteer Service Award

In May of 1996, Lynn Hardy, Director of Duplin Home Care and Hospice, nominated me in the category of Health for one of the Governor's Awards for Outstanding Volunteer Service. Her application read:

This eighty-year-old woman retired seven years ago from a long career of public service and has since accumulated this record in volunteering in service to the people in her area:

1. Seven years with Duplin Home Care and Hospice

2. Three years on the Board of Directors for Duplin Home Care and Hospice

3. Three years as a volunteer with Lenoir County Home Care and Hospice

4. Last two years on the Duplin County Quality of Life Task Force created by the County Development Commission

5. Six months on Duplin Partners for Health, continuing around another one to one and a half years to complete

6. Four years investing in Keep America Beautiful materials giving anti-litter programs, conducting and funding anti-litter poster contests in schools.

7. Duplin County Nursing Home Committee, one year

8. For the past fifteen years has given humorous and inspirational talks to Senior Citizens groups, emphasizing exercises, good diets, humor and positive attitudes as the secrets to good health in old age.

9. Seven years of serving as counselor and advisor to people in her area needing home health and other health services

SUMMARY: Around fifteen to twenty hours spent weekly, Duplin, Lenoir and Wayne Counties.

Governor's Award

for
Outstanding Volunteer Service

This is to certify that

Christine Williams

is hereby awarded the highest designation of appreciation for distinguished volunteer service to the People and the State of North Carolina, and is to be granted and extended all honors and courtesies provided by this Office, entitled thereunto by this certificate of recognition and appreciation.

_____
Governor

August 28, 1996
_____
Date

Governor's Award for Outstanding Volunteer Service

Stephen Ministry

The Stephen Ministry was founded in 1975 by Dr. Kenneth Haugh, a St. Louis, Missouri pastor, who remains its executive director. The ministry is non-denominational. There are now Stephen Ministries in sixty-two denominations in all fifty states and ten foreign countries.

Reverend Jack Benfield, pastor of Westminster United Methodist Church in Kinston, taught the required twenty-five, two-hour sessions every Thursday night, beginning the first Thursday in September 1996, and going through February 1997. There were six members in the class. Graduation was the first Sunday in March 1997. We were presented certificates and a Stephen Ministry badge, which admits us to hospital rooms and intensive care units.

Our county health director was interested in taking the course, so she spent Thursday nights with me and we traveled to Kinston together.

I especially felt I could use some advanced training in working with terminally ill Hospice patients and their families.

I knew Reverend Benfield many years ago through his ministry in Kenansville, where he pastored his first church. He has taught many Stephen Ministry sessions in his church. He is an excellent instructor, making every lesson come alive with special meanings.

Subjects covered were: listening skills, learning how to recognize and express feelings, the best use of Christian resources, specialized ministry skills, working with the elderly, the depressed and the suicidal, assisting the terminally ill, those experiencing grief due to a loss or divorce, et cetera, and those facing changes in family situations.

There was also instruction on "being professional," "crises theory," "confidentiality," and "biblical resources for Christian caring," all of which have proven meaningful and helpful.

Now that I'm eighty-two and just about the oldest person around, I seem to be the one person who has learned to listen the most. And surely, there is an ever growing range of people with problems just looking for someone who has endured and weathered storms in life. So, I needed to take the Stephen Ministry course and get any other help I can!

My best listening is with the neglected elderly and the terminal ill. When I'm with the neglected terminally ill, I can only think about how lucky I am to be up, active, and going. When I'm with the terminally ill, I cannot dwell on my own pain, because the person I'm trying to serve is so much worse off than I am.

Left: Julie Fields, American Indian sister of my first Hospice patient stands on the front porch of her run-down shack where "He considered The Lillies" before he died.

In 1994, Evelyn Devane presents the Duplin County Hospice Volunteer of the Year plaque to me.

Right: Summer of 1995—A sad time as persons who attended the final reunion for the beloved B. F. Grady School, which had been the center of our rural school district since 1928, visit before demolition begins. Ninety-year-old Louise Wells, a former teacher, talks with Edgar Wells, also a teacher, in the right foreground.

New state of the art K-8 B. F. Grady school occupied fall of 1995, widely known for contining excellent staff and parental support. $38,000 was raised at the 1996 Harvest Festival.

The Kinston Arts Study Club at a farewell party for the member on the front row (wearing pearls) who was leaving Kinston to be near her only son.

The Mount Olive College singers invite me to join them on stage at my eightieth birthday luncheon.

My son, Melvin, presents my portrait to The Duplin County Board of Commissioners to be hung in the County Courthouse.

1995—To Alaska on the Nordic Prince. *Left to right: Dr. Paul Bolin, his mother and my long-time friend, Sarah, myself and Dr. Bolin's wife, Linda, with snow-capped mountains in the background. This is the only place I've ever visited that was more beautiful than the color pictures I had seen of it.*

Milton, his son, Senol (in the U. S. Army) and his daughter, Betty Whaley Thornton in 1995.

Scarlette and Melvin

Melvin and Scarlette's only child, Stephanie, with her husband, Brian Childers, and their sons, Collin and Cody.

Cody at three years old.

Collin at two years old.

Collin Childers, age three, standing, and Cody Childers, age four, seated.

Dennis Waters, Jr. teaching his brother, Michael, to walk.

Dennis Waters, Sr., father of two of my great-grandsons, Michael, left, and Dennis, Jr., right.

Michael Waters, age four, playing at Grandma Christine's house on a very cold day.

Dennis Waters, Jr. on the same very cold day.

Left: Krystal Smith, age fourteen, Jennings Smith, age fifteen, and I have refreshments on my front porch and talk about their new venture into East Duplin High School's ninth grade.

Right: Amanda and Lee Ann Tyndall try out their new golf cart on Grannie's front lawn. They are very good neighbors.

1997
Duplin County Finishes 39th Year as North Carolina Leader in Agricultural Income

In early 1959, a special fifty-page magazine was published depicting the growth in agricultural income in Duplin County.

Area newspapers also blazed these headlines on their front pages:

"Duplin County Leads North Carolina In Total Agricultural Income In 1958, At An Estimated $44,705,647."

All those responsible for this achievement took a bow and agreed that our county had reached the height of agricultural progress. Expanded growing of chickens and turkeys had made the biggest income increases.

We in the Register of Deeds Office felt rewarded that we had been a part of the agricultural income progress by developing a system of recording farm production loan papers while the farmer or lending agency representatives waited. Thus speeding disbursement of loan proceeds.

Every year since 1958, Duplin County has continued to lead North Carolina in agricultural income as our farmers have been rapidly changing their operations.

Now at 1997 year's end, reports of the Duplin County and State Cooperative Extension Staffs and the North Carolina Department of Agriculture show a new high total agricultural income in Duplin County of $631,970,413 reached in 1997 with 56.5 percent coming from livestock and poultry and 43.5 percent coming from field crops.

In 1997, the 732 mega-size hog operations garnered $263,782,718 and the 230 big poultry farms which sold $221,577,161 in poultry products and $20,249,656 in eggs played a great part in the expanded income.

Not only did the 1997 agricultural income keep Duplin number one in North Carolina but it placed Duplin in the top twenty-five counties in the whole United States!

Industrialized Hog Growing Replaces Farm Hogs

It is interesting to note that the Duplin County Farm Magazine published in 1959 stated that in 1958, seventy percent of all Duplin farmers were growing hogs. Each farmer farrowed his own pigs, fed them, and took them to the local hog market on his own farm truck or a trailer that he pulled behind his farm truck. Then, just a few years ago, came the "Gold Rush" to industrialized hog operations with open waste lagoon cesspools, the foul odors, and the swarming flies. So, in 1997 Duplin County had only 732 hog growers and most of these were the industrialized ones.

The flies that breed in the fresh manure in the hog houses are not the ordinary house fly type which can be lazy and easy to swat. They are fast-moving zipping and zapping flies that can out-travel a swatter, sometimes for several minutes.

Some hog growers are greatly reducing fly breeding by frequently pressure washing the fresh manure out of the corners of the pens where the hogs are kept, thus flushing it out into the lagoons. But because of the added expense many growers say they won't pressure wash often enough to control the fly infestation unless it is mandated by law. Some hog suppliers have fly control chemicals available to their growers but chemical use is not mandated.

I have a beautiful white oversized rural mailbox with my name and address on it along with humming birds and flowers made into the cover. On all sunny days, when I visit my mail box, the white top is accommodating a convention of flies which seem to be taking a rest and making a decision as to which way they will go to their destination.

I have been to the homes of some terminally ill patients when the flies seemed to be intolerable. Some hog growers and their neighbors just seem to endure the flies making little or no efforts to control them. They appear to accept them as a permanent pest.

Others have sticky hangers just outside their doors to serve as prisons to catch flies trying to venture into their homes.

I use a large electric fan just above the glass table on my front porch near my front door. But I find such an outside fan will last only two years.

One neighbor has an electric insecticide dispenser located in her kitchen that squishes out liquid fly killer at regular short intervals into her big kitchen-den area. The noises it makes are very distracting. The wife of one big grower told me they have such an insecticide dispenser under their carport focused at their back door where their two small children go in and out frequently and let flies in the house.

One big hog grower told me that soon after his family moved into their magnificent new house with all white woodwork, the pesky flies so spotted up the beautiful white wood that it all had to be washed before they worked out any plans for fly control.

Just before my eightieth birthday party, I went to a noted cake maker to learn the cost of two hundred individual cakes. A big hog farm had located near her. The cakes she was baking smelled delectable. But her kitchen was so invaded by the zipping and zapping flies, I just asked her prices and came home and baked two hundred cakes and froze them for the big day.

My party was at our new school cafetorium near a hog farm. The school custodian sprayed flies in the cafetorium on Saturday but had to spray again just before the party on Sunday.

It was understandable that some Duplin County farmers who could afford to build modern facilities to accommodate mega-size hog operations would do so. But it was surprising how many non-farming professionals were interested, such as the county sheriff, some other county officials, attorneys, and business people who had never been farmers.

So open were the arms of Duplin County to the new industrialized hog operations that non-farmers from other counties came over to Duplin to put in operations and helped to make Duplin the number one hog producing county. Two of the largest such operations in the part of the county I live in are owned by non-farm professionals from adjoining Lenoir County.

When my next door neighbor put in his first four of a final sixteen hog finishing houses each holding seven hundred hogs, he said to me "When you smell something, just consider you're smelling greenbacks." His sixteen houses accommodate seven hundred hogs each, making a total of 11,300 at all times. These produce as much waste as 22,600 humans. And his is a small operation compared to some.

On 11 June 1998, one hundred people attended a hog waste conference in Raleigh sponsored by a group of civic and political leaders. News reports on this meeting stated that researchers present affiliated with the hog industry and those who are not, agreed only on one point and little else. The one agreed point was: "Making broad judgments about the health effects of corporate hog farms on eastern North Carolina communities is impossible without further scientific study." And adequate scientific study has been slow in developing!

Field Crops and Other Farm Income

In 1997, Duplin County income from all field crops including vegetables and berries was $123,958,873. Then there were smaller amounts from nursery and greenhouse sales, forestry, beef and dairy cattle, other livestock, milk, wool, honey, fish, and horses.

Duplin was ninth in North Carolina in tobacco production with five hundred growers producing 19,260,147 pounds of the golden leaf on 11,009 acres grown on 1,239 different farms which averaged $1.80 per pound.

I am reminded that when I helped sign up the first Duplin County Tobacco Acreage Reduction Contracts in 1933-34, there were over four thousand farmers growing tobacco. Many grew only four acres and used one log or wood-frame curing barn, stoking its brick furnace four to five days and nights with wood logs.

Now, these sad-looking, abandoned tobacco curing barns are our daily reminders of a bygone era as they dot the countryside. Their use has been replaced by efficient thermostat controlled gas fired bulk or box curing barns.

Since the time I was a child helping to set tobacco plants in the sharecrop fields using a wooden peg and pouring water from a cup around the plants, there has been a great evolution in all practices in the growing of tobacco which still remains the king of all cash crops, netting around two thousand dollars an acre.

We had to struggle with pulling weeds out of the cold, damp, tobacco plant beds sown in outside soil. Now, farmers use hothouses for growing tobacco plants with one house setting one hundred to one hundred fifty acres of tobacco in the fields.

Mechanical plant setters carry a water supply and set eight rows at a time using seated migrant workers. Chemicals have replaced the hot laborious tasks of picking green horn worms and suckers from the tobacco growing in the fields.

The old back-breaking job of cropping the matured tobacco leaves from the matured stalks is now done either by migrant workers sitting on mechanical harvesters, or by men walking and stripping all the leaves from the stalks at one time and throwing them into a ventilated metal box pulled by a tractor. One man stands on the box and stomps the leaves down to save space. Then the metal box is placed in a box barn where the tobacco is cured.

The tobacco auction markets now open in July. The cured tobacco is removed from the barns, put directly into burlap sheets and taken to the auction market, sometimes the same day.

Gone is the drudgery we endured in tying the cropped leaves on sticks for curing, piling the cured sticks of tobacco into a pack house to await sorting into four or five grades, retying the graded leaves into small bundles and putting the bundles on smooth sticks to be transported to the auction market later in the fall of the year.

Also gone is the era of tenant-landlord and sharecrop farming. Now, tobacco growers for many years have paid a per pound fee to lease tobacco poundage allotted by the government. Most of the five hundred county tobacco growers have some poundage allotments of their own and lease some from other farmers. Our Congress still considers changes in the tobacco production program.

And now in 1998, organic tobacco is beginning to gain favor. While it takes much more attention to grow, it sells for four dollars a pound instead of the $1.80 for that grown with chemicals.

Era of Contract Farming

Farmers have gone almost totally to contract farming with their hogs, poultry, sweet potatoes, cucumbers, and some other crops. They have profited by the changes from the old outmoded uncertain prices. Now they know what prices they can depend on!

Poultry—The Biggest Turkey Processing Plant in the World

Turkeys

Duplin County raises more turkeys than any other county in North Carolina. Carolina Turkeys, Inc., located in northern Duplin County is the largest turkey processing plant in the whole wide world.

This half-million square feet of thriving activity receives and processes from 75,000 to 80,000 turkeys every twenty-four hours. These birds come from a sixty mile, five county area. This plant is Duplin's largest employer with 2,100 full-time workers. Of these employees, 1,155 (55%) are Hispanic, 735 (35%) are African-American, 42 (2%) are Asian, and 168 (8%) are white. The white are mostly in management or clerical positions.

Unskilled wages begin at $6 an hour, can go up to $7.25. Benefits include retirement and health insurance. Carolina Turkeys, Inc. owns seven hundred rental mobile homes for its employees. All management personnel reside in next door Wayne County, mostly in the Walnut Creek Country Club area.

The research and development kitchen and laboratory facilities of the turkey plant employ six persons with master degrees in food science and one with a doctorate in food science.

Improved, delectable turkey products are continually developed for worldwide markets. Only twenty percent of sales are in whole turkeys.

Once when I arrived for a visit with a friend in Decatur, Alabama, her delicious entree was prepared from a package labeled "Carolina Turkeys, Inc."

Shipments of Carolina Turkeys products are made not only to all parts of the United States, but to Mexico, Canada, South Korea, England, Germany, Spain. Russia, and other countries.

Dennis Pittman, vice-president of Carolina Turkeys, in charge of human resources, contributed to this information.

Chickens

Since 1953, Duplin County has been raising chickens for a chicken processing plant in Rose Hill. Now Duplin is the county in North Carolina producing the most chickens.

The one aspect of chicken production that has been hardest for me to understand is the large number of poultry houses built in the 1950s and 1960s which now stand run down, abandoned, and neglected, detracting from the view of the countryside in our county. Many of the old chicken house roofs, which were usually made of crimped tin, have fallen down. Some whole houses have collapsed.

The owners of the valuable land upon which these awful looking relics of the past remain, cannot make use of the land as long as those non-useable structures stay on the land. One can often see these "eye sores" located near well kept farm dwellings and yards.

Surging Income Brings Landscape and Population Changes

The search for better jobs and a better life has brought hundreds of Mexican families to all of southeastern North Carolina in recent years and especially to Duplin County. The welcome sign has been out in Duplin County to these families because of the continually growing agricultural enterprises of poultry, swine, cucumbers, and sweet potatoes.

For many years, Mexican men came for work as migrant laborers, but more and more of them are bringing their families as a permanent home.

Duplin County schools report that in 1997, 11% of the county's 8,300 public schoolchildren are Hispanic. But, according to current county birth records one-third of the babies being born in 1997 are Hispanic. Five years from now 33-1/3% of the public schoolchildren entering kindergarten may be Hispanic with 33-1/3% African-American, and 33-1/3% white.

In 1998, we have 650 students in my local B. F. Grady K-8 school with 175 Mexicans. This is 27%. Some of them must be taught separately because they do not yet know enough English to join the regular classes.

So great is the influx of Mexicans that our community college is teaching English as a second language to Hispanics. But, for a long time most Hispanic public schoolchildren will go home to parents who speak little English and who will not be active in school activities and school support. I took ten Spanish lessons and retain few words.

As the new Mexican arrivals find permanent homes, the culture, language, even food they are bringing with them is altering the landscape of Duplin County and the surrounding region. We often see big trucks delivering goods to the Mexican stores which have sprung up in Pink Hill and most other towns. All area supermarkets now carry a full line of Mexican foods.

An Hispanic church uses a vacant store building in Pink Hill and several such buildings are being used for churches in other places in this county.

But, near the turkey plant, the Mount Olive First Baptist Church purchased a vacant store building and sponsored an Hispanic Mission in that building a decade ago. My brother-in-law built a steeple for the store building. The Mount Olive church paid an Hispanic minister twelve thousand dollars a year to be the pastor. As the mission grew, it took over the pastor's salary. Now the Mission has outgrown its first church building and the Mount Olive Baptist Church and others erected a big new church in 1997. This church is now making such great progress and will probably soon be self-supporting.

I visited this church once when their band was practicing for worship services and I was surprised at the number of musicians participating and the enthusiasm they display.

Mobile Homes

Most Mexican families live in mobile homes which are also changing the Duplin landscape. Before the arrival of the Mexican families there were already a goodly number of mobile homes in the county.

From 1 July 1996 to 30 June 1997, the Duplin County Electrical Inspection Department's reports show 907 mobile homes inspected for occupation and only 114 new traditional homes. This trend of only one new traditional home being occupied compared to eight used or new mobile homes has been going on for several years and this is contributing to our landscape changes.

Mexicans Need Medical Help

The Duplin County Health Department reports the percentage of residents attending health clinics in 1997 runs from 15% to 85% Hispanic.

My next door neighbor asked me to drive the pregnant wife of a Mexican farm worker twenty-four miles to Faison for a doctor's visit. I drove her without charge, which is my policy for taking people to a doctor. I was surprised at the free medical service she was entitled to receive. From then on the neighbor asked me to take her for monthly visits to a gynecologist in Kenansville, fourteen miles away, so I arranged for her monthly appointments to coincide with my monthly garden club luncheon meetings. I dropped her off at her doctor's office on my way to the garden club meeting and picked her up on my way home. One day I was almost home when I realized I had forgotten to pick her up.

I was brought up to believe that the gypsies who camped across the road from us when we were children were "strangers within our gates" and as such were neighbors. So, perhaps I had to be a good neighbor to this girl.

I had also been brought up to believe we should love our next door neighbor as we love ourselves, so when my next door neighbors asked me to help this girl living on their farm, I had to oblige. After all, here was a young woman whose first baby had died after her husband had left her in Mexico and had come to my next door neighbor's farm. Now she was having a problem pregnancy and needed help.

The Duplin County Social Services Office and the County Health Office have each had to add a Spanish interpreter to their staffs.

Most Mexicans find life here, even with low agricultural wages, better than what they could find at home in Mexico. Some describe work in the poultry plants as, "Work, work, work, with freezing fingers. Still it's better than any job we could get back home." Most describe their overall situation here as "happier than back in Mexico."

Trucks on Duplin Roads Resulting in Accidents and Deaths

In 1949 to 1953, Governor Kerr Scott, himself a farmer, set about to fulfill his campaign promise of getting North Carolina farmers out of the mud and put them on paved roads to market their farm products. The only way Governor Scott could pave the farm-to-market roads was to pave them just as they were, curves, unsafe intersections, and all other problems. These paved roads were a heaven on earth for the farm trucks, pickups, and family cars.

Then came Duplin County's phenomenal expansion of poultry, hogs, contract growing of sweet potatoes and cucumbers, with big tractor-trailers hauling feed, market chickens, turkeys, hogs, sweet potatoes, and cucumbers on little paved country roads designed for farm trucks, pickups, and family cars.

Probably the worst of all our rural accidents was in November 1994 when Betty Hatch Whaley, a young teacher at our local high school, her sister-in-law, Rachel Hatch, a fourth grade teacher at our B. F. Grady Elementary School and Lois Hatch, Betty's mother pulled out of SR 1502 at Scott's Store five points intersection into the path of a big tractor-trailer loaded with sweet potatoes on SR 1500. All three were killed instantly.

All three ladies were my close neighbors and friends. I played bridge with Rachel. They had been shopping at the Carolina Turkeys Outlet Store.

I have watched Governor Jim Hunt take quick action if he really understands a bad situation. So, after the funerals of the three dear, dear ladies, I sent him a copy of the long obituaries for each. He gave the accident account to his highway supervisor and very soon excellent safety measures including blinking yellow and red electric lights were installed on all five intersecting roads as well as islands were erected adjacent to the five point intersection at Scott's Store.

Our quality of life task force invited our County Highway Maintenance Supervisor to meet with us to discuss plans for improving the safety of our county rural roads. But the great problem that remains is that our farm-to-market roads were not designed for use by the great number of tractor-trailers they are accommodating. So, there is no good solution on the horizon of the foreseeable future.

Pigs Produce Duplin County's First Billionaire— Wendell Murphy

The October 1997, annual edition of *Forbes* Four Hundred Richest persons in the United States featured Wendell Murphy on the cover caressing a little white pig.

Wendell had not only become Duplin County's first billionaire and one of the four hundred richest people in the country, he had become the largest pig farmer, owning 275,000 sows with six million hogs at varying stages of growth from birth to packing house.

Live hog prices in 1997 were up around fifty percent over the past three years to $135 a head. *Forbes* estimated Murphy Farms in 1997 netted something like $150 million on $775 million in revenue.

But success and wealth hasn't changed Wendell Murphy. He's the same affable, attractive man he was when I first knew him. This was after he graduated from North Carolina State University and was teaching high school agriculture at an annual salary of $4,080. He was trying to make some extra money on the side by having a few people grow pigs for him in outside mud pits sprinkled with plenty of corn.

One of his growers told me Wendell would arrive at five o'clock in the morning to vaccinate pigs or check on them before going to teach school. He was learning the hog growing business with around three thousand hogs scattered around on a few farms. To serve them, he had his first small feed mill.

During the ten years when he served in our state legislature, he was greatly expanding his hog business and kept in almost constant touch with it by a phone in his legislative office or in his Raleigh condo. But he was a very effective legislator, always finding time to listen to and understand the concerns of the people he represented. I was at the state legislature many times regarding laws affecting the offices of the Registers of Deeds and I saw the high esteem in which his associate legislators regarded him.

In spite of his uncommon success, he still takes time to hug old friends at funerals and other gatherings and ask how they're doing. Monetary success hasn't changed his spirit of charitable giving. Not only when his university alma mater needed a new sports arena did he respond, but he also responded when Mt. Olive College needed a new cafeteria, or his local high school needed new band uniforms. I have known Wendell's mother, Lois, since she was just a young girl. She has always been his heroine, even more so since his buddy, his dad, died a few years ago. Her long-time friends say her change to wealth hasn't changed her in the least. I recently saw her eating collards and pork backbone with friends at the famous Beulaville Wagon Wheel restaurant where four hundred pounds of the favorite greens are consumed on their weekly "collard day."

Wendell's wife, Linda, is charming and talented. She has served as organist and choir director for the Rose Hill Baptist Church many years. She was a Hospice volunteer with the terminally ill for a time. Linda is the kind of person who can help your food digest with laughter and light conversation if you're lucky enough to meet her for lunch at a favorite restaurant. She laughingly says she feels obligated to give an excuse when she feeds Wendell a meat other than pork since he makes their living from pork production.

Changing Pig Farming from Low Tech to High Tech

When Wendell Murphy left his high school teaching job to become a full-time contract hog producer, he moved toward high technology. He went "full-hog" when he hired a team of nutritionists and engineers to regulate comfort temperatures for his hogs from farrowing to market; used ultra-sound machines to determine if sows at his 125 hospital-like sow farms were pregnant; increased the number of pigs born by his sows to twenty-two per sow a year; and produced one pound of meat for every three pounds of feed while typical pigs consume four pounds of feed for every one pound they put on.

He has continued to bring in talented outsiders such as a logistics manager from GE, a chief financial officer from Hershey foods, and the former president of Champion Spark Plug maker, as his president.

When Murphy Farm pigs are fifteen to eighteen days old, they are moved to the next contract farm where they stay until they reach fifty pounds which takes about fifty days.

Then they go to a finishing farm where they stay for twenty-one weeks to reach their market weight of 250 pounds when Murphy's tractor trailer trucks deliver them to the packing house where they qualify for premium prices.

Murphy Family Farms uses eight hundred contract growers in North Carolina, Iowa, Oklahoma, Kansas, and Illinois.

The contractors receive varying prices depending on the pigs' stage of development. More growers were anxious to join in Murphy's pig growing when the 1997 North Carolina State Legislature imposed a two-year moratorium on new hog operations.

Pigs are now the biggest Duplin County and North Carolina cash agricultural product. In 1997, the Duplin County tax collector listed Murphy Farms, Inc. as having the highest tax value in the county and paying the biggest tax bill of $520,634 on $66,502,596 property valuation.

In addition to Murphy Farms, several smaller swine contractors operate in Duplin County and in other Eastern North Carolina areas. By July 1998, Murphy owned hog operations in a total of nine states.

Surplus Pork Shows Up in Early 1998

When the serious 1998 surplus of pork became a reality, and contractors were selling to slaughter houses for thirty-three cents a pound with costs of production amounting to forty cents, Wendell Murphy became concerned not only for himself but for his eight hundred growers. Riding out a loss of seven cents a pound would present a challenge that would not be easily overcome. But he and his team would give the situation their best efforts.

River Landing

Early in 1997, Murphy Family Farms held an all-day open house for the public at its newly developed 1,500 acre gated golf community near Wallace, North Carolina, called River Landing.

It is hard to believe the beauty and grandeur of such a perfectly landscaped community with its streams, waterfalls, bridges, streets, green lawns, and championship eighteen-hole golf course designed by Clyde Johnston of Hilton Head, South Carolina.

When I once visited Hilton Head there was no part of its development as beautiful as River Landing. There was no bridge to compare with the beauty of the Old European style wrought iron and brick main bridge, a focal point in River Landing. A golf pro shop is in operation. A club house with dining facilities is planned. Harry (Pete) Murphy, one of the two brothers/owners in the Murphy Family Farms hog operations is in charge of this development. Several new and beautiful homes were already under construction during the open house. Life in River Landing is simple and as peaceful as the river it overlooks.

Residents who don't care for golf can walk to their favorite fishing hole, watch the sunset as they paddle a canoe on the Northeast Cape Fear River, or take time to watch birds or squirrels.

Later on, when all plans have been completed, they'll be able to lounge at the side of a sparkling pool or play tennis and cap off a perfect day with a delectable dinner at the planned club house.

Life at River Landing offers a great mix of solitude, recreation and enjoying relaxing in the great outdoors.

Headlines of the Hog Story (1995-1998)

During 1995-1998, as Duplin County marched steadily to become the number one hog producing county in the United States, the Murphy Family Farms reached number one status as the country's biggest hog grower, and Duplin County citizens appreciated what the hog industry brought to the local economy, a groundswell of protest over expansion arose which has led to great debate.

Radio and television airwaves have carried frequent commercials by hog producers portraying themselves as protectors of the environment.

Here are samples of headlines which have blazed across local and state newspapers and appeared in national magazines, such as *U. S. News And World Report* and *Forbes:*

Duplin Advances In Swine. Hogs Produce Twice As Much Waste As Humans

Hog Empires Grow Up In Small Towns

Pig Farming Has Gone High Tech, And That's Creating New Pollution Woes

Proposals Bar DEM Inspections Of Hog Farms

What's That Smell? It Ain't Roses, But Money

Serious Violations Found During Probe Of Onslow Hog-Waste Spill

Onslow Is Among "Badlands"

Violations Cited At Model Hog Operation

Critics Take Aim At Pork Industry Advertisements

Hog Heaven—And Hell

Hog Lagoon Spills Have Been Major Sources Of Pollution In 1995

No Winners In Board Of Health Decision On Hog Situation

Lawmakers Work To Change Law

Of Politics And Pigs

Inspections Find Improper Operations

Highlighting Hog Woes

Duplin County Commissioners Hold Evening Session-Hog Pollution, Other Issues Discussed

Foes Of Hog Farms Make Their Feelings Felt

Valentine Loses Hope On Key Hog Issues

Hog Industry Tones Down Anti-Regulation Rhetoric

Public Wants Action, Hunt Warns

Hunt Wants 2-Year Hold

Hunt Proposes Moratorium

People Bus To Raleigh To Share Concerns

Tougher Measure On Hogs Clears Key Hurdle In Senate

In A Pig's Eye—Duplin County State Senator, Charlie Albertson, Has Ignored Public Concern With A Maneuver Temporarily To Exempt The Many Hog Farms In His County From Inspections By Water Quality Regulators

Special Provisions Subvert Democracy

State Won't Exempt Duplin From Hog Rules

Strict Hog Measure Gets Final OK

Moratorium Unable To Halt Hogs—Before A Ban On New Hog Operations Takes Effect, North Carolina Officials Allow The Number Of Swine In The State To Hit 10 Million For The First Time (Waste Produced Will Be Equivalent To That Of 20 Million People)

Builders Big Losers In Moratorium

Group Sues Farm Affiliated With Murphy Family Farms

Heavy Rains Test Waste Lagoons

Hog Group May Be Political Committee, Legislator Says

Hunt Wants Hogs To Keep Their Distance

Hog Farmers Headed For Lean Times

County Plans To Use Health Rules To Control Hog Farms

Livestock Farmers Protest—Duplin County Commissioners Approve Inspection Fee Regulation

Duplin County Upholds Hog Farm Rules

Chrysthine

Watson To Seek Recount In Race

Hog Clock Is Ticking

Board Prepares For 1999 Lifting Of Moratorium

Hog Processor Criticizes State Regulator's Terms Of Sewage Permit

Election Reflects Past And Future—Hogs And Votes

Fund-Raisers, Hog Farmers Squealing At State Inquiry

Errant Witnesses Set Tone For Hog Hearing

Brubaker Denies Linking Hog Rules To Gifts

Brubaker Cleared Of Charges

Legacy Of A Hog Scandal—Hearing Raised Issues That Linger

Mystery Donations Revealed—Hog Farm Gifts Total $29,500 Unreported

Megafarms As Neighbors

Hog Farms' Rapid Growth Outstrips Government's Ability To Control Them

According To A Senate Study, A Single 50,000-Acre Hog Farm Being Built In Utah Could
    Produce More Sewage Than The City Of Los Angeles

Slaughterhouse Freeze—An Agreement To Limit The World's Largest Slaughterhouse To
    24,000 Hogs A Day Is A Victory For All Concerned About The Cape Fear River Region.
    It Could Help Control Long-Term Growth Of The Hog Industry

If Pork Industry Wins State House Race, Region Is Big Loser

Health Hazards Affecting The Animal Confinement Farm Worker

State Politics Wallows In Dirt—More To The Elephants Vs. Hogs Story Than What's Been Told

Experts, Residents Discuss Problem Of Hog Waste

Hopeful On Hogs—A Forum Focusing On Health And Environmental Problems Associated
    With Hog Waste Gives Hope That North Carolina Is Poised To Make Progress Towards
    Ensuring A More Benign Hog Industry

State Election Board Orders New Election For Rep. Watson; Likely To Be Sept. 15

Watson To Get Another Chance—The State Board Of Elections Invalidates The Primary Vote
    In Which The Republican Legislator Lost To A Challenger Backed By The Hog Industry

Rep. Watson To Be Commended

Research Cited As Lacking On Hog Waste

State Orders New Vote In Duplin Race—"My Concern Is, Given The Obvious Disregard For
    The Law That Has Occurred In Duplin County, How Can The Citizens Of Duplin County

Believe The Outcome Of The Election When Law So Basic Has Been Violated?" Said Larry Leake, Chairman Of The State Board Of Elections.

Manning Defeats Watson in Second Primary

Manning Loses to Russell Tucker

Duplin's Exceptional Cooperative Agriculture Extension Staff

When I was a child, the one county agricultural extension farm agent and the home extension agent made great impact on us as children in the school 4-H clubs and on our parents as advisors on farm practices.

The farm agent would go out into the field where Daddy was working and talk to him about fertilizers, seeds, and the cultivation of his crops with the one-row horse and mule plan.

The home agent visited our school once a month and gave 4-H demonstrations on such topics as sewing, caring for clothes, and cooking. It was at one of these lectures that I saw the home agent demonstrate how to make a fruit cobbler with an easy to remember recipe that I still use: One cup of self-rising flour is mixed with one cup of sugar. One cup of milk is added. Then one quart of any kind of berries or fruit is added and the cobbler is ready to bake.

Neither home economics nor agriculture classes had been added to our schools as part of the curriculum when we attended.

When I went to work for L. L. McLendon, farm agent, in December 1933, he had no assistant and there was only one home agent. There was no secretary.

In early 1959, when the fifty-page magazine describing how Duplin County had first reached the highest agriculture income in the state in 1958, there were five dedicated men and three enterprising women on the county extension staff.

The men were Vernon Reynolds, county agent, and Jim Bunce, Lawerence Reece, Ralph Sasser, and Bill Jasper. The women were Alta Kornegay, home agent, Jean Huie, and Annie Lois Britt.

Later, Annie Lois Britt became the first woman Duplin County farm extension agent and gave commendable leadership in our growing agricultural economy.

After 4-H clubs were removed from the public schools, Duplin County's extension agents continued to provide instruction to the community 4-H leaders and members resulting in great 4-H achievers.

In 1997, the county cooperative extension staff is headed by Ed Emory and Jo Ann Williams with a total of eight professional farm and home agents, four secretaries, and eight part-time technicians. The continually growing agricultural economy has placed great demands on the extension staff.

For example, in 1996, the staff was called to train all of the county animal confinement workers in the provisions of the new State Animal Waste Management law in a period of just two months.

The extension staff now has both a swine and a poultry specialist. A poultry and swine laboratory performs important functions in diagnosing diseases and giving advice.

Duplin County has always been fortunate in having exceptional qualified, energetic and interested extension personnel who inspire our farmers to progress.

Now the work of the cooperative extension staff has been expanded to touch the lives of our people in many areas in addition to farming.

Above: A typical field of tobacco ready to be harvested.

Left: One of hundreds of old flue cured tobacco barns which dot our countryside. They gave way to "bulk" curing barns and now to "box" curing barns.

Right: My neighbor, Anthony Smith, in front of his complex of thirty-two "Box" tobacco curing barns. He grows four hundred acres of the golden leaf using two year-round farm laborers and seventy migrant workers during harvesting season. No mechanical harvester is used. The migrant workers strip the leaves by hand from whole stalks, throw them into ventilated metal boxes pulled by a tractor. Filled boxes are placed directly into the "box" curing barns automatically heat controlled. Two large green houses produce his tobacco plants for field setting. Sheer hard work and attention to details are his trade marks.

Left: Modern farm home of Anthony and Sonya Smith, parents of three pre-school children. Sonya is a counselor at our James Sprunt Community College and keeps Anthony's farm books. One of her college duties has been to represent the college on our county Quality of Life Task Force.

Murphy Family Farms of Rose Hill, said to be the biggest swine producer in the United States.

Carrolls of Warsaw produces not only swine but turkeys.

Brown's of Carolina, of Warsaw, owned mostly by Smithfield Packing Company.

A modern pig nursery which produces 3,000 week-old pigs each week, amounting to 156,000 annually. It is as modern as hospital baby nurseries, even using ultra sound to determine if sows are pregnant.

An average modern 8-house swine complex for growing out swine to market weight. Each house accomodates 700 hogs for a total of 5,600 at all times.

Carolina Turkey Processing Plant—the largest in the world—in Duplin County near Mount Olive. It processes 75,000 to 80,000 every 24 hours, employs 2,100 people and ships to world markets.

THE RICHEST PEOPLE IN AMERICA

1997 Edition
$5.95 (Canada $6.95)
www.forbes.com

400 Forbes

Getting
rich
off
low tech

Motels

Bad debt

Garbage

Parking

This little piggy
went to market
and made
Wendell Murphy
a billion

Wendell Murphy, the first recognized Duplin County Billionaire, on the cover of the 1997 Edition of Forbes *Richest 400 People in America.*

My "Trip" to Georgetown University Family Center in Washington, D.C. by Way of a Thirty-Minute Video

In June of 1997, Mary Catherine Bass from Magnolia, a clinical social worker, who had been interviewing some of the cancer patient families in our neighborhood in an effort to try to help us understand more about the unusually high numbers of cancer deaths in our area, asked me to do a thirty-minute video with her.

Mary Catherine completed her postgraduate work at Georgetown University Family Center and belonged to a research group there which had asked her to present a program on her work in studying diseases in agricultural areas.

Since this is a subject of great interest to me and since I had been working with our Duplin County Partners for Health in studying our high number of deaths from cancer, diabetes, stroke, and heart disease, I was happy to oblige.

The audience for this video to be shown at the Family Center would be a research group made up of family therapists of high educational levels and professional expertise from all over the country. These people largely have no comprehension of what it is like to live in an agricultural area and see the struggles of those who work so hard to provide people nationwide with an adequate food supply, nor do they have any knowledge of the agricultural practices which create health problems. Most of the audience had absolutely no knowledge at all of farming or what goes into food production.

The reason Mary Catherine asked me to help with the video is that I was almost eighty-two at the time and still very active in many endeavors in spite of the reality that I came from a family plagued by cancer and high blood pressure. Too, I live in a part of our county where I seem to be the third oldest survivor. One of the two older than I lives in a nursing home. The other one is not very active.

During the taping of the video, she asked me questions about my decisions as a teenager to eat a diet heavy in fruits and vegetables, to exercise daily, to enjoy humor and laughter, to do for others with no expectation of payback, and to believe in a power greater than myself.

We talked about how these decisions validate what is now considered "new" in science and medicine—the mind, body, spirit, and attitude connection to one's health.

The research being conducted at the Georgetown Family Center is particularly interested in studying how one's habits, beliefs, and attitudes affect one's health. These are things which have long been obvious to individuals, but modern science and medicine are just now beginning to officially recognize their effects on the health and activities of individuals.

It was encouraging to learn from Mary Catherine that the Director of the Family Center, Dr. Michael Kerr, was impressed with our thirty minute chat.

In the video, Mary Catherine and I talked about how the population in the agricultural areas is changing right along with the environmental changes. We talked about how finding ways to adapt to both environmental and population changes are important and necessary to healthy living.

It was gratifying that the Georgetown University Family Center audience was complimentary and appreciated our video on health problems in our changing agricultural environment and changing population.

Helping Eat Four Hundred Pounds of Collards

Retirement nine years ago brought more opportunities to enjoy "collard day" at the Wagon Wheel Restaurant in Beulaville, eleven miles away.

On the last Wednesday I participated in this southern delicacy of collards and backbone, there were six senior citizens at the next table who had journeyed eighty miles from Bethel to enjoy "collard day."

People from Raleigh, Wilmington, and Jacksonville drive to this three stop-light town on Wednesdays to enjoy a "collard heaven" outing.

The hard work in preparing four hundred pounds of the southern treasure begins on Tuesday when Bo Carpenter, owner, has some ladies come in and check each collard leaf for bugs and worms and wash them through six or seven cold washes.

Bo's seventy-four-year-old mother-in-law, Zannie Atkinson, and two other ladies come in around 10:30 every Tuesday night and stay until around 8:00 on Wednesday morning, cooking the collards in eight barrel-sized pots.

Visiting the Wagon Wheel Restaurant on Wednesday anytime between 11 A.M. and 8 P.M. gives one a good opportunity to not only enjoy collards and backbone on the regular five dollar luncheon buffet, but it's a good place to see friends and acquaintances and faraway collard lovers.

Tuesday was "collard day" from 1968 when Zannie Atkinson and her husband opened up the restaurant until 30 November 1997, when Bo Carpenter, present owner, decided to close the restaurant on Mondays and Tuesdays and have "collard day" on Wednesdays.

The Mount Olive Senior Birthday Club

Many years ago, my sister and her husband and several other couples from the Mount Olive Baptist Church, formed what they called a Neighborhood Club. They went out on some Friday nights to eat and sometimes met in the homes for Christmas parties. I soon became a regular part of this club.

As members of the group became older, the club evolved into what they call the Birthday Club, going to the Southern Belle Restaurant to eat on the Friday might nearest a member's birthday with each person paying for their meal ordered from the menu, for around four dollars.

Only one of the original couples is now man and wife, because the other men have died. But a new couple has joined and it's just great to have two men now.

The restaurant owner, Gaynelle Brock, allows us to bring in our own birthday cakes with accompanying small paper plates.

Sister Alma makes our reservations at the Southern Belle and calls by phone to remind everyone. Being a member of this club for a long number of years has been a real treat. I get to have a nice visit on many Friday afternoons and nights with Alma and enjoy her delightful friends.

Most of the Birthday Club members are from the First Baptist Church JOY Club, Just Older Youth.

Upon arrival, each member presents a birthday card to the honoree. The card is sometimes comical, sometimes sentimental, sometimes handwritten, sometimes purchased especially for the celebrant, and sometimes from a box of cards—ten for one dollar—with a personal note added.

After we dine, funny stories are shared. The stories are sometimes about the honoree, but most always about "old people" doing "dumb things."

All of us look forward to the fun and fellowship and the internal jogging we get in laughing with this group of lively seniors. Each birthday party reminds us how fortunate it is have reached another milestone.

Each party helps us to muster our resources and head for another birthday among friends who seem like loving members of our extended family.

Age Eighty-Two—A Very Good Time to Start Playing Golf

All of my life I have never sat still for very long at a time. There always seemed to be a reason to get up and move often.

But in March 1997, when I started writing this book in long hand checking and verifying data and had to stay ahead of Beatrice Sheppard's typing of my scribbling with corrections and revisions, I had to stay put for hours at a time or I would have no typing for her to do.

Beatrice was seventy-eight years old and would be transferring from her community college to East Carolina University at Greenville on 17 August as a junior. I needed to have a good portion of the first draft finished before she left. I would then be responsible to write and type the remaining parts of the book in addition to editing and retyping parts of the entire book.

While I had continued my early morning exercise routine, my remaining hours since March had been spent sitting. And by the first of August, I was getting stiff!

My salvation came when suddenly Alta Kornegay and Doris Chestnutt, two Garden Club friends, asked me to join them in free golf lessons being taught at James Sprunt Community College to senior citizens. They needed another golf student! And taking golf was just what I needed!

For two semesters, we played with the supervision of an excellent coach and I practiced on my lawn in between by hitting balls into a pine tree area and then retrieving them.

Every aspect of playing golf proved to be perfect breaks from searching and verifying data, interviewing people, taking pictures, identifying and mounting them typing, editing, and retyping portions of manuscripts.

The fifty-nine-year-old coach was patient with old ladies who were tackling a new game. Two twenty-year-old community college students joined the class for the second semester. They treated us as gently as if we were their grandmothers.

The well kept fairways make walking a joy. The greens around each of the eighteen holes were like fresh cut velvet cloth. So perfect are they that its hard to step off them and start toward the next tee.

As summer came on, we found that eight o'clock in the mornings once a week proved to be the perfect time to continue this game that had so filled a need for more exercise and a need to enjoy the great outdoors in the freshest time of the day when the birds and squirrels are most active and the dew is still on the grass, and everything seems right in a world of perfect nature.

We will be able to adjust our playing times according to the seasons to get the most out of this seemingly perfect game that provides so much fellowship and fresh air along with exercise and a little skill development.

Pink Hill, North Carolina—Looking at the Past and Present

Since 1938, except for the World War II years in Wilmington, my home has been two miles west of the 650 population town of Pink Hill, on N.C. Highway 11 toward Kenansville.

Through the years, when it has been necessary to wear a name tag at meetings or conventions and show Pink Hill as my mailing address, or whenever I had to fill out papers showing my address as Pink Hill, people stare and ask: "Where is Pink Hill?"

It is hard to understand how so much curiosity and conversation is evoked by the name "Pink Hill." My usual reply is: "It's in eastern North Carolina, between Rose Hill and Snow Hill."

Then, if stares get more pronounced, I explain: "It is a wonderful little town of 650 people, located in a vast farming area between Kinston, Camp Lejeune Marine Corps Base, Wilmington, Fort Bragg Army Base, and Seymour Johnson Air Force Base at Goldsboro." I usually add, "I don't really live in town. I live two miles west of Pink Hill toward Kenansville, in the suburbs."

By this time they have usually decided they've known someone stationed at one of the named military bases or they've had some connection with one of our North Carolina beaches or coastal areas.

The name "Pink Hill" just seems to fascinate strangers. It also fascinates people who have ever lived in the area, because it is a most unusual community in the richest agricultural section in our state.

Pink Hill is on the line between Duplin and Lenoir counties. All of Pink Hill is in Lenoir County, except three houses and two mobile homes which straddle the line separating the counties.

The town was named for the patches of "pinks," flowers that once grew in abundance in the area, especially at a nearby plantation named "Pink Hill." The original post office which first served the little village of Pink Hill in 1847, was not actually in the same location as Pink Hill is today.

In 1900, during the heyday of the cutting of the longleaf pines which made this area famous, a railroad was put in from Kinston to Pink Hill and the town of Pink Hill was moved to its present location to be near the railroad tracks.

In 1918, the railroad was extended sixteen miles to Chinquapin, mainly to haul the longleaf pine logs and lumbering products through Beulaville and Pink Hill and on to Kinston.

This was the time when the network of small railroad lines was installed in the Chinquapin area to accommodate the great number of sawmills and turpentine stills which had sprung up. This was the railroad on which my parents, my baby brother and I rode in 1921 from Chinquapin to Kinston to have my tonsils and adenoids removed at Parrott's Hospital, while my older brother and my sister stayed with neighbors.

Prior to the extension of the railroad to Chinquapin, the logs and other lumber products cut in that area had to be hauled fifteen to twenty miles from the forests in the Chinquapin vicinity to Magnolia, which had been the shipping center of lumber products since the Wilmington to Weldon railroad was built through Magnolia in 1840.

By 1929, the cutting of longleaf pines had diminished and logging could be accommodated by the new roads and motor trucks. So, the railroad tracks from Kinston through Pink Hill and Beulaville to Chinquapin were removed.

Pink Hill has always been known for two main attributes: Its hospitality which flows like a river through the town and its people and the great amount of business going on in the town.

The town has a most unusual, longtime Business and Professional Club, acting as a volunteer Chamber of Commerce. This club has promoted such projects as telephone, electric, water and sewer services, better streets, an annual town Christmas parade, and a Boys and Girls Club.

This Business and Professional Club hosts an annual Appreciation and Awards dinner for the volunteer fire and rescue units. Tickets to this dinner are $12.50 and are sold by the club members to the community residents. The profits are divided between the fire and rescue departments. It is a heartwarming sight to see our business and professional men and women cooking and entertaining these public servants who are always on call and serve fire and rescue emergencies so unselfishly.

Participating in the membership and activities of this club was one of my retirement goals, which has proven enjoyable and rewarding.

Visitors to Pink Hill can enjoy browsing in a museum owned by Wilbur Tyndall, retired John Deere dealer. The museum displays a collection of thirty John Deere tractors and generations of farm memorabilia dating back to 1929.

An Unusual Trait for a Small Town

In addition to the traditional attributes of the hospitality of its people, and the great amount of business going on in Pink Hill, another most unusual and admirable trait is regularly displayed which is not always present in small towns.

There is a prevailing attitude of welcome, pride, and joy at seeing people come to Pink Hill and become successful in business. There are many, many outstanding examples of how this open minded trait has worked well for new enterprises and the town.

Teachey's Supermarket—An Up from the Ground Story

Teachey's Supermarket has been a most interesting example of the business opportunities in Pink Hill.

Remus and Gaynelle Teachey grew up attending the rural B. F. Grady School in Duplin County, not far from Pink Hill. Remus worked at different times in the grocery departments of both big Pink Hill general stores which served Pink Hill for a long number of years. These merchants sold most everything needed by townspeople, area farmers, and other citizens. They sold not only groceries, but dry goods, hardware and appliances. One of these general store merchants also owned the Allis Chalmers farm equipment dealership, and the other owned a Ford automobile dealership. Both stores and their dealerships closed a few years ago.

Remus had learned the grocery business while working at the general stores and learned it well. For several years now he has owned a thriving grocery supermarket in Pink Hill, where quality and good prices prevail amid well-stocked shelves and modern display equipment. He also owns a supermarket in nearby Deep Run.

Gaynelle took a business course and went to work at the local bank where she served thirty-eight years. Since her retirement from the bank, she is seen daily in the grocery supermarket, being Remus' helpmate, working in the office, assisting customers when needed, preparing bank deposits, and allowing the customers to enjoy her friendliness and charm.

These are two people who have never changed as their hard work and ingenuity have changed their fortunes. Remus does such civic minded gestures as supply some four hundred ribeye steaks for the annual Fire and Rescue Appreciation dinners, donate computers for the Pink Hill and B. F. Grady Elementary Schools, support Hospice, the Boys and Girls Clubs, Boy Scout projects sponsored by the Business and Professional Club and all other good causes.

The most unusual attribute of this couple is that they can often be seen chatting in their friendly, unassuming manner with their customers at the supermarket. Customers appear to regard them as old friends.

There is another first-class grocery supermarket in Pink Hill, owned by a Kenansville man who also owns supermarkets in Kenansville and Beulaville. He and his wife work at Kenansville and he makes visits to Pink Hill and Beulaville. He inherited his Kenansville market from his parents, who were my close, lifelong friends.

A Far-Reaching Furniture Store

Since 1976, both the outside and inside of Jones Furniture Store in Pink Hill has been a great source of pride to local residents and all of eastern North Carolina. Customers regularly come from a one hundred mile radius. The half-block long, snow white building with its bright purple awnings catches the eye, whether being seen in passing on the street or in the store's frequent television ads on Greenville's Channel 9.

Inside are friendly, down-to-earth Cletus and Jo Ann Jones. They live in rural Duplin County. Jo Ann took a beauty culture course, but soon abandoned the beauty shop to join Cletus in the booming furniture business after he had closed his barber shop and gone into the retail furniture business. Later, their only child, Wendy, and her husband, Chris Turner, joined the Jones furniture venture.

The rambling areas of the store are filled with beautiful and practical displays of good quality, attractive living room, den, bedroom, and dining room furniture.

The Joneses advertise that they keep in stock one hundred Lazy Boy chairs and eighty eight-way, hand-tied sofas. They are quick to tell customers they sell only furniture that will hold up and hold up their furniture does!

Their most far-reaching sale was to a local bride who bought a considerable amount of furniture from Cletus and Jo Ann, to be shipped by the U. S. Army to Germany where she was joining her husband at his military post.

The way the Joneses use their honest "straight shooting" in everyday life is illustrated by the only time Cletus served on a Duplin County jury. He came by my office in the courthouse when the trial had ended and related his shock and dismay. The jury's inclination was to give a squatter six acres of Bill and Ruby Carlton's land which the squatter had fenced in and was using as his own along with his small parcel of land adjoining the Carlton's. There was no question about the Carlton's or the squatter's property lines.

When the jury retired for their deliberations, a consensus began to emerge among the jurors: The Carltons were big, well-to-do absentee landlords and the poor little farmer had only a small plot and needed the six acres of the Carlton's land.

It took the "straight shooting" and honesty of Cletus to help the jurors understand that "big" and "little" had nothing to do with what was "right" and "wrong."

The jurors returned a verdict in favor of the Carltons.

Bill and Ruby were old friends of our family. They spent time during their "courting days" swimming with us at the nearby Cooper's Mill Pond. Bill owned a big farm at Warsaw where, after marriage, they operated a country store. Upon retiring, they moved to Hollywood, Florida.

The Town Library

About a decade ago, when the town's small public library needed expanding, Mr. and Mrs. T. J. Turner and T. J.'s brother, Graham, donated a large house in the center of town, across the street from the bank. The new library was named for the Turners' mother, Etta Jones Turner.

The library is consistently the one most bustling place in Pink Hill. It is a computerized branch of the Neuse Regional Library and can secure books and other library materials from the central library in Kinston.

The importance of the Pink Hill Public Library and its impact on the children is so vividly portrayed in the story of Lee Heath when he was a third grade student at the Pink Hill Elementary School.

Lee's teacher assigned the students to write a paper: The Most Famous Person Who Ever Lived Around Pink Hill.

Lee wrote his paper on Mrs. Sabra Waller and Mrs. Jeraldine Hill, who have served at the Pink Hill Library since it was moved to its present quarters. These two ladies are famous not only to Lee, but to the hundreds of boys and girls, men and women, who frequent the library. Mrs. Waller and Mrs. Hill are thoroughly familiar with every bit of knowledge available in the Pink Hill Library and its associated resources, regardless of the medium. They are famous for being genuinely helpful to patrons of every kind and description who frequent the facility in their pursuit of knowledge.

To be considered famous by anyone is an achievement, but to be labeled famous by a sincere child in the search of knowledge must be among the highest of all achievements.

A Couple Who Believes Laughter is the Best Medicine

If you hear a couple of senior citizens coming down a hall giggling like a couple of little schoolchildren, it just might be Julia and Aubrey Turner. They can nearly split your sides telling about such simple incidents as being ready to depart from the Kinston airport and not remembering whether they left their electric coffee pot on or not.

He is a retired businessman and she was a schoolteacher. They make jaunts to country music shows and other entertainment events whether they're in Branson, Missouri, Myrtle Beach, South Carolina, or in Kinston or Kenansville. They see fun and laughter in most daily aspects of living.

I once read that when we progress to the point where we can't laugh, especially at ourselves, it's time to go on. At the rate Julia and Aubrey live and laugh, I just don't ever expect them to go on. They won't find time between laughs.

Town Government

In 1998, the town of Pink Hill is still known for its longtime sound, conservative, and efficient government by an elected mayor and three commissioners.

Handsome young Leslie Turner, an assistant district attorney was elected mayor in 1997. James Thomas, Nerey Wall, and Anthony Mitchell complete the team. The town council gave a city tax reduction for 1997.

Carol Sykes has served as Town Clerk-Administrator and Finance Officer for twenty-five years. Her duties have ranged from handling the town's public relations, to dealing with slow tax, water and sewer payers, to chasing stray cows out of citizens' gardens.

Pink Hill

Carol Sykes, town clerk, stands in front of Pink Hill Town Hall and EMS building on a hot "Dress Down Day."

Mrs. Geraldine Hill and Mrs. Sabra Waller, librarians, with Lee Heath, a high school student. When Lee was a Pink Hill third-grader, he was assigned to write a paper on "The most famous person who ever lived in the Pink Hill area." He wrote on "Mrs. Hill and Mrs. Waller." Lee knew where the most action was and he gave them credit.

Pink Hill

Gaynelle and Remus Teachey in front of their busy supermarket.

Jo Anne Jones and daughter, Wendy Turner, in front of the far-reaching Jones Furniture Store. Their husbands are delivering furniture.

A Little Journey Through Some Duplin County Towns

Beulaville

The famous Wagon Wheel Restaurant in Beulaville where 400 pounds of southern collards are served every Wednesday, year round. Diners can have a choice of fresh pork backbone or sugar-cured ham with their collards and a choice of many other vegetables and desserts from the $5.00 buffet. Newspaper reporters from as far away as Charlotte, N.C. and the Associated Press have visited and published articles on this unusual phenomenon. The publicity forces regular diners to go earlier.

Beulaville

1873 Post Office—The records of the Post Office Department in the National Archives show that the post office in Beulaville, Duplin County, North Carolina, was established on 13 May 1873 as Snatchette, with Calvin Thomas appointed as postmaster on that date. Its name was changed to Beulaville on 23 March 1874. Calvin Thomas was still postmaster at that time. Some of the later postmasters have been Ada Williams, John George Kennedy, Earl Gresham, Tommy F. Bostic, David Stevens and the 1997 postmaster, Muriel Culbreth.

New, modern Post Office Building erected in 1997. (Pictures and data supplied by Sarah Bolin).

Faison

The old Faison Train Depot. It is now a beautiful and much used town library and museum.

Left: Cates Pickles of Faison was established in Duplin County in 1929. Cates has 270 full-time, year-round employees. They also employ 250 seasonal workers when their 800 acres of Duplin County contracted cucumbers and peppers and 5,000 acres contracted in five other east coast states are harvested.

Right: Magnolia Hall at Faison was built in 1853 by Isham Faison. It was later owned by a Williams family. During the Civil War, it served as the secretarial headquarters for the Federal Army.

1998

A Glimpse into the

Town of Magnolia

A 1998 glimpse into the town of Magnolia would let a visitor see that the people of that town have always had great community spirit and pride. They have worked hard and together to try to overcome low wages for work in agriculture, with only a small measure of success. They have worked against many other odds to help their town remain a lovely and functional place to live.

When their high school grades were combined with James Kenan High School seven miles away, near Warsaw, the middle school students were sent seven miles in another direction, to the E. E. Smith School in Kenansville. Their elementary classes were carried to a new Rose Hill-Magnolia School four miles away in still a different direction. The people of Magnolia felt they had lost the heart and soul of their community when they lost their school.

In spite of the losses of much of their population and their school, Magnolia remains a delightful little town.

When the last population count was made in 1994, the non-white population was forty-seven percent of the 747 residents. It is estimated that the 1998 population is close to eight hundred, with the non-white percentage remaining at forty-seven percent.

A modern town hall serves as the center of town activities. It is staffed by a town clerk and a policeman. The town enjoys a brick community building with a kitchen.

Volunteer fire and rescue units, using modern equipment, are housed in upscale brick buildings and serve the Magnolia area

Two town recreation programs operate part-time.

Water, sewer, and garbage services are modern and efficient.

I recently gave a program at one of the meetings of the integrated town garden club which works on beautification projects for the streets and the highway entrances.

A library, located in an old store building on Railroad Street is staffed with volunteer assistants.

The people of Magnolia have always been a religious people. There are several churches where the residents get strength and spiritual inspiration.

The continuing burgeoning poultry and swine industries provide badly needed jobs, though most laborers still realize little in the way of job security or benefits.

Since Dr. Corbett Quinn retired and his associate moved his practice to Beulaville, Magnolia residents lack medical services and must seek care in Kenansville, Rose Hill, or Warsaw.

The following article copied by permission from a June 1997 issue of *The Wallace Enterprise* newspaper, clearly portrays the 1997 prevailing spirit of the people in the town of Magnolia:

Organized and Ready to Go . . . Magnolia Children Work to Make a Difference in the Community

The children of Magnolia worked hard in the heat on Monday cleaning up a yard that had been neglected since Sedell Crawford, owner of the house, passed away.

These children are members of the 4-H and were on their way to a meeting when they passed by the yard and noticed that it had become overgrown since the former occupants of the house had passed away. "Mrs. Crawford used to keep her yard neat and clean," one of the youngsters commented. The others chimed agreement.

Magnolia Police Chief L. S. McLean was on a call on the same street and said, "The girls stopped and asked if they could clean up the yard." Chief McLean also added, "The neighbors had been complaining about the yard being grown up."

When these children began cleaning the yard a little after noon, other children came to help.

Chief McLean said, "This builds character." McLean also stated, "Stopping crime begins with the younger generation."

These young people worked hard throughout the day and even had a little help from their congenial Chief of Police. They did their best to get the yard back in the shape that Crawford had it before her death.

"The house will not be vacant much longer," Chief McLean said. "Someone plans to be moving into the house soon."

Children who helped throughout the day were Jermila Sloan, age 6; Harry Sloan, age 14; Sharon Sloan, age 12; Davon Sloan, age 12; Kristy Sloan, age 11; Melissa Edwards, age 11; Megan Edwards, age 7 and Marquite Edwards, age 13.

These children said that they have nothing else to do and the would be happy to clean up anyone's yard.

A Good Place to Retire

In 1997, Reverend John Andrews and his wife, Nancy, retired after serving the Magnolia United Methodist Church. After evaluating what they were looking for in a retirement home, they settled in Magnolia.

Reverend J. B. Helms, a former Magnolia United Methodist minister, and his wife, had already made Magnolia their retirement home.

The railroad still runs through Magnolia's two-block main street in 1998.

Magnolia's library is staffed by volunteers.

Right: A private school in the 1800s. This building was moved to the center of town and served as the elegant home of wealthy John Croom.

Rose Hill

The famous "World's Largest Frying Pan" is displayed on the town square. It was created for use during the annual Poultry Jubilee which attracts great crowds.

Edd Dudley Monk, who was one hundred years old in 1998, with his sister, Etlar Mainor, with whom he lives. Their family and mine worked together in tobacco and cotton from 1922 to 1932 and we have remained the closest of friends. Etlar taught me to loop tobacco fast and to pick one hundred pounds of cotton a day.

Wallace

The Wallace U. S. Post Office.

The Wallace Thelma Dingus Bryant Library, the center of Wallace activity and culture.

The entrance to the new and beautiful gated community of River Landing, near Wallace, developed and owned by Murphy Family Farms.

Wallace

Stunning mural painted on the tall Cavenaugh Building in Wallace in 1997 by resident artist, Theresa Brooks Elias.

Warsaw

A 1997 view of one of the two blocks of Warsaw's Railroad Street where the young people socialized on Saturday afternoon during the depression. I worked in Fred Maroon's dress shop during my high school years and daddy sold pork barbecue on Saturdays on the street.

Warsaw

The Bowden Hotel on Railroad Street across from the town's two blocks of stores. It was the hub of activity during the great railroad days. Empty for years, it is now used for Mexican housing.

The L. P. Best house in Warsaw has been restored to all its 1884 glory, now a veteran's museum. When we moved to the Hines farm in 1922 the annual veteran's parades had already started and we went in our buggy. I have missed very few since. Every one makes me glad to be an American. Warsaw has become famous throughout the U. S. as having honored its veterans with a parade longer than any other town.

Warsaw

The monument in the Veterans' Square on main street is a constant reminder that Warsaw honors its Veterans.

This building was the Kenansville Post Office during my elementary school days where I saw the signs about "When Jesus Comes." Attorney Robert L. West moved it seven miles to Warsaw in 1972 where it has served as his law office.

A marker two miles west of Warsaw on Highway 24 adjacent to the office of Carroll's Food.

My Feelings Now and My Look to the Future with Expectations

Now, in my eighty-third year, I am grateful for having been allowed to outlive every known active family member of both sides of my short-lived Whaley and Thomas ancestors and contemporaries.

I am especially grateful that life is still full, rewarding and exciting.

I am truly glad that after eight years of prodding by my son, Melvin, I have finally taken time to examine scrapbooks, notes, and manuscripts and do the needed research to use two dozen free-flowing Pentel rolling writer pens to sling out stories about my family and events which shaped my life through good times and bad as a sharecropper's daughter in Duplin County, North Carolina.

I am grateful for my friend, seventy-eight-year-old, widowed, Beatrice Lillico Sheppard, who completed two years of study at Craven Community College by February 1997 and transferred to East Carolina University as a full-time Junior 20 August of 1997.

She spent a good part of every week for six months with me, to type pages as I finished writing them. Without Beatrice, I could not have completed this book, because of a problem caused by repetitive motion to my right wrist in the long clean-up after Hurricane Fran last fall. Without our laughter and our enjoyable banter for much of six months, the book couldn't have become a reality.

The Debts I Owe as I Face the Future

The people who have loved me and people I have loved have been constant reminders of how much I owe to so many people.

When we bought our first television I saw a ninety-three-year-old woman being interviewed, who was asked: "What do you do for a good time?" Her answer: "Oh, I run errands for the old people in my neighborhood."

That's when I set my goal to try to live to a ripe old age and run errands for old people and others.

Most of my life has been made up of memories of people helping me. So I feel that I owe so much to so many people and to people in general. There is no way I can ever repay even the interest on what I owe people for the help I have received.

I have lived to learn that we cannot sometimes prevent tragedies that happen to us, but the way we react to what does happen seems to determine our own happiness and the quality of our time on this earth.

Some of us are given the opportunity to be here a long time and for this we owe much service. As I get older, I realize that the most rewarding work we can do is to give of ourselves and our means to others where we don't expect anything in return. The more we give, the more joy we awaken to each new day!

Some Lessons I Have Learned from Other People

I can never enumerate the many people who have taught me lessons which affected my life. But here are just a few. If your name is not mentioned, please know I am thankful for any you may have taught me.

From Mother, who was a pillar of strength, though she lived with poor health every day, I learned to keep faith and hope when it seemed the world was crumbling around me. I went twenty-five years being afraid to admit my marriage wasn't working, afraid it would affect my ability to earn a living. She was my anchor, though she had been responsible for my not marrying Ivey.

From Daddy I learned to be diligent and meticulous in every task, to be honest and to take pride in producing good results of my labor. After I lost brother Rdell in 1935, then Daddy in 1948, and Mother in 1968, of all people I have been most fortunate to have had brother Milton until 1995 and to still have sister Alma and sons, Melvin and Glenn. All of them enriched my life.

Betty Whaley Thornton has taught me how great it is to have a niece, a niece who has always been like the daughter I never had.

Then, there is my only living nephew, Senol Whaley, serving in our Army and still loving his Turkish family as well as his American relatives.

Josephine McKee, Alma's twice-widowed daughter-in-law, has taught me that it is possible to keep on spreading love and cheer when cancer has taken two husbands and one of your eyes and you're without children.

From Dr. Norman Vincent Peale, I studied the power of positive thinking from the day he published his first book on the subject. Then I read every subsequent book he wrote and subscribed to all of his publications. The Kinston Jaycees sponsored his appearance at the Barbecue Lodge when there was a snow on the ground, but the snow did not deter me from going. I am an eternal student of spiritual books about positive thinking and taking control of your life.

From my friend, Dr. Donn Wells, I learned the value of a daily routine of non-strenuous exercises. He taught me that if we can't change the pain we must live with, we can keep all the other parts of our body strong and working by regular exercise.

From Garland Carr, my lifelong friend, I learned that tragedy can become a source of strength. When she stopped receiving letters from her husband after the Normandy invasion in World War II, she took her baby and spent a week with us in Wilmington. The day after she went home, she received the tragic news. Then she and her mother were in an automobile accident that took her mother and left her injured. Through the years, I am never with her that I don't feel that I am a better person for having been in her company.

As to my good friend, Louise Wells, I watched her living to ninety-four gracefully and loving every person on her horizon. She taught me to be a good traveler, whether on a one-day cruise from Ft. Lauderdale to the Bahamas or a seventeen-day trip to China. She said she felt rewarded for teaching the ten commandments to her fifth grades even when the children were repeating in unison one day: "Honor thy father and thy mother that thy days may be long upon the land which the Lord thy God giveth thee" and one little boy stood up in the back of the room and said, "Miss Wells, Miss Wells, He ain't give us no land yet." But she lived to see this boy get a good education and get some land with a fine home and a swimming pool.

I have learned from studying many people that holding on to anger, resentment, and hurt takes up room in your heart and does not leave enough space for love. Forgiveness turns you back to laughter and joy in living. I have learned to feel sorry for people who cannot forgive. But, most of all, I feel sorry for people who have an inferiority complex which drives them to tell themselves that the way to building themselves up is to tear someone else down. This habit of tearing others down seems to be much harder to break than to quit alcohol, drugs, gambling, adultery, or any other undesirable habit. They seem to live on the "high" they create for themselves by spreading malicious gossip in an effort to hurt others and they become addicted to the point they must have someone to tear down. If they are asked to stop, they retaliate and pretend to be crucified. They have failed to find joy in spreading love. I have watched these people in their last days and they never seem to live happy sunsets. And if the sunset is the most beautiful part of each day—then I am trying to make the sunset of my life the most wondrous part of my life by forgiving and letting go and feeling sorry for those people who have not found the joy of reflecting happiness.

From my dear friend, Sarah Bolin, I have learned there is more to life than being a smart business woman—there is going with a friend before Thanksgiving to purchase poinsettias for shut-ins so they will have a full month to enjoy them before Christmas. There is going together to run-up turnip fields to buy bushels of turnip greens to share with shut-ins and friends and to freeze for a year's supply. There is sharing cucumbers, sweet potatoes, and any other vegetables you happen to acquire. There is driving each other for eye appointments. There is sitting silently together in waiting rooms during tedious surgery of family members when you don't want to talk. And traveling together on short trips and on longer trips to Florida or Alaska. There is sharing confidences, knowing they are "locked in." There is the side-splitting laughter that comes from driving up to a Hardee's pickup window and telling the attendant you forgot to ask for the senior discount when you placed your order and having the attendant say, "You didn't have to tell me. I could tell at the loudspeaker you were two old women who couldn't make up your minds what you wanted."

From my friend, Ruth Spell Herring, I learned the meaning of having a close friend for more than sixty years—to date together, to work together through two careers, to swap Sunday dinners every third Sunday while your children were growing up and to learn the sadness of seeing her health fail and see her fade away.

Narcie Turner taught me the joy of having a friend to share memories of our growing-up years, knowing mutual Warsaw friends and acquaintances, and the fun of revisiting childhood landmarks!

Dovie Penney taught me how to see all of Walt Disney's Epcot in one day and how to have fun traveling. She taught me how to find laughter in politics. But she also taught me that cancer cells can grow in healthy looking persons as well as in puny looking ones.

Tom Yates, personnel director of a big corporation, L. S. Guy, our county superintendent of schools, and Grey Morgan, a bank president taught me that in spite of pressures connected with one's position, it is possible to always be very human and take time to converse with old friends.

Hattie Lee Turner taught me that even if you know where the next meal is coming from, that's no excuse not to keep a weed from growing in your vegetable garden and freeze or can every single surplus vegetable you have except the ones you give to neighbors. She taught me that to outlive your parents' ages you must work every hour, keeping your body in shape, that you must love all people and always be there to cook delectable meals, not only for your own family, but for every neighborhood family going through sickness or bereavement.

Ruth Wallace taught me there are younger friends who can be trusted with your inmost thoughts and friends who never change though times and circumstances change.

Ethel Edwards, my longtime friend, taught me that though your husband delivered your many babies and could give you only aspirin and a Pepsi Cola to bring you comfort, and though he didn't get their birth certificates recorded, there will always be someone to help you file their certificates when the children really need them. So, it's right to love your husband when he does the best he can.

She also taught me that if your husband is on his death bed and you learn Social Security has found a flaw in your marriage, you can put him in the back seat of your car and take him to the register of deeds who will issue a valid license and get a Justice of the Peace to perform a legal ceremony and sign the license as a witness so you can draw Social Security. So, don't despair.

My longtime friend, Ellen Huddler, taught me how refreshing it could be on busy days to have her sweet smiling face come in almost covered by her homemade gingham bonnet with the top of her dress usually held together by a big safety pin instead of having wasted time in sewing on buttons and making button holes. Her long skirt always contained five yards of gingham and it took three to make her gathered tie apron which she proudly wore at all times. She would come in to share little visits as long as she lived and always took me back to the early American days of "sweet little old ladies" who brought nothing but joy to all the lives they touched.

Lynwood Turner taught me to always "look at the meat of a coconut before making a decision on the outside only." His wife, Grace, taught me that there are still people who never think too highly of themselves, but they are the "salt of the earth." They never seem to get really excited over circumstances and events, but they are thrifty and wise and true friends.

Evelyn and T. J. Turner taught me that there are still sweethearts forever and that life together can get more lovely after the first fifty years.

Young Alice Smith Scott has taught me many lessons. Among them, she has taught me how meaningful friendships between young and old people can be and how much old people can benefit from these friendships, even when the old person is slow at learning bridge!

Belle Stroud taught me it is impossible to figure out a bridge problem and carry on a conversation about another subject at the same time.

Alda Duff Kennedy and her husband, Cleo, have taught me how great it is to have one active, wonderful first cousin left in your old age.

Marsha Brewer and Marie Hill taught me there is virtue in listening with a loving, sympathetic ear to frustrated persons and realizing they need nurturing, too.

Edd Dudley Monk and his sister, Etlar Monk Mainor, taught me that friendships formed doing tedious chores in harvesting tobacco during the Great Depression last forever, even when you're one hundred years old.

Geraldine Aldridge Tucker taught me that consistency in all things is the bedrock of a good life.

Adelaide and Milton Rice, who moved from New Jersey twenty years ago, in 1977, taught me it is possible to move to a new location at mature ages, find true friends, get involved in such efforts as Friends of the County Library, a garden club, raising horses and enjoying a new life on thirteen acres of a portion of North Carolina, which has been called "the goodliest land under the Cope of Heaven."

My longtime friend, Sammie Williams Carter, taught me there are no handicaps that can keep one from enjoying a family, a child, a grandchild, and a good life of great service as editor of three local newspapers, while smiling through it all.

Jo Cameron Jones taught me how to find love and laughter in spite of circumstances. For years she inspired her high school English students to achieve beyond their beliefs in themselves. Now she enjoys her family and still serves her area with her newspaper abilities. She remains a good person with whom to laugh and cry.

Duplin County's Wendell Murphy, who is reputed to be the world's biggest swine grower, has shown me and many others that it is possible to be effective, successful, rich and famous, and never lose touch with the people, always having an ear to listen.

I remember so vividly one time when he was our state senator. A Registers of Deeds bill was being heard in a senate committee of which he was not a member. I had talked with Wendell about the bill and he had monitored it. He was the only senator present who was not a member of the committee. When he had entered the committee hearing room and took a seat, a good feeling had swept over me. I knew his presence would make a difference.

The State Registers of Deeds' legal counsel and I were the only persons present interested in the bill, except Wendell. The committee had significant questions which I was able to answer. The bill was given a favorable report and was enacted into law.

As I Look Ahead

Since I was born in 1915, there have been more advancements in science, medicine, and technology than during all other times since the world was created. And I have enjoyed observing every one of them as they have made our lives easier.

There has also been the creation of more dangerous weapons and more forms of pollution disrupting the ecological balance of all living things, including our own lives.

There is much work to be done in the Twenty-first Century by those who want to work on our problems and I hope to be part of the action.

I am learning to take time to savor the color of the sunset and the friendships that have enriched my life.

I have learned that life is about loving and being loved, finding meaning in what I think and what I do every day.

I am learning to enjoy relaxing more, seeing more good in people and listening more.

Above all, I have learned three things:

1. To look forward to each new day.

2. To seek truth.

3. To keep faith in myself, faith in righteousness of a cause, and in the promises of God.

There has never been a time when I did not feel the presence of a power greater than myself. Life has granted me release from the worries over circumstances that I cannot change and given me peace of mind and heart as I reflect on the past and face the future at eighty-three.

I give thanks—

For all of the peaceful hours I have spent,

For all of the beauty I have seen,

For the food that has fed my body and soul,

For friendships gone and those to come,

For those who loved me when I needed love the most,

For the courage to face the days ahead with great expectation and hope.

Appendix:
Good Old Days Recalled
by Former Duplin Man

Reminiscing—Little Stephanie Williams of route 2, Pink Hill listens as her great uncle, Milton J. Whaley, of Portsmouth, Virginia, formerly of Duplin County, and her grandmother, Duplin Register of Deeds, Christine Williams, who is Whaley's sister, reminisce about the "good old days" of the 1920s and 1930s in Duplin County. Whaley, who was attending a high school reunion in Kenansville Saturday night, is also the brother of Mrs. Norman Anderson of Mount Olive. He tells about his childhood days in the accompanying story.

The good old days of walking two miles to a one-room school house, carrying lunch in a tin lard bucket for himself and three siblings, and of wearing patched overalls and cropping tobacco by hand were recalled during the weekend by Milton J. Whaley.

Whaley, a native of Duplin County and brother of Mrs. Norman Anderson of Mount Olive and Duplin Register of Deeds, Christine Williams, was in Kenansville to attend a reunion of several high school classes.

He is attending Tidewater Community College in Portsmouth, Virginia, where he is a Dean's List student majoring in Human Behavioral Sciences. Whaley retired as a Chief Warrant Officer in 1959 after serving in the Navy and Air Force. Prior to entering college, he served the United States as a technical representative in Turkey, where he taught the Turks the operation and maintenance of diesel electric power plants.

Whaley reflected on the Duplin farm days of the 1920s and 30s in a term paper he recently completed at college. Following is his story about

A Sharecropper's Son

I was born in Magnolia, North Carolina 8 April 1914, the son of Mack Whaley and Genet Thomas Whaley. At that time Magnolia was a booming town that had sprung up on both sides of the railroad. Its economy revolved around two enterprises. One was the shipment of Tar, pitch, turpentine and lumber from the harvest of long leaf pines. The other was the quart cup and crate factories which manufactured wooden cups and crates used for the shipment of strawberries to the northern markets. Flower bulb growing was looming on the horizon. The quart cups were put together in the homes by the women where they were paid a pittance for their labor. The thirty-two quart crates were made in the factories by the men who usually received fifty cents a day.

Another choice which became available to poor people as a way of life was sharecropping, defined by Webster as "to work the land for a share of the crop." Since tobacco was one of the highest crops in money value, my father and mother decided to try this.

All of the foregoing information was related to me by my parents. I witnessed Magnolia's economy in action many times when I was a youngster during our family's horse and buggy visits back to Magnolia to see our relatives.

My first recollection of being branded as a sharecropper's son was when I was going to a one-room school at Chinquapin where the teacher taught seven grades in our one room. My younger sister and I walked to school while I carried our lunch in a metal lard bucket made up of whatever mother could prepare from the farm products we had grown.

The first three sharecrop houses we lived in were at Chinquapin. All of these houses were made of wood weather boarding with only one layer of outside walls—no inner walls and very little in the way of partitions. Only one fireplace in each house burned wood for heat. I remember so well how we almost froze in winter and how our parents would warm bricks in front of the fire, wrap them in cloths and put them to our feet as they tucked us in our home-made feather beds in our cold room.

My father's reputation as a tobacco farmer rose because of his careful attention to all details of growing, curing and preparing his tobacco for competitive markets. He was sought after by landlords.

We had lived in three different sharecrop houses at Chinquapin by the time I was in the third grade at school. Then we moved near Kenansville, the county seat, into what we thought was an absolute "mansion" because it had a dining room, small kitchen, and three bedrooms, all partitioned off. Above all, there were real inside walls made of tongue and groove wooden ceiling boards. We needed three bedrooms, one for mother and daddy which would be our family room because it had the only fireplace, a bedroom for the two boys we now had and one for the two girls. There was never any running water and we only had electricity one year before I joined the Navy. But, oh, those inside walls!

Our "mansion" has stood empty and abandoned two miles west of Kenansville on N.C. 24 for many years but I always visit it when I visit my two sisters in Mount Olive and Pink Hill, because it still holds many, many memories for me—some happy, some sad.

My two sisters and I went to school in Kenansville, two miles away. My younger brother attended school until he died of Hodgkins disease at age fifteen. We still walked the two miles to school until I was in the ninth grade and I still looked after our lunch in the tin lard bucket until I graduated. Walking to school in all kinds of weather seemed to make us healthier than our parents.

The Kenansville school was small but we had the standard eleven grades. Most of the students' parents were independent farmers.

Due to the lack of money to wear better clothes, I always felt we were marked as sharecroppers' children. We wore overalls which usually had neatly sewn patches and gingham dresses made by our mother who was a fine seamstress. We always had just one dress outfit reserved for Church activities and special occasions. Our clothes were always shabby, but always very clean and well ironed by mother's old smoothing iron that was heated either in front of the fireplace or on our wood-burning cook stove. Mother once said: "You can't help being poor, but you can help being dirty."

Life went on year after year working hard after school and all summer from dawn to dusk. We received half of the selling price of what we produced which brought very little when we sold it. One year, the price of tobacco ran in the ten to fifteen cents price range.

Social life was mostly going to Church every Sunday and visiting neighboring sharecroppers. Big social events for us were popping corn or pulling home-made candy in winter with the peanut poppings in spring. Due to my parents' policies of honesty, hard work, cleanliness, love thy neighbor and Church attendance, we were accepted by some of the wealthier families and invited to their parties when other sharecroppers' children were not.

Some variations to our social life were provided when Daddy would take us to the Medicine Man shows each fall or to a summer tent revival. And he never missed taking us to the Warsaw 11 November World War One Victory Parade with its accompanying carnival where he always gave us a few pennies to spend.

Through hard work, often when I knew they were sick, our parents saw us through high school and wanted us to go to college, but this was impossible.

Although my father's life was cut short in 1948 and mother died in 1968, they both lived to see my two sisters and I living a better life than they did. They considered this a reward for all they had tried to do for us and we loved them dearly for their efforts.

For Reference

Not to be taken from this room

NORTH CAROLINA ROOM
NEW HANOVER COUNTY PUBLIC LIBRARY

N C R